THE OMG CHRONICLES

THE OMG CHRONICLES

One Man's Quest to Discover
What God Means to People
All Over the World

Peter Rodger

HAY HOUSE, INC.
Carlsbad, California • New York City
London • Sydney • Johannesburg
Vancouver • Hong Kong • New Delhi

Published and distributed in the United States by: Hay House, Inc.: www.hay house.com • *Published and distributed in Australia by:* Hay House Australia Pty. Ltd.: www.hayhouse.com.au • *Published and distributed in the United Kingdom by:* Hay House UK, Ltd.: www.hayhouse.co.uk • *Published and distributed in the Republic of South Africa by:* Hay House SA (Pty), Ltd.: www.hayhouse.co.za • *Distributed in Canada by:* Raincoast: www.raincoast.com • *Published in India by:* Hay House Publishers India: www.hayhouse.co.in

Editorial supervision: Jill Kramer • *Project editor:* Alex Freemon
Design: Nick C. Welch

Library of Congress Cataloging-in-Publication Data

Rodger, Peter.
  The OMG chronicles : one man's quest to discover what God means to people all over the world / Peter Rodger. -- 1st ed.
     p. cm.
  ISBN 978-1-4019-2845-2 (tradepaper : alk. paper) 1. God. 2. Religious adherents--Interviews. 3. Rodger, Peter, 1965---Travel. 4. Oh my God (Motion picture : 2006) I. Title.
  BL473.R64 2011
  200.92'2--dc22

                              2010026585

Hardcover ISBN: 978-1-4019-2845-2
Digital ISBN: 978-1-4019-2942-8

14 13 12 11   4 3 2 1
1st edition, March 2011

Printed in the United States of America

*This book is dedicated to my father, George Rodger,
who taught me how to wield a camera; to my mother,
Jinx Rodger, for being a pillar of strength; to my
father-in-law, Abdesalam Akaaboune, who taught me
how to go with the flow; and to Soumaya, my wife;
and Elliot, Georgia, and Jazz, my children, for putting
up with my absence, even when I was at home.*

CONTENTS

PART III: CATCHING BUTTERFLIES

PREFACE

There's a hushed silence. Many people are sitting expectantly in a room in a foreign land. It's hot outside. They are all different—different people with different sensibilities—yet they all have made the effort to be here. They are waiting for me. It's so quiet, I can hear their breathing.

The presenter has uttered my name. This is my moment. I bound down the steps to the podium. I have to say words, to strangers, to shadows, to people . . . to the audience I have thought about for three years. Now they are here, waiting patiently for me to say something.

I take the microphone and look out. All I can see are anonymous shapes. Yet I know that each shape cloaks an identity—a discerning thinker; an individual; a mother, brother, sister, wife, husband, lover, friend; an intellect; an enjoyer of food. I take a breath and start speaking: "I cannot think of a more appropriate place to launch a film entitled *Oh My God* than here in the Holy Land."

I am in Jerusalem, and I am launching my film amid the hubbub of it all: the claims, the disdain, the walls, the hurt, the pain, the history, the thorns, the corruption, the disruption, the diggers, the seekers, the policemen, the peacemakers . . . the Holy Land.

I have spent three years—and all my money, time, and energy—traveling across 23 countries asking: "What is God?" And now here I am, presenting my movie for the first time at the Jerusalem International Film Festival in the Holy Land. But is it really the Holy Land . . . or the Land of Holes?

—⊘—

INTRODUCTION

What Is God?

I was on a ski lift at the Deer Valley Resort in Utah when the idea came to me. I was watching incredible vistas of bright white slopes slowly and silently unfold below on a perfect winter's day. The sun was so bright, bouncing off the wedding-cake folds of fresh snow, that it flared my goggles. The overpowering beauty of the earth beneath me inspired me to mutter to my friend, "God—this is like—God-kissed."

"Hmm," she agreed without thinking.

I pondered my statement for a while. It had seemed so natural, so easy, and instantly understandable as it had tripped effortlessly off my tongue. But what exactly did it *mean?*

We had been attending the Sundance Film Festival. I had been working for years to get an independent film off the ground, and I had just heard that my financing had fallen through.

"You know what I should do," I announced, rather than asked. "I should make a film asking people around the world, 'What is God?' That would be really cool."

My fate was sealed.

I HAVE AN EXTREMELY ACTIVE MIND that gets bored very easily. I have always tried to fight this, but I realize it's a battle I'm never going to win. So I've developed a strategy to keep myself from becoming insane with boredom when I'm in positions of imprisonment—for instance, going out with people with whom I don't want to be. My strategy is . . . *napkins*. Since paper napkins are always available, whenever I feel a fit of boredom coming on, I grab a few, pilfer a pen from a bartender, and entertain myself by inventing little adages. Consequently, I literally have stacks of napkins from all over the world, filled with meaningful phrases (well, meaningful to *me,* that is)—many of which can be found at the beginning of the following chapters.

But there's one adage for which I wish I could take credit. A bizarre psychic enlightened me to it in London years ago. Crippled, he would hobble into a darkened room on a weird contraption, then proceed to wag his head about and glaze his eyes until he entered a trancelike state, at which time he would start to "become" a spirit called Ishmael. I'm not sure whether it was Ishmael talking or the psychic—but this is what he said: "Yesterday's breath is memory, tomorrow's breath is contemplation, but the air in your lungs now is what is keeping you alive."

I like that statement. It has a certain ring to it, and it became a source of strength for me throughout the entire project.

Ever since I completed my adventure, many people have asked me why I dropped a successful career as a director of commercials and advertising photographer to pick up a camera and travel for so long asking people, "What is God?"

My semi-ersatz reply is that I was fed up with the childish school-yard mentality that permeates our world—I call it the "My God is greater than your God" syndrome—where we have grown men slamming airplanes into buildings, shouting, "God is great!" Where we have the Reverend Pat Robertson saying that the nation of Haiti was devastated by a large earthquake because its people "made a pact" with "the devil." Where we have the constitution of a country (Iran) dictating that its supreme leader is "God's representative on Earth." And where we have people blowing themselves up and murdering innocents because they believe it will buy them a place in heaven.

But before I start sharing this adventure with you, let me tell you a little about me. I'm a curly-headed Brit who moved to Los Angeles with my family in 1996. And, dare I admit it, I am now middle-aged, although I still feel like a teenager. I am deeply addicted to traveling, experiencing new adventures, and discovering new places. I was heavily influenced by my late father, George Rodger, who was a photojournalist and taught me how to see in a photographic, visual-storytelling way—a privileged education that I then nurtured into a career. I love food and have always been fascinated by people. I'm an Aries, and have a tendency to jump into things based on gut instinct, which has caused me trouble on more than one occasion.

I grew up in an Anglican household and went to church every week. I attended Sunday school and was baptized and confirmed. I was brought up to believe that God was this kind, fatherlike spirit in the sky in the image of man; and if you wanted to go to heaven (which was a really nice place) when you died, then you had to behave yourself on Earth and abide by His rules.

It never occurred to me to question this upbringing until I started traveling extensively and was introduced to other cultures. Then, when 9/11 happened, I realized that a lot of what goes on in the name of God seems to be diametrically opposed not only to what I had been taught, but also to what the prophets of all the main religions preached. It wasn't until I started to study the world on a more spiritual level that I began to realize that so many of us were as conditioned as I had been. Suddenly, the whole concept of God just didn't seem to make any sense to me anymore.

What kind of a world would my children grow up in? In an age of oversaturated information . . . awareness, understanding, tolerance, and ultimately peace were being threatened by religious dogma, barbaric actions, and polarized opinions. Knowledge seemed to be flowing at an unprecedented rate. Wisdom seemed to be ebbing at an unprecedented rate. It seemed that truth was becoming diluted by too many voices all keen to reference the name of God to further their own agendas.

But what exactly *is* God? Does anyone really know?

It was this yearning that must have bubbled to the surface that sunny morning in Utah, and as the weeks passed, the desire to find out what other individuals around the world thought about this contentious issue took root and began to grow. There are so many conflicting ideas about God, as well as so much sensitivity. I wanted to know why everyone gets so riled up about this entity that means different things to different people. Perhaps if I posed the same set of questions to a diverse group of men, women, and children, some light could be shed upon this ancient conundrum.

So in 2006, without any financial backers, I took a line of credit out on my house (which in those days was actually increasing in value) and went out into the world to ask these questions. I did an intense amount of reading and research. I knew I couldn't make a film about what people thought God was without embracing the major religions and visiting the Middle East. I wanted my journey to unfold organically, with one thing leading naturally to another. I asked all my friends and family for suggestions and introductions, and most of the people you will meet in this book came as contacts from that process. Since there was no way I could accomplish the whole journey in one trip, I let circumstance take its course and did it in chunks—so I could at least come home from time to time and make sure my family wouldn't forget who I was.

I had no idea when I started just how long the process would take, or that it would culminate in my penning the work you now hold in your hands. *The OMG Chronicles* started on day one with a journal that became the germ for these written words, but it was the excitement and the hilarity of circumstance that made writing this book as important, if not more important, than the film itself. There was so much said by so many wonderful people that couldn't be expressed in a 98-minute documentary, so the book quickly became an opportunity to delve deeper and experience the layers of the world in which we live, as well as feel the hearts of those with whom we share our lives.

But most of all, it is the behind-the-scenes adventures—and misadventures—that make *The OMG Chronicles* such a wonderful extension to *Oh My God*. So much happened during the making of the film that obviously had no part in the movie itself, but which added much color to the backstory—from how I got to each place; to the people with whom I traveled; to the sometimes poignant, occasionally unbelievable, and oftentimes downright hilarious characters and experiences I encountered along the way. Some made me laugh, some made me cry, but all of them, in their own ways, contributed something unforgettable to this journey.

But back when my journey started, I had no idea of any of this. All I knew was that there were two things driving me: one was a question that no one, to my knowledge, had ever answered satisfactorily; the other, I'll confess, was a desperate need for adventure and escape. I yearned to shoot the world through my own lens, as opposed to the one commissioned by a client. And perhaps, too, I was a little unhealthily motivated to do something to serve, and cultivate, my own ego. That was the air that was in my lungs—those were the desires that were keeping me alive—and it gives me great pleasure to share this journey, warts and all, in the following pages.

When I started out, I thought it would be fun to have a six-month adventure. . . .

Nothing could prepare me for what I found.

PART I

INTO THE UNKNOWN

CHAPTER 1

The Leap

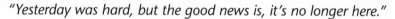

"Yesterday was hard, but the good news is, it's no longer here."

— NAPKIN #1

God, couldn't you have made me go on a different day?

There was no turning back, it seemed, as I made my way to Los Angeles International Airport to board a flight to London and then on to Tangier, Morocco. I was finally off on my adventure. I had forsaken my career, mortgaged my house, and leased a whole load of camera equipment, planning to travel around the world to ask all sorts of different people, "What is God?" Was I absolutely barking mad?

It was mainly frustration that had driven me to make this "leap." Why on earth would people blow themselves up, slamming airplanes into buildings, shouting, "God is great!"? What did suicide and murder have to do with an entity that all the prophets and belief systems around the world seemed to indicate was a father figure of compassion? Why did people use God's name to induce fear, and unhealthily enhance their own nefarious political agendas? Why does any human being have the right to tell others that they're going to go to hell after they die because they aren't members of the right club? *"My God is greater than your God. Worship my God and you will be saved when you die!"* Where were all those people who acted with benevolence, charity, and *compassion* in God's name?

I really wanted to find out what people had to say. Would they agree? Would they disagree? Would they disagree to agree? Perhaps they would agree to disagree. By asking diverse individuals from as many places as possible across the globe, perhaps I could shed some light on this age-old question.

There was no doubt it was a daunting exercise I had set for myself. The world seemed so large, with multiple permutations and combinations of ideas, differences of opinions, and belief systems—and the first problem was, where was I going to start?

My wife, Soumaya, was from Tangier, so it seemed sensible to wet my toes in territory that was not only accessible through her family and their connections, but also exotic. Soumaya's father, Abdesalam, had put together a great itinerary for me and was going to get all sorts of interesting characters together to appear in front of my lens. All I needed to do was pack the cameras, get on a plane, and go.

But the date I chose to travel, August 10, 2006, was the day after the British police had busted a group of terrorists attempting to take liquid explosives onto planes bound for the United States with the intent of blowing them up in the name of my protagonist. The skyways were in turmoil. It was the first time in aviation history that you couldn't take any hand luggage on board. You could only carry a see-through Ziploc bag with ticket, money, and credit cards inside. No books, no pens, no cell phones, no computers, no water, no duty-free items, no jewelry (and no ego). I had just one Claritin pill with me (because planes make me sneeze all the time) in one of those individual foil blister packs that are impossible to open. They found it. They made me swallow it in front of them before they let me board the plane.

I'd been filming around the world for years, and there was a golden rule: always take your film stock (or these days, tape stock and hard drives), lenses, and camera with you on board in case the baggage goes missing. This usually requires copious amounts of charm, time, and teeth clenching with polyester-clad airline staff. In 20 years of traveling, it had never failed—until today, when they refused to allow carry-on luggage aboard and then made me swallow my antihistamine.

So when I arrived in North Africa, everything—from the leased camera equipment, tapes, lenses, chargers, laptop, cell phone, and my research material with all my handwritten notes and quotes; to the little gifts I had brought for my family and friends; to my socks, shirts, shoes, and my soul . . . every last item that had been in the hold of the British Airways aircraft—had vanished, never to be seen again. As I stood by the carousel, poised for the grab, waiting for my baggage and equipment to slide through the hole and inch toward me on that squeaky black tacky rubber belt, it slowly dawned upon me that my documentary film was already over before it had even started.

My mind revisited that favorite adage I heard from that psychic in London years ago: "Yesterday's breath is memory, tomorrow's breath is contemplation, but the air in your lungs now is what is keeping you alive . . ." *Not without a camera!* I thought, hyperventilating. Had I upset Him so badly that my equipment had been taken from me? The irony was not lost on me. I was a victim of those would-be terrorists spouting His name. Perhaps this film wasn't such a good idea, after all. What was I doing? What had I done? What was I *going* to do? I didn't even have a toothbrush.

WITH SHATTERED DREAMS AND EXPLODED EXPECTATIONS, I had to endure the torture of being in a colorful foreign country with endless filming opportunities that couldn't be captured, because everything I needed to make the film was gone. Instead, I found myself bartering for boxer shorts in the bazaar. I couldn't even fly home early, as the aviation world was reeling from the latest security upheaval.

Even when I finally arrived back in the U.S. dressed like someone out of *Hideous Kinky,* it took almost two months of intense work to get compensated, purchase new equipment, and program it. I endured a streak of bad luck where just about everything went wrong: my mother, who lives in England, broke her arm when she was hit by a car as she was walking home from the post office; my friend's brother collapsed in Chechnya and died (poisoning was eventually ruled out); and I was booked for speeding and got a parking ticket in the same day. I soon wondered if someone was trying to tell me something.

But no. I decided that all these events were telling me that I simply *had to make this film.* The world had gone crazy! There seemed to be no direction anywhere, for anyone, anymore. No one's decisions were making any sense. Wars were being fought based on lies. People had been stripped of faith because there no longer seemed to be any boundaries between politics and religion, or even church and state. Major beliefs had been shattered by science, yet the believers had become more fanatical. People everywhere were suddenly angry, about *everything*. Knowledge was becoming dangerous. Lack of knowledge was becoming explosive. Stories and parables were being undermined; the spin had no web, no sense, no direction, and no course. People were holding on to their past and their social and formal educations, clutching on to their religions and beliefs and passing the buck onto answers they had been conditioned to regurgitate, without questioning who, where, what, or why. People were now drifting at the whim of previously unimagined forces, like the Internet and overcontrolled media. The liberation of freethinking had suddenly released the controls on our lives. God had become questionable. Religion was becoming fanatical, fundamental, or nonexistent. Were the ones who were really manipulating the world beginning to lose their grip because of undeniable questioning, or were they just beginning to take control? Who really knew? And who were "they" anyway?

I decided that the events I had just experienced had nothing to do with God, nothing to do with anything . . . but they had a lot to do with me: they had strengthened my resolve to make this film, and my faith in the project was rekindled. In retrospect, I realize that when I did finally manage to start filming, I hit a wave of fortuitous timing that never would have occurred had I not been derailed.

Perhaps there's a reason for everything.

AFTER A FEW WEEKS OF HELL, I found myself on Monday, October 2, 2006, surrounded by cases of brand-new camera equipment . . . and waves of anxiety. Today was the day I was going to start— again—on the documentary. Not wishing to repeat myself (or history), I had decided to begin the shoot with a road trip from Los Angeles to New Orleans and back. I wasn't going alone, though. I had persuaded my friend Patrick Ellis to accompany me as my producer and overall support mechanism.

Patrick is a character. Supremely intelligent, fluent in many languages, and a relentless smoker, he's a cross between Patrick O'Brian's Dr. Stephen Maturin from *Master and Commander* and Keith Richards. I often wonder if he just likes to challenge statistics, or if he's trying to prove something by conducting his life excessively as a rebuke to convention. A chameleon who spends his life on the road, working internationally as a producer, he was the perfect partner for this adventure. I didn't have to explain stuff to Patrick, and Patrick could explain stuff to *me*. His main job was to organize where we were going and whom we were to interview. He spent lengthy periods of time glued to the phone setting up interesting people and places for us to film.

My other companion, Alexander van Bubenheim, was the antithesis of Patrick. A large Bavarian who is a black belt in karate, with a fondness for knives, guns, skydiving, wine, and women, he constantly gets himself into trouble by uttering politically incorrect statements at the most inappropriate moments. An Aries through and through (just like me), he's compulsive, tough, tortured, and above all, a talented composer (although by looking at him, you would have guessed a completely different career). Because of his military, don't-mess-with-me aura and many a verbal faux pas, Alex soon earned the nickname *Colonel Boobs*.

The waves of anxiety that accompanied me throughout the trip stemmed from the reality that I had absolutely no idea what I was trying to do. The only thing I knew was that I was doing it—whatever *it* was. I drew comfort from the movie *Indiana Jones and the Last Crusade,* in which Indy has to cross a nasty ravine by taking a leap of faith. We learn (in the movie) that if one *believes* one can cross, one can cross, but Indy stares perplexed at the ravine, which appears to be both unrealistically deep and impossibly wide. But he isn't fooled; it's an optical illusion, for there's a bridge, but it has been camouflaged, painted to look just like the rock strata of the ravine wall behind. Clever Indy throws sand on it to reveal its presence, and then strides confidently and safely across to the other side.

I felt rather like this myself that day and was desperately trying to change my perspective so that I could reveal my own bridge to safety, yet all I could see was an extremely wide gap. Why was I doing this? But here I was, with everything packed and ready to go; it was too late to turn back now. I felt like Frodo Baggins in the Shire without a Gandalf. Then I realized that stepping out into the unknown was what it was all about. How cool was that? Let the current take you . . . and if you believe it's taking you where you want to go, sit back and make sure you do what you need to do; record the journey professionally, visually, artistically, and succinctly so you can share it with the world.

It had been time to go for hours, but we had already missed our self-imposed deadline of departure. We stuffed the equipment into my SUV and said good-bye to my wife, Soumaya, and my children, Elliot, Georgia, and Jazz; and off we headed toward New Orleans and a long, long journey into the unknown.

By the time we finally hit the I-10 freeway heading east, it felt good—very good.

There was another character (of sorts) among our crew: "Agnes the navigation system." She had such a polite, kind, patient voice and was never rude, even after a wrong turn. She was a constant oracle of direction. She would talk to us from time to time, even when she didn't really need to, just to reassure us that we hadn't gone wrong. She never raised her voice. She was our female HAL.

We took turns at the wheel all day and into the night. The idea was to drive nonstop until we arrived in New Orleans; spend a few days shooting there; then meander slowly cross-country through Louisiana, Texas, New Mexico, Arizona, Nevada, and back to California. Our route would be guided by what we learned.

It was documentary-filmmaking time. The problem was, Patrick, in a Keith Richards moment, decided to swallow the whole contents of one of those multicolored truck-stop caffeine-pill packages. They kept him awake for a good while, but then he started to feel a little poorly, and his eyesight went squiffy. Instead of keeping him alert and on top of things, he went into a caffeine-induced, spasmodic-twitching mode. Alone in the backseat, riddled with angst and unwilling to disturb me, he courageously kept his plight to himself.

Baffled by the incessant scratching and writhing going on back there, I would occasionally inquire if he was all right, but before I had even finished asking, he would cut me off at the pass with a tightly clipped "Yep, fine." In fact, every time I started to formulate a word, he would quickly butt in with a "Yep, fine."

Colonel Boobs had made it very clear that, owing to his eyesight, he was a daytime driver only. So I ended up taking the wheel most of the night, until the beautiful rays of the desert sun started to peek over the horizon and it was light enough for the Colonel to see. It was a very long night for me. My mind wandered everywhere, from pondering the true color of the paint marks on the road to what the work crew had been thinking as they operated the machinery laying them down on a highway 3,000 miles long. I wondered what their opinion was about God.

In the middle of the afternoon of the second day, we pulled off the freeway for gas and found ourselves in a different world—on the back roads of Texas. The gas station was also the general store of a hick town called Roosevelt, population 19. Finally I was about to start filming the first frames of the documentary. Giddy with excitement and feeling like a cowboy putting my gun together, I assembled the camera, hitched up my pants, and moseyed on in. I interviewed most of the locals; and to my dismay, I realized I had bitten off so much that I could barely move my jaw, let alone chew.

I hadn't realized how hard it was to formulate questions in my head and then ask them succinctly in a way that the interviewee could understand, while at the same time controlling the light and exposure levels on a complex camera that I'd never used before because it had only just been invented. And that was without the added handicap of having driven nonstop for two days and a night. I felt like a nervous young virgin—extremely keen to do the deed, but scared into impotence.

And everyone said the same thing: "I believe in God."

"Why do you believe in God?"

"I always have since I was a kid."

"But what *is* God?"

"God is everything. God's in here," they'd avow, tapping their hearts.

"How do you know?"

"Because I feel it—because I believe it. I live my life for Him."

"But have you ever met Him?"

"Not yet—I hope not—I'm not dead yet! I don't think!" They'd chuckle.

"So you think you will meet Him when you die?"

"I hope so. I lead my life with the values I believe will send me to heaven when I pass on. I hope to meet Him then."

Wow, I thought. *Here's conviction, faith, a code of life—everyone's saying the same thing.* They were all very generous people, but were any of them really thinking for themselves? Or had they just been conditioned by their upbringing to say this? Were their beliefs and expressions of faith really coming from their hearts, or had it been implanted—and if it *had* been implanted, by whom?

We left the gas station with invitations to come elk hunting in November when the season started. We would always be welcome in Roosevelt.

WE DIDN'T GET TO NEW ORLEANS IN ONE HIT. None of us had understood the vastness of the United States of America. Figures, particularly zeros, don't adequately illustrate the reality. You have to drive across the U.S. to truly understand that the country is *absolutely massive;* it goes on for miles and miles—especially the Lone Star State. We copped out at 8:30 P.M. in Seguin, Texas; ate some extremely unhealthy food; and hit the hay in a cheap motel.

CHAPTER 2

Louisiana

"Falling is fine—it is the landing that causes the pain."

— Napkin #2

We arrived in New Orleans at dusk and checked into Le Richelieu Hotel. New Orleans had been falling for years (as far as crime, poverty, and the shameful ostracism of its minority citizens were concerned), but it was very evident as we drove into town that it had landed with a very hard bump. Or rather, the wrath of Katrina had visited its shores with frightening impact, exposing all the social weaknesses and stigmas concealed beneath the glittering facades of Mardi Gras, Jazz Fest, and Bourbon Street.

It had been just over a year since the disaster, and the city I had once known so well, having filmed here many times, was no longer the same. The sense of dispossession and emptiness was palpable; people trudged the streets as if through treacle, that *look* of aftershock still tattooed onto their brows. The "It is what it is" resignation uttered by so many lips was evident in their movements and actions. The core and heart of the Big Easy had been sucked dry; its very soul flattened. The Big Easy had turned into the *Big Difficult.*

Even the music in the French Quarter seemed to have lost its rhythm and soul. Its presence felt like an echo of performances past, as if it was only there for the few tourists and not being played by musicians for musicians in a musicians' town. New Orleans was a sad place now, a poor facsimile of its former self; but at least the food was still good, and the locals put on a brave face and welcomed us in true Southern style.

Katrina became a character in my film. She had swept through; made a lot of noise; and left a huge trail of devastation, desperation, disappointment, and anger in her wake. Although physically long gone, she was mentally immortal. I wanted to know how she'd affected the survivors' thoughts about God.

THE FOLLOWING MORNING WE SET OUT to shoot the storm damage. It was a wake-up call. We drove past block after block that on the surface looked normal. It was only when we got closer that we realized the houses were all derelict on the inside, abandoned and empty. The lights had gone out on this part of the city, and there was no one at home.

It soon became obvious that large chunks of the area had withered and died, and become ghost towns. There were malls full of stores with no windows, their contents still spilling out into the parking lots like the scattered entrails of a disemboweled horse.

We entered the Lower Ninth Ward. This was the place we'd heard so much about—the point where the levee had broken and flooded all those poor people's homes. Houses that had been picked up and plunked down on top of cars were still there today. The only things left lurking in the soil were anger, horror, and a whole load of unanswered questions. You could feel the despair, the anguish, and see the once-prized items of clothing hanging in ripped-open wardrobes, waiting for owners who would never return.

I wedged the camera on the running board of the SUV, and Patrick drove slowly down the deserted streets as I shot the graphic shapes of neglected retail. Colonel Boobs donned his special digital microphone and captured the echo of emptiness in department stores still stocked with goods that the looters hadn't felt worthy of looting.

Later that afternoon, as the sun was painting graceful rays upon inelegant destruction, we came across a charismatic African-American man, named Nathaniel, clearing the last of the debris from the yard of his friend's house. He ranted and raved as he chopped dead branches with a blunt machete. He wasn't angry, though. He praised the Lord! He revered God.

The storm damage wasn't caused by God, he said. It was caused by the breaking of a levee that was built by man. God sent the storm as a lesson to force the evil folk to pull up their socks; expose their indulgent, weak ways; and make them atone for how they'd chosen to conduct their lives.

No, Nathaniel wasn't angry with God; Nathaniel *thanked* God.

"You're born with nothin'—naked and free. When you die, you can't take any material things with you, like this house or my 1972 Cadillac. You can only take what's in here . . ." He tapped his heart. "And I'm thankful to God for sending us this lesson. He could have made it a lot worse. He could have made the waters 60 feet deep instead of 20, but He didn't. I admire what He's done!"

I rather admired Nathaniel's strength of character. His resolve was based on his faith. That was sufficient for him, and God seemed to be working for him.

Nathaniel continued: "I'm a firm believer that you're not gone until ya time. If it was time for me, I wouldn't be here right now talking wit' you." He pulled himself up to his full height, and his eyes stared intensely. "You have to live a good and righteous life. But it's not gonna be stress free. Livin' is stressful. It's according to how you adjust to it and deal with the situation. This is stress, here," he said, gazing at the devastation surrounding us. "Looking at the city is stress, but we're not gonna be stressed for the rest of our lives. We have to face reality to deal with what happened, pick up the pieces, and move on with our lives. That's what we need to do, and that's what I'm prepared to do. Thank you."

By the time we finished, a harvest moon hung over the Ninth Ward like a silver-gold pendant—a beacon of light that never changes, illuminating a very changed world below.

We returned to the relative opulence of the French Quarter and ate somewhere jolly, loud, and cheap—to expel the gloomy spirits of all that we had just witnessed. Everyone gets down from time to time, but in the face of what I was witnessing, it made me feel ashamed for not appreciating how privileged I am.

THE NEXT DAY, PATRICK HAD ORGANIZED an appointment with a popular minister called Doctor Clay, who lived out in the suburb of Kenner, Louisiana. Doctor Clay was supremely devout, oozed genuine benevolence, but was not quite as colorful as our friend

Nathaniel with the blunt machete. But amid the monotony of his dialogue we occasionally came across little pearls of wisdom.

I asked Doctor Clay about God and time.

"God is not in time's hand; time is in God's hand," he said. "Before there was a beginning, there was God; and there's not a suggestion that God Himself had a beginning process because He's not a product of the beginning process, but rather, before the beginning began to be, He already was."

That night we found a fantastic bar with a great band, where I zoned out to the most exquisite blues guitar mixed with soul. Here the musicians played music for musicians. It made me wonder: *Perhaps God is music, or music is God?* It's certainly a language that everyone can understand.

Our next port of call was the Upper Ninth Ward, where the majority of the homes also had been rendered uninhabitable by the floodwaters. Much of the area was deserted, as there was very little in the way of accommodations. Those who were left lived in little white FEMA trailers, parked in the backyards of houses with uncertain futures. Many homes had been burned down as a result of feuds fueled by anger, jealousies, and despair. Every front door sported a spray-painted red cross, creating four segments in which the date of city inspection, the name of the district, the initials of the inspector, and the number of dead bodies (either human or animal) that had been discovered on the property had been scribbled. It reminded me of the stories of the days of the great plague in Europe. It was a chilling sight.

Whenever we came across human beings, I would ask to talk with them, but they all turned me down. They'd had enough of news crews. They were fed up with white people sticking cameras in their faces. They were still in shock a year later, their eyes glazed over with a permanent film of anger and hurt. They had no money, no jobs, no possessions, broken promises, and innumerable letdowns; they were victims of corruption, and there was no sign of a better future.

We came across a group of kids, the Offray brothers. They were full of life and full of pain. They all looked way older than they were. The youngest, about eight, stood on the porch of his dilapidated house. I asked him, "Whereabouts do you think God was when the big storm hit?"

He replied, "He evacuated to another city in the sky."

"So while Katrina was here, God wasn't here?"

"No," he answered definitively. Then he added, "I wanna give a shout-out to ma mama. I wanna give a shout-out to ma dadda. I wanna give a shout-out to ma sister and"—he hit his chest—"God, right here in my heart." He kissed his fingers and held them to the heavens. "Rest in peace to ma uncle, ma cousin Danny—he dead. Just wanna give a shout-out to ma whole family." He kissed his fingers again. A car alarm went off in the distance. He crossed himself. "I love You, God. I'm in the Sixth Ward right now. Come and see me. Peace." And then he turned away.

THERE IS SOMETHING UNIQUE TO LOUISIANA. A melancholy accentuated by the wailing cries of distant trains, a humidity that declares its presence on good folks' walls, that peels paint and sits heavy in your lungs as you fight off the heat. There is a sexy romance about the South—immortalized by Anne Rice and dramatized with the blood pouring over Lisa Bonet in *Angel Heart*. You can cut the vibe of the South with a knife. If you sit still in the swamps and listen to the critters, nature is the embodiment of the light and the dark, the primal ooze, complete with cottonmouths, water moccasins, and alligators. No wonder the blues bubbled up from these murky depths—man's expression of bringing light out of the dark, spirit out of despair, heady notes to ease the hearts and souls of generations of the displaced and abused. The blues was alive—very much alive.

CHAPTER 3

Road Trip

●

*"The good thing about a small tank is that it
doesn't take much to fill it up."*

— NAPKIN #3

We left New Orleans and headed northwest across Louisiana toward Shreveport and back into Texas. The weather closed in, and so did my mood. Had I uncovered enough in Louisiana? I'd wanted to find crazy Cajun *Deliverance* types out in the swamps who only spoke French and spat all the time, or venom-tongued white supremacists spouting some crazy biblical distortion; but other commitments called, and we had run out of time before we'd even scratched the surface.

I didn't shoot that day. I just stared out the misty windows, listening to the swish of the tires on the road and the air pushing through the gap of my semiclosed window, wondering if any of the footage we'd shot was any good.

To say that I felt uncomfortable would be an understatement. My stomach flip-flopped almost in time with the *kathunk, hum, kathunk* of the wheels on the road. It was the same butterfly-in-the-stomach sensation that had visited me off and on over the years, whenever I was feeling particularly stressed. And I was feeling stressed so often lately that I had started to refer to my flighty abdominal companion as *Mr. Chou.* Mr. Chou and I would become the greatest of friends over the next months and years as this project consumed and almost drowned me. I named him Mr. Chou because he reminded me of a parable:

> Once upon a time Chuang Chou dreamed that he was a butter-
> fly, a butterfly flitting about happily enjoying himself. He didn't
> know that he was Chou. Suddenly he awoke and was palpably

Chou. He didn't know whether he was Chou who had dreamed of being a butterfly or a butterfly dreaming that he was Chou. Now, there must be a difference between Chou and the butterfly. This is called the transformation of things.

(Parable 2:14, *Wandering on the Way: Early Taoist Tales and Parables of Chuang Tzu,* Victor H. Mair, trans.)

. . . And such was the relationship between me and my own Mr. Chou.

BY THE TIME WE GOT TO AMARILLO, my stomach had settled down. We pulled into the parking lot of a world-famous restaurant called The Big Texan Steak Ranch. It lived up to its name. Here, everything was *big*. They offered a 72-ounce steak, which was free if you could finish it all. I personally found the whole concept of gluttony obscene.

But our waitress was a gem. Her name was Sally. She was 18 and very smart. She was wearing shorts, a red scarf, and the ubiquitous Stetson. We talked about what we were doing. She started telling us about her best friend, Cody, who was just back from Iraq, and their mutual childhood friend who had been killed by an IED (improvised explosive device) on the road to the airport in Baghdad on the day he was meant to be flying home. Cody had returned without him, and couldn't sleep. If he did sleep, he would wake up screaming every 20 minutes, so after work Sally and her sister would go over to Cody's to help calm him when this happened. She hadn't slept for a month, but it was the least she could do for her friend.

As Sally was telling us her story, a man who was about 6'3" and 55 years old stood up at the next table and said, "Miss, when you see Cody, would you please tell him we're thankful for what he did out there," and then he burst into tears. He hugged Sally and cried like a baby, sobbing into her red scarf. When the man pulled himself together, she used it to dry his eyes—a big Texan in the Big Texan steak house, in tears.

Later she explained to me: "You know, we never really understand why someone dies, but we're always told it's because it was his time. Now, serving the United States and the Army is a great honor for some, and especially to die doing it, but it hurts so much when someone is so close to coming home and you know that it was just a few hours before their mom could hug 'em one last time, or their sister could give them that kiss on the cheek that they've been wanting for a while.

"It's hard for Cody to deal with. It's hard for me, 'cause I don't know how to react to the way he acts now. But it's harder for him because he was close to it, and so when he asks why, there's no real reason to tell him besides 'It was his time'—because that's what we were told. That's how we lived our whole life."

"And where do you think God comes into that equation?"

Sally gritted her teeth and licked her lips. "Ahhh. You know that's a real hard question. He's the person that put us here and takes us away. God giveth and God taketh away. So the only thing I can say is, I believe he was put on this earth for a reason, and maybe that was to show light to others; he had the pride that all of us should have—he died for our country. Maybe that was his sole purpose. Maybe he had lived his full life, and God said, *Okay, now it's time for you to come home with Me.*"

"Have you learned from that loss yourself?"

Sally thought very hard. "I have. It's hard for me to take, seeing as I'm going into the Army, that many of us die for a war; but are we dying for our country, or are we dying for someone else's? That's the question that's hardest for me to answer than anything else."

THE NEXT DAY WE RAN INTO A STROKE OF LUCK. We found Bernie and Charlie Stokes—the husband-and-wife owners of the Panhandle Gunslingers gun shop. Charlie was a trip—she was about five feet nothing, with straight hair and a smoker's laugh.

I shot her (excuse the pun) in front of a rack of more than a hundred semiautomatic weapons. A devout nondenominational born-again Christian, she told me that God was her protector, her everything, her provider, her best friend. God was everything and the reason for being. When I started questioning her on the correlation between God and arms, she became quite animated.

"The only time God's people have been disarmed was when they were in direct rebellion against God, so you can see that I'm not in real rebellion, because I have lots of arms." She chuckled with a throaty, emphysemic wheeze that just seemed to keep on coming, bubbling out of her lungs.

"If you look throughout history, God has always supplied people with what they needed—food, arms, whatever—and so I can't see how you can be against God's word when it's written throughout history that God has given you, ah, his armor."

"As a spirit-filled, born-again Christian, how do you regard other religions?" I asked.

"God is not a religion, and so I don't care if you're Baptist or Methodist or nondenominational or Catholic or Jewish; I believe that the only way is Jesus Christ, and if you don't believe in Jesus and he's not your Lord and Savior, then you're not saved."

"Do you think there's one God, then?"

"Absolutely."

"Do you think there's one God for the Muslims and the Jews and the Hindus and the Sikhs—the same guy as yours?"

"No."

"And why do you think that?"

"Because those people cut Jesus Christ out of it."

"So you feel your God is valid as a born-again Christian, but others, including Allah, for the Muslims, don't really come into the equation?"

"No. To me God is God, and you can define God in many ways, but my religion says the only way to God is through Jesus Christ; and they cut Jesus Christ out of their religion, so are they going to heaven? No. Not by my point of view."

"Now, getting back to your business and selling guns—guns were made originally to kill people. They are weapons—"

"May I correct you just for a moment?" Charlie interrupted me with a big sheepish grin.

"Yes. Please."

"Guns are not *weapons*. Weapons are anything that's used for offense or defense, which can be a screwdriver, can be a knife—ah, the most common domestic-violence weapon is a screwdriver because everybody's got one. Guns are firearms, they're guns, they're . . ." She paused, looking for the right word. ". . . tools. Not weapons. We don't use the *W* word," she finished with another long, wheezy chuckle.

"So, they're for sport?"

"Yes."

"Even that M15 behind you?"

"That can be used for personal defense, but it's not a weapon. It's a tool. Just as a screwdriver can be used to build a chair, but it can also be used as a weapon. It's what's behind it, not what it is."

"So, getting back to God and very highly dangerous sport utensils that could be used in unsavory manners, does that make you look at your clientele in a specific way, because, obviously, you don't want to sell any of your nonweapon guns for bad reasons?" I asked.

Charlie let out a guffaw. "'Nonweapon guns for bad reasons'!" The laugh lasted even longer this time. "We have to do a background check on every firearm that we sell so that we know we're selling guns to law-abiding citizens. Criminals do not come into gun shops to buy guns. Criminals steal guns. I would say that probably 98 percent of the people that walk in here buy a gun for personal defense or sport."

I decided not to ask her about the other 2 percent.

I liked Charlie a lot, even though I didn't agree with her views. She went on to explain that the only reason guns weren't mentioned in the Bible was because they hadn't been invented yet.

"If they *had* been invented, do you think David would have used a slingshot against Goliath? No, he would have used an M15!" Charlie leaned toward the camera . . . "You know, when you're talking about weapons, Cain slew Abel with the jawbone of an ass!"

I WAS HAPPY WITH WHAT WE FILMED IN AMARILLO. We hit the road again, speeding toward New Mexico, and reached the town of Gallup at sundown. We checked into a hotel and went in search of food.

We dined in a typical hick bar/restaurant with blaring country music. A beat-up Native American entered and walked over to our table. He didn't look very well. He explained that he'd been taken ill and had been in the hospital, but was now hitching his way back to his reservation. I bought him dinner. You could see the life slowly ebb its way back into him as he ate. He was a kind, proud man; and it pained him deeply to have been lowered to a position of begging.

Patrick, Colonel Boobs, and I adjourned to the bar. There, I got talking to a very articulate young man by the name of Evan. College educated, Evan chewed tobacco incessantly, only stopping to spit a wad into a Styrofoam cup in between sips of beer. I was amazed how he could keep the tobacco intact in his mouth, while sucking beer past it.

Once I started to interview him, it became evident that he was surprisingly smart. He rattled on about man and God and what we've been told to think and what his own views were; and then he stopped, leaned into the lens, and said, "Peter, I'm gonna ask you a question in reverse: Are you doing this film for yourself, or are you doing it for God? Is it your will on Earth, or is it God's will? That's the question you need to ask yourself."

I couldn't answer that one. But maybe at the end of the journey I would be in a position to do so.

As Springsteen's "Born in the U.S.A." blasted out of the jukebox, I was thinking about the chemical reaction of Evan's chewing-tobacco strands being broken down by saliva—and if copious amounts of Bud sped up the reaction or slowed it down—when a man tapped me on the shoulder. He had a foreign accent. "I couldn't help overhearing your conversation earlier," he said. "What a fascinating idea, to ask people about God."

I asked him where he was from, and he said he was Palestinian. *In Gallup, New Mexico? That's a first,* I thought. "That's a long way from home," I said.

"I don't have a home . . . well, Gallup is my home," he replied.

I wasn't actually glancing at the drink in his hand, but he must have thought I was, because he immediately raised his bourbon glass and said, "I know. I've just broken Ramadan." Ramadan is an Islamic period of fasting, during which it is forbidden for

Muslims to smoke, or ingest any food or liquid in the hours of daylight. Drinking alcohol throughout the 28-day period is a crime punishable by imprisonment in even the most liberal of Muslim countries.

"I couldn't help it," the man admitted shamefacedly, before going on to explain that he had just been betrayed by his own brother and had ended up at the bar.

He put his hand out. "I'm Antonio Tutarro. It's a pleasure to meet you."

Antonio talked about the Palestinians. He felt there was an uncanny resemblance between the plight of the North American Indians and what was going on with the Palestinians in the Middle East today—even though they were different cultures in different lands.

"If greed can make two brothers fight like we did, then no wonder it causes conflict within a dispossessed, dysfunctional, and persecuted people like mine," he added. We agreed to meet at his home in the morning for an interview.

"AGNES" TOOK US UP SQUEAKY-CLEAN WINDING ROADS, dotted with identical single-story houses with massive air-conditioning boxes on their roofs. It looked as if the architect had simply photocopied his plans and distributed them around the neighborhood like an outdoor ad campaign. The SUV's wheels swished to a different tune on asphalt as black as coal. Agnes announced our arrival at Antonio's house.

Inside, Antonio's mother was busy roasting lamb. It smelled delicious. Even though none of the family would be eating because it was daylight, they were preparing a special gastronomic celebration for us. I set up the camera, thinking how fascinating it was that making this film had opened doors to experiences that I could never have invented—little windows into people's lives.

Antonio's father, Mario, sat down at the end of the table. A sensible man dressed in an impeccable suit, he said he wanted to tell us something before we began filming. In a gravelly voice that quivered with emotion, he recited a poem he had written:

"You have to know that we are guests on this land—we who live will be joined by others, while many have already passed. We all leave with empty hands—so do good things and leave aside all that is bad. Only your goodness will go up high, and your goodness will be your only gateway to your eternal life in the heights of heaven and paradise."

He looked as if he was about to cry.

A Guns N' Roses song suddenly blared out from the copycat house next door. I would have given my eyeteeth for a quick peek into that house, just for contrast. Would there be some tattooed, oversized youth having a hit of crystal methamphetamine while Mom was bleaching her wig and worrying about cellulite cream? I wondered what it would smell like—cold French fries and gray hamburger patties? Probably not lamb. I shook myself out of the daydream and gently sat Antonio down in front of the lights.

He said, "I would like to see the whole world live in harmony and peace, and promote peace all over the world.

"It's been terrible, because 9/11 has made all the Muslims look like terrorists. All look like suspects. And it's not going to stop for a long time. Because there is a fear that everybody that has that [Muslim] belief might one day do something bad and harm this country, which is absolutely not true. We all came to this land to have a better life. We ran away from dictators and occupations, and we came here for a better future. And now we are getting the same treatment as in the third-world countries.

"What scares me the most is, what if something again happens in this great country? And that question always runs in my head, you know: 'What's going to happen to us?'"

The family seemed tortured and upset that they were treated differently because of their religion. Despite their sadness, however, they were welcoming and open.

I'm still not sure why they had Italian names, but the lamb was delicious.

SINCE IT WAS VERY IMPORTANT TO EXPLORE the thoughts of indigenous populations in this film, we headed off to Arizona, where we had been invited to attend a Navajo festival and powwow. Patrick enlisted his old friend Lorrie Mannie, who belonged to the Navajo tribe, to guide and translate for us.

The full grace of planet Earth began to unfold; the Arizona desert was truly breathtaking. Mile after mile of exquisite landscape unfolded before our eyes: big skies, wide-open vistas stretching to eternity as we purred our way along empty roads, punctuated occasionally by a polite Agnes reminding us how far we had left to go.

Tuba City is a nothing town filled with mobile homes scattered across sparse hillsides as if they had been planted by a paintball gun. Deep in the Navajo reservation, it was the place the tribe would congregate, sell their wares, and have fun. I had visions of a native elder, sitting alone with the elements, chanting and singing songs about the sky, the rocks, the spirits, and his affinity with the earth and everything. Instead, we found ourselves in the middle of a flea market, surrounded by sad, forlorn faces, proud around the eyes, but downcast like a cloud before a squall.

Covert glances followed us as we wandered across the scorched, stony ground, examining the assortment of Stetsons, rough silver belts, and turquoise jewelry that was on sale. We were the only white people there, it seemed. I felt ashamed by history and the stark contrast between the reality and the stories, folklore, and films like *A Man Called Horse* that had influenced me as a child. I felt guilty that my forefathers had purposely distributed blankets infected with smallpox to kill off the indigenous population under a rancid deception of benevolence, hundreds of years before. I also felt sadness and the resignation in the tribe present today—a clash of cultures, a clash of civilizations, the conflicts of man.

We ended up in a parking lot with three mumbling old ladies who were not only all over the age of 90, but, bizarrely, were also all named Mary. They only conversed in Navajo, and despite our sophisticated microphones, it was impossible to hear a single word over the cacophony of constantly revving pickup trucks and the pattering sound of stones being scattered by kids doing wheelies on two-stroke dirt bikes, drowning out anything that Mary, Mary, and Mary might have said.

When one of the bikes stalled, giving Lorrie the chance to understand and translate a few words, I knew it was time to go back to the drawing board. We would have to do some proper research in order to find a Native American who could sum up thousands of years of culture in a few words, and looked good and sang and had . . . feathers. According to Lorrie, Mary or Mary or the other Mary had said that if we wanted to find out anything about God, we should *read the Bible; it was all in that book.* I just stared blankly.

"Didn't you know?" Lorrie quizzed me. "Most of the Navajo have converted to Christianity."

Now I understood why they were all called Mary.

I felt a familiar fluttering, as we politely said good-bye to Mary, Mary, and Mary.

Idiot! I berated myself. Did you honestly think you could just bumble around in an SUV across America and actually run into the things you had created in your head, and then film them quickly and succinctly within a short time frame, and without a proper budget?

It was slowly becoming apparent that this film would take a lot longer to make than my naïve, gung-ho Aries mind had projected. And I hadn't even started on the rest of the world yet! *Abandon now, or be imprisoned or broke—or both—for years!* a voice of reason boomed in my head. How right it (I?) was. But just as I was beginning to sink beneath this overwhelming realization, my attention was distracted by a loud yelp from Patrick.

"Shit—shit and double shit!" My first thought was that he'd stepped on a rattlesnake. It was much worse than that. While we had been filming, Patrick had set up camp on the tailgate of a large pickup. "Shit, shit, shit," he repeated.

"What is it?" Colonel Boobs and I chimed in unison.

Patrick pointed to an empty space.

"The pickup has gone."

We stared blankly at him.

"My file with all the release forms was sitting on it!"

There was a momentary pause, then . . . "Shit!" I exclaimed, as the realization dawned. My investment, along with the last three weeks of work, had just disappeared across Tuba City on the back of a pickup truck—without those release forms we would never be able to show the film!

Patrick read my face. "Yes, I know!" His eyes had started popping.

"Shit!" I declared again (too stunned at that moment to notice how my vocabulary seemed to be shrinking in direct proportion to the dire nature of our situation).

"Lorrie—hold the fort!" I yelled as, like the Three Stooges, Patrick, Colonel Boobs, and I immediately dove into the SUV. "What did the truck look like?" I panted.

"It was green," cried Patrick.

"No it wasn't—it was red," corrected Colonel Boobs.

"It wasn't red. It was dark green with mud all over . . ." Patrick argued.

"A tap . . . it had a tap logo thing on the side—*that* was red!" Colonel Boobs exclaimed indignantly. "I'm Bavarian, remember— I don't miss a trick."

"You're right," Patrick agreed. "Plumber's truck! A red and green plumber's truck." We rounded a corner into the main pow-wow event area to see a natural amphitheater-shaped hollow in the desert; and there, distributed like large bees on a sea of honey, were *about 2,000 pickup trucks*. I pulled to a stop.

"Anyone got any ideas?" I calmly asked.

WE HAD ADJOURNED TO THE LOCAL GAS-STATION CAFÉ. The coffee didn't calm Mr. Chou, but I drank it down anyway. The sun was beginning to set as all three of us sat side by side, elbows resting dejectedly on the Formica. For a while we just stared out, saying nothing.

Patrick finally broke the silence.

"I could go back . . . I know where they all are . . . just retrace our steps and get them to sign them all again. I could fly—you know . . ."

We all knew that was an expensive, time-consuming task; and anyway, we had footage of people from all over the place whom we had just *happened upon,* and their addresses were—*on the release forms!*

We ambled out of the café. I felt the same way I'd once felt years before when, while shooting a Bacardi advertising campaign in the Caribbean, I'd left the entire production float of $200,000 in cash in a plastic bag on an outdoor table at a beachfront restaurant in Antigua. I hadn't even noticed it was gone until the next morning when I was getting ready to take a flight to Saint Kitts. I'd returned to the deserted restaurant at sunrise and found the bag with all the money intact on a shelf behind the bar. The gods had been smiling on me that day.

I wondered where they were now.

Then I spotted the image of a faucet on a truck pulling out of the main parking lot onto the highway.

"Guys . . . !" I shouted. "Tell me that isn't a red tap! Come on!"

We dove back into the car and blasted out onto the road, weaving in and out of the cars and pickups being driven by the reservation's population as they started to head home. Soon we caught up to the green and red tap truck . . . and there, believe it or not, on the tailgate was the unmistakable shape of Patrick's file, as if it had been glued in place.

"It's still there! I can't believe it!" Patrick's eyes bulged.

"Step on it, ja!" said Colonel Boobs.

"We'd better catch him before the freeway!" I proclaimed.

I honked and fishtailed, flashing my lights—but the driver obviously didn't have any mirrors or couldn't hear or both, because he just carried on toward the looming freeway access ramp.

"You've gotta get him before the ramp!" Patrick yelled. "The faster he goes—it's gonna—"

Too late! Before Patrick could finish his sentence, the file flew up into the air and landed splat on the highway, scattering pieces of paper everywhere. I watched aghast as, just like a scene out of one of those awful movies in which the robbers' cash falls off a building and all the kids frantically grab armfuls of it, our release forms instantly became airborne. But those pieces of paper weren't worth anything to anyone—except us. I stopped the car in the middle of the highway, blinkers on.

"Boobs, you hold off the cars behind . . . we'll collect!"

I'll never forget that sunset . . . the Colonel holding back the traffic, Patrick and me running all over Route 160, Tuba City, picking up release forms.

Looking at them today, I can't help chuckling when I see the imprint of a faraway pickup's tire.

CHAPTER 4

India

"The best paths are those that are untrodden,
but actually lead somewhere."

— NAPKIN #4

I was feeling more than a little nervous as Patrick and I drove off to LAX on October 21, 2006. All I knew was that we were going to India—beyond that we were essentially traveling blind, and the last time I had gone through this exercise, I had checked in my equipment, never to see it again.

My angst was compounded by the fact that the last few days had been a nightmare. Our arms were sore and swollen from every type of injection you can possibly imagine—cholera, typhoid, tetanus, meningitis, Japanese encephalitis, and hepatitis—all at once. We were taking pills for malaria, and all sorts of other prophylactic paraphernalia that couldn't have been doing my head much good.

We were flying Air India to Delhi, via Frankfurt—coach— and we hadn't had time to recover from our drive back across the States. We couldn't afford to take Colonel Boobs with us on this leg of the trip.

"Come and join me and Mr. Gill in Raipur, in Chhattisgarh," Chandi Duke Heffner had said to me on the phone a few weeks previously, when I was setting up the trip. The adopted daughter of billionaire Doris Duke, Chandi had used her wealth to help humankind in India. She was a philanthropist, but not just a check writer; she was the down-and-dirty, in-the-trenches type who wasn't afraid to roll up her sleeves and help 275,000 impoverished villagers in Uttar Pradesh battle malaria, chikungunya, and an epidemic of tuberculosis, as well as treat their animals to prevent cross-contamination.

Chandi and I had been connected by a mutual friend. All I knew was that Mr. Gill was a very prominent policeman and worked closely with Chandi as a trustee and organizer for her project. "I'll have you picked up at the airport—allow a month of your time." That was all it took. Now we were on our way, and I had no real idea what we were in for.

My superstitious fears of banned carry-on luggage proved unfounded, and we managed to board the flight without incident. I had taken another leap of faith, and now here we were on the plane—with the camera safely stowed in the overhead bin. I sat back in my seat, soaked in sweat, as oversized women in saris brushed past, wafting overwhelming clouds of petunia oil in their wake. I realized it was going to be a very full flight. I pulled out my copy of Dawkins's *The God Delusion* and started to read, elbows tucked in tight against my ribs.

After a change of planes in Frankfurt, we arrived some 25 hours later in New Delhi—at 4 A.M. We walked out of the airport into the hot, muggy air; and I breathed in those familiar Delhi fragrances of wood smoke, smog, and leaded-gas fumes. I was glad to be back. India is one of my favorite countries, and it made my whole body tingle with excitement and adventure.

We drove in an Ambassador taxi to the Imperial Hotel, where American Express Travel had secured us a great deal. I loved this hotel; I had stayed there before. It was like stepping into the past. The service was exceptional, the food was very good, and it brought out the British in me. The walls were covered with exquisite art, most of it from the days of the Raj, and every room was beautifully furnished.

The hotel had been honored just a few weeks prior when George W. Bush had been visiting India and his people had bought out the entire place. But the management was still upset with him. They'd been expecting the President, the First Lady, and a good portion of the White House staff; what they got were 73 Secret Service sniffer dogs and their handlers, who'd had the hotel's staff running around delivering Kibbles and mashed lamb for jet-lagged canines. The manager still hadn't recovered from the insult.

After a nap and a good breakfast on the terrace, it was time to fix a silly mistake. In my rush to leave, I'd neglected to pack properly. I had literally forgotten my trousers, apart from those I wore on the plane. I complained to Patrick that I still felt groggy, and the last thing I wanted to do was run around Delhi shopping. I should have known that Patrick would have the answer.

"I've got just the thing!" he declared triumphantly. An evil grin split his face as he pulled out a package from his pocket. Never one to give up on a quest, Patrick had apparently continued his search for the perfect "driving aid" throughout our entire road trip across America. I eyed him suspiciously, as pictures of the trembling wreck, twitching in the backseat of the car on the I-10 freeway, flooded my memory.

He must have had the same thought. "No, it's okay—it's just ephedrine," he reassured me.

A once-popular over-the-counter cold remedy and decongestant, ephedrine was now a controlled substance in many states— but not, apparently, in Texas, where a delighted Patrick had stocked up on enough of it to keep an entire army moving.

Ninety minutes later I was marching through a bazaar like an overwound toy soldier on steroids. Locals watched in bewilderment as—eyes popping, head snapping from left to right like a Wimbledon umpire counting volleys, and lips smacking in a vain attempt to eke saliva out of dry glands—I strode past stalls piled high with every type of merchandise one could imagine (not to mention a few pieces one couldn't).

"Must have cargo pants . . . gotta be cargo pants somewhere. . . . What about here . . . ? What about there . . . ? Look, Patrick— let's check that one out . . ." I rattled on at machine-gun speed, all traces of jet lag having been chased out of my body by the system-revving, appetite-suppressing, stimulant effects of the ephedrine. No wonder the FDA had banned its use as a dietary supplement!

At one point I could have sworn I heard Patrick reciting Kipling. Since he was walking and talking just as fast as I was, I had little doubt that he had partaken of a "driving aid" or three.

If our arms had flapped any faster, we would have flown. Then I found the stall.

"You got cargoes?" I chomped in the kind vendor's face—so close I could smell the cardamom he'd been chewing. "Cargo pants, you know . . . pockets, lots of pockets. I need lots of pocketsies so I can put things in, good for batteries . . . and lenses and, er, adapters. Oh, and must have buttons—for pickpockets, see . . . ? Gotta be secure. No fuss. Cargo pants? Got any? Yep? Got any?" The man cocked his head to the side and looked at me sympathetically. My diatribe fizzled.

"Perhaps sir would like to come inside?" he offered politely.

"For a moment there I thought you were going to call him 'my precious,'" smirked Patrick.

I bought six pairs, most for $3 each, but I stretched to $5 for the green ones with extra pocketsies. The vendor folded them very well and packed them in a canvas bag while I sipped chai, jiggled my leg, chomped some more, and drummed my fingers. The kind man thought I was mad—and so did I.

"I think I need to swim the Channel," I said to Patrick back at the hotel, but the pool was closed. We had a croquet match instead.

It wasn't easy crawling out of bed the next morning to catch a 5:30 flight to Raipur. I made a mental note to not take ephedrine again (except in dire need), and especially not while trying to purchase cargo pants.

Raipur is situated in the state of Chhattisgarh—a three-hours flight southeast of Delhi. It is off the beaten track and certainly not a tourist destination. It was also under siege by a violent group of insurgents called Naxalites—but we had no idea of that at the time.

As the plane taxied to a stop on the smoldering tarmac, the captain asked us all to remain seated. Seat belts were to remain buckled. I peered out of the scratched plastic inner window to see six police vehicles—jeeps filled with machine-gun-bearing commandos—surrounding the air stairs.

"Something's going on," I whispered to Patrick. There was a cracking, sucking sound as the exit door opened and hot air wafted aboard, immediately followed by four crisp police officers, two of whom had automatic weapons draped over their shoulders. The officers whispered to the steward, who picked up the intercom, cleared his throat, and announced: "Would Mr. Rodger and Mr. Ellis please make themselves known to the cabin staff."

A guttural Scooby-Doo–esque throat burp emanated from Patrick. "I can't remember doing anything out of line," he whispered out of the corner of his mouth.

"Those pills—they're not like *roofies,* are they?" I demanded to know.

"What are roofies?"

"You know, date-rape drugs, where you can't remember stuff the next day."

"Lordy! I hope not . . . what do you think we did?"

"I don't remember much after you knocked Mountbatten's head off with the croquet ball."

"They wouldn't put us in jail for that."

"It might have been valuable . . ."

"Maybe if it was a statue of Gandhi, but not Mountbatten."

"What about the pills, then? If they're legal in Texas, it doesn't mean they're legal here. Where are they?" I spat out.

"Some in my pocket . . . couple of boxes in the camera bag," Patrick confessed guiltily.

"Oh, great!"

"They look like aspirin. Don't worry."

"Mr. Rodger . . . Mr. Ellis—please make yourselves known," blared the voice over the speaker.

We took a deep breath, smiled timidly, and stretched up our hands. The officers with the automatic weapons stood guard as two of their companions marched over to our seats. Then, to our surprise, they broke into wide grins and saluted us.

"Mr. K. P. S. Gill is waiting for you, sir . . . sir. We will carry your hand luggage."

"Oh! Oh, er, yes. Yes, absolutely," I said, as we pulled ourselves together. "Hello, there—yes, er, I'm Peter and this is Patrick."

"We are very honored to have your acquaintance, sirs—most honored."

They shook us warmly by the hand; and to the bewilderment of the other passengers, collected our hand luggage, of which, owing to my previous experience, there was rather a lot—camera case, still-camera case, tape case, lenses, film, computer case, sound case, and so on. Refusing to allow us to carry anything at all, they stumbled along behind us, like two Passepartouts struggling along in the wake of Phileas Fogg in *Around the World in 80 Days,* while we marched down and were ushered into a purring, white Ambassador car with a red flashing light on the roof and bulletproof windows.

To this day, I am amazed by the efficiency of our arrival in Raipur—before we had deplaned, the police had already isolated our checked baggage and loaded it into the back of a jeep. And, mercifully, it was all there!

Officers closed in around us, police jeeps revved, sirens blared . . . and suddenly we were speeding across the tarmac at breakneck speed, through security gates flanked by more saluting officers, and out into the hustle and bustle of Raipur Airport road. Chickens scattered, children stared, whistles blew, and more officers saluted us through red lights on a frenetic journey that only slowed to allow a cow (cows are sacred in India) to cross in front of us, before we zoomed off again.

"So, remind me, who is Mr. Gill again?" Patrick asked me.

Our motorcade burned into police headquarters—a massive compound that was extremely well guarded. Past a blur of parade grounds filled with marching officers, firing ranges, and recreation areas, our convoy sped through bustling police activity into another well-guarded inner enclosure with a sign bearing the words OFFICERS' MESS. We pulled up in a peaceful driveway surrounded by barracks on one side and the single-story "mess" on the other.

Patrick and I were shown to a room on the ground floor that opened out onto the gardens. It was basic, very clean, and smelled strongly of mothballs. Birds chirped everywhere. A ceiling fan circulated warm air around. Although it seemed as if we'd already spent a whole day getting here, it was still only 9 A.M. The officers invited us to make ourselves at home while they went to get our breakfast, after which we would be taken to meet Mr. Gill.

Patrick turned to me with a bemused look on his face. "I thought we were coming to see a lady called Chandi Duke Heffner."

"We are . . . and Mr. Gill," I said.

"But who is Mr. Gill?"

"A friend of Chandi's. She said he was very interesting, and he would be very helpful."

"Did she tell you who he was, or where we were going?"

"Not really."

"Or why there are so many guns everywhere?"

"He fights terrorism and is the former head of the Indian Police Service," I admitted.

"Oh . . . okay . . . jolly good." That made total sense to Patrick.

Breakfast arrived, and we sipped sweet chai to an accompanying choir of parrots.

An hour later we were escorted across the compound to meet our hosts. I had a bottle of 25-year-old Macallan scotch tucked under each arm; Patrick carried a box of Belgian chocolates.

There was a lot of saluting and "Hello, sirs" as we were led to a room in the officers' mess. Our escort rapped politely on the door. We heard a muffled "Come in," and the officer disappeared inside. Patrick and I waited . . . and waited . . . and waited . . . until finally the door squeaked open and we were invited in.

There before us stood a very tall Sikh man sporting a majestic-looking light pink turban; a blue starched shirt; and the most enormous handlebar mustache atop a beard that had been expertly bound, doubled back, and tucked up into the rear of his turban.

Distinguished was far too pedestrian a word to describe Mr. Gill. With his deep-set eyes, and bushy brows that quirked with a contained humor that only the privileged were entitled to experience, he was like a blast from the past. Soft-spoken and modest, he was clearly a man whose word one could depend on. Despite the elevated position he occupied (as we soon came to discover), he exuded an air of toughness, yet was without arrogance. I later learned he was one of the most well-read and informed men I had ever met. Beside him, looking equally magnificent, stood a smiling, elfin lady immaculately dressed in an embroidered silk sari. Mr. Gill and Chandi welcomed us in.

I felt a little awkward at first, not knowing quite what to make of our hosts. With his economical way with words and inscrutable manner of silent observation, there was little doubt that Mr. Gill had perfected the art of intimidation.

In my nervousness, I found myself talking a little too much to fill in the gaps.

By contrast, Chandi, a wonderful communicator, was expert at putting people at ease; her conversation was always stimulating and entertaining. It wasn't until later when I'd gotten to know him better that I discovered that Mr. Gill was a truly funny man, with a sense of humor so dry that it verged on combustible. Despite that, I addressed him as "sir," because I always felt as if I was back at school in his presence. It was immediately clear that Chandi and Mr. Gill, bound by a professional common goal to make the world a better place, were 150 percent dedicated to their cause.

And bringing single-malt scotch with us could not have gone down better, since it immediately established the fact that Mr. Gill and I had something in common. As Chandi was a teetotaler, Mr. Gill was very happy with two liters of the "golden nectar" instead of one.

We hadn't been in the room very long when Mr. Gill suddenly pronounced, "So let's go. Are you ready?"

It was a sign of things to come.

Fortunately, I'd had the foresight to assemble the camera after breakfast, just in case we had to shoot something fast. The one thing I learned very quickly was to never keep Mr. Gill waiting!

The motorcade started up. There were seven vehicles: two jeeps of armed officers in the front, the white Ambassador with the bulletproof windows and red flashing light on the roof (which I soon learned was Mr. Gill's special vehicle), an SUV for us, and three chase vehicles carrying commandos with machine guns taking up the rear. I had absolutely no idea where we were going or what we were doing. Our convoy simply took off, like bats out of hell, sirens blaring again.

So why the guns? We soon found out that Mr. K. P. S. Gill, former director of the Indian Police Service (the Indian equivalent of chief of the CIA), was the chairman of the largest antiterrorism think tank in the world—the South Asia Terrorism Portal. Although semiretired, Mr. Gill is the first person the Indian state governments pull in when problems arise. He was responsible for eradicating terrorism in Assam, Punjab, and Gujarat; and was now here in Chhattisgarh to rid the rural area of the terrorism of the Naxalites—a Maoist extremist group that was dedicated to undermining the political infrastructure of India. The Naxalites were going from village to village, cutting off people's heads and arms, and saying, "Join us or the same will happen to you." The situation had become so bad the previous spring that the local police forces in the area had fled, leaving the Naxalites free to commit their atrocities unchecked, until the BJP (Bharatiya Janata Party) government had brought Mr. Gill in to stamp out the problem. He was now known locally as the *Peacemaker.*

It felt a bit strange to be in a foreign land, miles from anywhere, in a region that was not only without any tourist hotels, but also devoid of all *foreigner* infrastructure, under the auspices of a couple of people I'd never met before. But it felt very good, too, to have Mr. Gill and Chandi pulling out every stop to help us.

We drove through village after village. Whenever we stopped, we were warned to stay in our vehicles until the area had been secured. I later found out that parties had been sent ahead of us to clear the surrounding fields of possible snipers. Once we had the all clear, I was told I could film anything I wanted to, so we just picked up the camera and went around asking villagers, "What is God?"

Suddenly, halfway through an interview, we were summoned back to the vehicles by wide-eyed officers with a sharp: "Mr. Gill is ready to leave!" (Translation: *if you value your life, do not keep Mr. Gill waiting!*)

After driving for about 90 minutes, we arrived at Champaran Temple, where Mr. Gill was greeted like royalty. The inhabitants were so happy to have his help; he was a hero figure to them. Striding through the temple with his bodyguards and escort, he cut a fine figure with his large stature and pink turban. Music came from everywhere . . . along with bells; chanting; and children squealing for Mr. Gill's autograph, with their parents watching proudly, crying for joy. So many of these people's fates were in his hands—it was the stuff of folklore, and he carried it off very well.

The Indian people are by far the most universally polite group of human beings you could ever meet. Yes, we all know about the tourist areas where you get swarmed by children screaming for baksheesh (money), and horror stories of poverty-stricken kids being mutilated by evil Fagin-esque heads of begging teams—or even their own parents—in order to elicit pity and therefore bigger handouts. But out here, off the beaten track, where tourism doesn't yet exist, there was none of that—just honest and open kindness. Of course, that might have had something to do with the fact that we were traveling with 35 heavily armed commandos, but you really can't fake an earnest look of respect; a sincere "Pleasure to have your acquaintance"; or a hospitality that's genuinely warm, gracious, and openhearted.

As holy men, called *sadhus,* with long beards and intense, sparkling eyes, glided by in strange garb, it struck me that India is the only place where I've found colors that aren't in the rainbow and which you can still see when you close your eyes. Their vibrancy is infused by the spirit of the people you encounter and listen to in song and conversation.

Shooting conditions were hard for me, what with having to constantly alter sound levels, compensate for the contrast between sunlight and shade, and film in uncontrollable environments filled with visual gems. *If only I could catch it all . . . if only the throngs would part . . . if only I were closer.* The other problem, of course, was that Patrick and I were also considered Very Important People; and thus everyone wanted to bless us, cover us with silk scarves, and load offerings of musk and nuts on us—so suddenly we, too, became subject matter and not just flies on the wall. It's not easy to shoot a ceremony when you're part of it. Finally, we were whisked away to private, quiet quarters; and the dignitaries of the temple were ushered in so that I could interview them.

I loved having Mr. Gill as a character in the film. He was so charismatic. One of the reasons for his success was that he was the only person who had managed to open a dialogue between the various religions in India. He had won the confidence of everyone—Christians, Muslims, Sikhs, Hindus, Jains. They all felt comfortable consulting him for advice. He had managed to break down the boundaries of religion and use the results to combat terrorism. I wished to break down the boundaries of religion in my film to promote understanding, tolerance, and world peace— so, for me, this was a match made in heaven.

Mr. Gill made no secret of the fact that the success of his anti-terrorism strategy lay in his ability to speak the same language as his adversaries—in short, he had no compunction about fighting violence with violence. Indeed, it was *the only way* to fight terror-ism, he insisted, despite the fact that some of the decisions he had to make pained him to the core.

That evening after a dinner of chapatis and dal, Mr. Gill opened one of the Macallans; and we talked way into the night about politics, religion, terrorism, and faith. The distant sound of gunfire punctuating our conversation brought home the serious-ness of Mr. Gill's mission in these parts.

Walking back to our quarters, I quickly checked in with Sou-maya on my cell. While I was on the line, there was a particularly loud exchange of fire out beyond our highly fortified enclave.

"What's that noise?" she asked.

"We're in India. You know how they love fireworks here," I replied. *Boom!* "Lots of pageantry." I could tell that my wife didn't believe me.

What a fascinating day it's been, I thought, as I drifted off to sleep that night to the sounds of distant gunfire and the rhythmic whir of the pre–World War II ceiling fan.

SINCE MR. GILL HAD TERRORISTS TO DEAL WITH the next day, he left us in the capable hands of Ragveer Singh, the chief of security for the city of Raipur.

Whatever we wanted to happen—could happen. A serious and deeply religious 52-year-old Sikh with a kind heart and high mor-als, Ragveer managed to balance his faith in humanity and in God with his professional responsibilities, in an elegant, subtle man-ner. I suspected that, to begin with, he felt a bit miffed at having to babysit a couple of crazy foreign filmmakers, but after spending some time together, he really started to "get" what we were trying to do with the film. We quickly became very good friends.

Having the head of security for the region as our location manager and *chief fixer* proved very beneficial. Nowhere else in the world could you turn up at a location, cast your movie, cordon off the set, and shoot for several hours without navigating your way through a mountain of prior planning, paperwork, permits, and pain. But with Ragveer, that's exactly what happened. And it couldn't have been more perfect.

With a security unit of armed officers in tow, Ragveer took us to a temple called Dudha Dhari, where we found dozens of pilgrims, all of whom were ascetically perfect for the shots we were hoping to capture. With Patrick as soundman, the bodyguards as grips (the muscle on a film set), Ragveer as our interpreter, and perfect lighting conditions to boot, we thought we had found filmmaker's heaven.

Then we ran into translation issues with the complicated parables and storytelling. Everything was so long-winded that it rendered most of the interviews unusable, so the day's filming became more cement than bricks, more color than substance; the footage was only as good as it looked and would have to support the narrative from another place. But I needed that kind of footage as much as the interviews themselves, and the more visual it was, the better—and these pilgrims were visually impressive.

To explain my philosophy as a filmmaker, I use the analogy of the surface of a pond. You see the reflection (the obvious message of the film), but at the same time you can perceive what lies beneath the water. The trick is to create—through shots, editing, and music—that layering so that you spin the audience away on a journey that is rich and filled with the essence that supports what's being said. I didn't want to make just another wobbly camera, home-video-looking documentary. I wanted to create a visual odyssey.

And with Ragveer, we could move where we wanted, when we wanted. I hoped to shoot Indian life, the layers beneath the pond—portraits, rickshaws, cows on the street, markets, faces, children, street signs, food, a smile, a hand, a pat on the shoulder, sadhus and mystics, and the evening light that graces the space—to bind the stories and the narrative of the film together.

Flanked by one of the bodyguards, Grippy Grip (so named by us because he was exceptionally good at his newly found vocation), I'd fly the camera through the streets, over cats, pigs, dogs, and cows; commandeer a rickshaw; and film the late-afternoon commute, with horns blaring, children giggling, and sari-clad moms ushering their offspring home from school. What I particularly *loved* about this place was that we were so far removed from the beaten track that I had no problems trying to frame out backpackers and white people, because there weren't any. This was pure India, India as it was and India as it should be: unspoiled, respectful, undiluted; uncorrupted by euro, pound, dollar, and yen.

But I also had to remember that I was in a privileged position. Grippy Grip was in plain clothes, and at one point Ragveer was off to the side. Patrick was behind me when a couple of police officers, on their beat, marched up to him.

"What are you doing? Who are you? Papers, please!" They were extremely menacing, hands clasping guns . . . pretty much what you would expect anywhere if shooting wild with a big, professional-looking camera.

But Patrick just pointed toward Ragveer and said, "We're with him."

I have never seen anyone melt so fast as those two uniformed officers. "Ah, okay, yes, absolutely . . ." Ragveer approached, and they snapped to attention, heels clicking. "Sir, yes—yes, sir—absolutely, sir." I soon had them on traffic control so I could get right up to the wheels of the rickshaws without getting run over.

We worked long into the night—blurred colors, coupled with the sounds of busyness, people like ants—an Indian night in a hot city, minds and souls going about their after-hours chores, full of buzz, energy, and lots of smiles.

"Do you think we're absolutely barking mad?" I asked Patrick later that evening as we tried to spot stars through a smog-laden sky.

"No . . . I think *you* are barking mad." He chortled.

At least there was no gunfire that night.

—⊘—

CHAPTER 5

Exploring Raipur

"It isn't until you shake and pound it about,
that milk will turn into butter."

— NAPKIN #5

I wanted to film a number of children of different religions and find out their views on God. Ragveer relished this task and found a school in Raipur—St. Paul's Church Higher Secondary School. Although the school was Christian, the children came from all sorts of religious backgrounds—Jains, Hindus, Muslims, Christians, Sikhs, and students from a number of religions with unpronounceable names.

Sirens wailing, our convoy of police vehicles skidded to a stop in front of the school's office. Ragveer politely asked to see the principal, who immediately received us in a room with pre–World War I ceiling fans, which scraped and hiccupped a wheezy existence but produced very little draft. Several cups of hot sweet chai and a lengthy conversation in English later, the principal, who was a very proper Indian lady with smiling eyes and a motherly face, was 100 percent on board. All the children would be required to write one sentence answering the question "What is God?" for their homework that night, and we were to return the following morning at 7 sharp to film their answers. (I shuddered to think how long it would take to organize something like that in the U.S.)

Still, it was no easy task. There must have been about 600 students aged 13 to 18 gathered in the school yard the following morning. It was very hot, yet they all looked fresh in starched blue and white uniforms. St. Paul's was coeducational, and there was an abundance of laughter and tomfoolery, but I don't think I've ever seen such an impeccably behaved bunch of children.

The teachers had them well trained. In step, they walked single file across the dusty, dry quad to congregate under an awning of corrugated iron that provided a stark contrast to the pillared, colonial architecture of the school's main building. They ignored Patrick, me, and the camera, which was a blessing, as that freed me up to get in really close so that I could capture their expressions as they chanted group prayers in English and Hindi.

The principal helped organize the interviews; and Patrick, who'd had a previous life running a school for handicapped children in England, put on his old headmaster's voice and, in a very British way, quickly had the whole situation under control. My idea was to lock off the camera (which means putting it on the tripod and making sure nobody touched it) with a great composition in frame. The background wouldn't change; then I'd have kids of varying shapes and sizes pop up in front of the lens and say their lines. Later, I would cut the scene together to provide a montage of ideas and expressions from a series of different souls, all dressed identically, but echoing different beliefs, reflective of their different religions, which would appear randomly against the fixed backdrop.

We lined the kids up in an orderly fashion; marked their position in chalk on the flagstones, eroded by the passage of many children's feet; and marched them in one by one, like a factory line, to speak from their hearts. It was remarkably efficient, worked like a dream, and the kids enjoyed it.

"What is God?" I asked.

"God is wonderful."

"He is amazing."

"He has given us many things."

"He has created the atmosphere, nature . . ."

". . . trees, mountains . . ."

". . . water . . . and air . . ."

". . . teachers . . . our parents."

"We, the human beings, are the most loveliest creatures of God in the world."

"I see God in myself."

". . . and I feel God in my heart."

"He is the Almighty. He is present everywhere."

"But when we disobey Him, He gives us punishment."

"I am a Christian."

"My religion is Muslim."

"I am a Hindu."

"Every religion has many names for God."

"But I think that God is only one."

"And we can say in different names."

The principal then chimed in: "That is the duty of we grown-ups, to teach the students the meaning of the Lord Almighty. God has not created religions . . . He has created humans."

"I am a Muslim," said a young girl.

"And I am a Hindu," said another.

"I believe that there is one God."

"I also believe that there is one God."

"Trust God, do good things, help others, love your neighbor," added the principal. "And these are the things through which we can approach God."

I enjoyed the school's positive and progressive attitude of unity. It felt so important to express this display of tolerance toward different beliefs. I knew at that moment, finally, I had something that would make it into the film.

A whistle blew . . . it was recess time. The staff excused themselves to go and have a chai break. I grabbed the camera to shoot some establishing shots, and the moment the adults disappeared, the children switched personalities. Suddenly, the neat and orderly *model* children we'd been filming turned into little rascals. It was a real-life *Lord of the Flies* moment—there were whoops of joy from cheeky boys who were climbing on top of one another, making human pyramids to wage war. There was so much giggling and excitement that I thought someone had slipped something into the school drinking fountains. Soon there was just a sea of faces, hands, and expressions as they rushed toward me, clambering over each other to present popping eyeballs to the lens.

I glanced over to see Patrick puffing his chest out and stretching his body upward in an effort to look more authoritative.

"Order, children, order!" he was exclaiming in his best John Cleese voice.

Of course, the kids ignored him. I was having such fun; I was no help at all. Crouching down, I pointed the camera up at the children surrounding me and spun it around in an effort to capture the kaleidoscopic frenzy of smiling expressions—humanity molded into one. Then a whistle blew, and just as if someone had thrown a switch, the clamor of voices abruptly ceased as, with lightning speed, the children instantly went back into their orderly lines and the conveyor belt started up again, carrying them off to their next lessons.

"COWS REPRESENT SACRIFICE. Without them, there can be no sacrifice. Cows are guileless in their behavior, and from them flow sacrifice and milk and curds and butter. Hence cows are sacred," says Bhishma, one of the strongest characters in the Hindu scripture the *Mahabharata*.

Bhishma also observes that the cow acts as a surrogate mother by providing milk to human beings for their entire lives. So, to Hindus, this animal is truly the mother of the world. India had offered to take in millions of cows destined for slaughter in Britain as a result of the mad-cow-disease crisis in 1996.

Ragveer had taken us on a mission. He'd been doing a lot of thinking about the project and wanted to show us some really holy cows. Not just ordinary holy cows, but ones that were so holy that they had five, sometimes even seven, legs. We'd been driving around Raipur for several hours in search of these nomadic herds that belonged to a group of sadhus who supposedly used the sacred cows' mystic powers to see into the future. However, it was getting late, Patrick and I were tired, and privately we were more inclined to believe that if there were such a thing as seven-legged cows, it was more likely to be a result of some weird mutation of mad-cow disease.

Suddenly Ragveer barked an order. The driver slammed on the brakes. The two police vehicles behind almost careened into us, and then we took off at breakneck speed across a field. We pulled up in front of a bright red mobile shrine mounted behind a motorcycle. There were all sorts of paintings, statues of deities, and effigies on the contraption; and beside it stood a wonderfully charismatic sadhu, also dressed in red. He beamed a toothless grin. Ragveer jumped out and conversed at length with him.

And then I heard excited voices. A group of holy men could be seen approaching. The red-garbed toothless sadhu gesticulated with glee. Ragveer rushed over in excitement. It was *a holy cow!* He had found them after all. I checked my camera; made sure there was enough power, tape space, and drive space; and quickly monitored the settings—I didn't want to miss this moment. My heart started racing. The group was almost upon us. Ragveer marched over to them and quickly signaled for me to follow. I was already shooting as I walked toward them as smoothly as I could. The colorful crowd parted to reveal . . . a holy many-legged cow.

It was a young cow, just north of calf, about four feet high at the shoulder. I stood there, stunned, as I looked through the lens and counted . . . one, two, three, four very normal-looking cow legs. I looked up at Ragveer, who, eyes wide and with both hands raised, was mouthing, *Wait!*

The holy men turned the cow around, and there, dangling from its left shoulder, were *two extra legs!*—well, leg-like appendages. About two and a half feet long, complete with hooves at the end, they hung down, absolutely limp, flapping uselessly against the cow's flank. They didn't appear to bother the cow, who seemed rather to be reveling in the attention.

"This is a six-legged cow, Mr. Peter! Very, very holy cow, this one, isn't it?" Ragveer pointed out excitedly. It was a bizarre sight. "Would you like to shake its leg?" he asked. "It's okay, you can. Very good luck."

After I had finished filming the cow, I put down the camera and picked up a hoof. The cow mooed. It was a strange sensation.

"Very holy cow. Very holy cow." Ragveer translated the sadhus' repeated mutterings.

I interviewed the red-garbed toothless sadhu. It was a protracted interview; it went on . . . and on . . . and on . . . and didn't make any sense to me. I couldn't understand how one question ("What is God?") could prompt an hour-long diatribe. I knew, of course, that it is a deeply layered question that's been asked for thousands of years, but this particular answer just . . . kept on coming. Finally, the sadhu stopped speaking, and Ragveer's gallant translation ended.

Smacking his lips, the sadhu fished around in the mobile shrine and pulled out a beautiful conch shell. He held it high and blew a melancholic cry that echoed across the fields, which was then echoed back to us by a somewhat higher-pitched response from somewhere far off in the distance. The sadhu stopped, stared straight into the lens, and smiled.

I cleared my throat and plucked up the courage to ask another question. Since Ragveer had said that the sadhu was a fortune-teller who gained his powers from many-legged cows, I simply had to ask: what did the future hold in store for the film I was making? Anticipating another lengthy response, I was shocked when the sadhu uttered one very concise sentence, delivered with absolute conviction, and then abruptly stopped speaking.

I looked at Ragveer, who obediently translated. But what he said was not what I wanted to hear at all.

"Is—is that it?" I stuttered.

The man did the classic Indian lateral shake of the head that stands for "yes."

Another shrill sound rent the air. We turned our heads to see a dusty mass moving across the fields in our direction. The orange-red disk of the sun was sinking into the ubiquitous Indian smog that hovered just above the horizon. I swung the camera around, just in time to capture on film the sight that was coming into view.

Squinting through a long lens, I watched the mass begin to separate into individual shapes.

"Well, are they centipedes or cows?" inquired Patrick.

"Somewhere between the two," I muttered, as my lens began to zoom in on the extra limbs flapping against the flanks of each approaching blob. Some had one, some had two, and some even had *three* extra limbs! *It's true!* I thought incredulously, as I prepared myself to meet my first seven-legged cow.

As the sun silently disappeared behind a distant line of frangipani tress, the sound of Ragveer's voice, translating the sadhu's prediction, echoed in my ears.

"The film will take a long, long time and will deplete all your resources," he had said, "but if you are patient, it will be worth it in the end."

"Holy cow! Very holy cow," muttered Ragveer under his breath.

CHAPTER 6

Adventures Around Chhattisgarh

●

"The best way to find a leak in the roof is to wait until it rains."

— NAPKIN #6

I was working on my computer in our living quarters when my attention was diverted by a huge commotion outside. Ragveer was barking orders, officers were scrambling to attention, and a convoy of police vehicles was tearing into the circular driveway. I poked my head out the door; it was like a military exercise.

A couple of senior members of Ragveer's staff rushed over to announce that we would be leaving in ten minutes sharp, and we were to pack for a few days.

"Patrick!" I called out. He'd been off exploring the compound.

"Something's going on," he remarked, as he came ambling toward me.

"Yep! We're leaving in nine minutes—with everything."

"What?"

"Moving out."

"Oh Lordy!"

I was halfway through a download; it still had eight minutes to run—and it is *not* a good idea to abort the transfer of valuable footage. I scooped up the equipment I'd been in the process of cleaning, shoved my clothes in my bag, and exchanged my sweat-soaked T-shirt for a clean one. The download-progress bar was still creeping across the computer screen.

"Sir, we're ready to load your baggage." A young policeman popped his head around the door, proving yet again that when they said ten minutes, they really meant seven.

Help! Nothing for it but to abort the download.

I slammed the computer closed and slid it into its case. Panting, disheveled, and suddenly extremely thirsty, we rushed outside, where 16 vehicles and approximately 50 commandos were waiting for us. Mr. Gill's white Ambassador was in front of the mess, door open, with a police officer standing to attention. Our SUV was behind. As always, I filmed the activity.

Mr. Gill's ever-present personal bodyguard was already exiting the building, which meant that we would be leaving—*right now!*

Mr. Gill and Chandi appeared, both dressed completely in white.

"We are going on an excursion north," Mr. Gill advised me.

". . . into insurgent territory," added Chandi, as they both disappeared into the Ambassador.

Our driver was smiling at us nervously, indicating that it was definitely time to jump into the SUV.

"I think we can safely deduce from this that at any given time we have to be ready to rock-and-roll with just a five-minute warning, don't you think?" remarked Patrick as we sank back into the seats.

"Better make that three," I added.

The journey lasted several days and was fascinating. I just let go and allowed circumstances to take their course. There was no knowing what would happen next or where we were going. We were surrounded by so much security that we were actually more restricted than free. But it was worth it; Mr. Gill took us to some amazing places and introduced us to experiences that few people are fortunate enough to have in life.

I was unsure what this had to do with our mission of asking people, "What is God?" but the more I got to know Mr. Gill, the more I realized not only how much I had to learn, but also how well he was preparing me to execute my plan. Not for the first time, I felt like Frodo. Mr. Gill was rapidly becoming Gandalf, Patrick was Samwise Gamgee, and the film was the Ring. I just hoped I wouldn't be called upon to throw it into the fires of Mordor.

At every stopping place—usually the police headquarters of the major cities in Chhattisgarh—the routine was the same: The most senior officers would line up in their best-pressed uniforms, heels clicked to attention, batons held stiffly under their arms. Mr. Gill and Chandi would get out of the Ambassador, flanked by bodyguards. The commandos would fan out before us, scanning the bushes in case there were any Naxalite snipers hiding out, waiting to get off a shot, and then Mr. Gill would inspect the officers. Patrick and I would trot along behind, into the inner sanctum of police HQ, where we would all politely sip tea and munch on biscuits imported from England. Mr. Gill would ask questions of the commanding officers, and everyone in the room would introduce themselves (including us) with a few words about what we were doing there. It soon became apparent that Mr. Gill had an uncanny knack both for remembering the tiniest details about his officers' lives and for putting them at ease.

"And Sergeant Boparai, how is Radha?" he asked.

"She's doing very well now, sir, after the surgery—thank you, sir."

"I hope the encounter with the cobra didn't upset her sensibilities."

"She was very lucky, sir. It was a glancing blow. She hobbled around for a little bit, sir. It was very difficult for her to get her bearings. And of course, she wouldn't venture outside again."

I imagined a plump officer's wife in a colorful sari, standing in a darkened room, staring out the window at the barrack gardens with a petrified frown.

"I imagine she probably navigated her way around the house in circles."

"It was harder than that for her, sir."

"How so?" Mr. Gill inquired with genuine concern.

"It became a problem of equilibrium, sir. Every time she tried to drink her milk . . . she would end up in it!"

Everyone laughed heartily. Especially me, when I realized that Radha was the officer's three-legged pet cat, and not his wife. "Poor, poor Radha. She doesn't know what has hit her, sir," the officer said, shaking his head.

"No, no, Sergeant Boparai. You should say, 'Poor, poor, *poor* Radha.'"

"Sir?" The sergeant looked confused.

"Because she is a cat . . . with three paws!"

The room erupted into laughter. Officers who just moments before had been terrified to the core at the thought of meeting the "Peacemaker" were now rocking backward and forward on their heels, guffawing. That was just one of the many gifts of which Mr. Gill was a master.

I WAS BROUGHT UP ANGLICAN. We lived in a beautiful village called Smarden, situated in the Weald of Kent in southern England between Dover and London. It was very reminiscent of the Shire from *The Lord of the Rings* (one of my favorite reading experiences)—without the Halflings, the wizards, and the underground houses, although it did boast many above-the-ground Elizabethan buildings made of wattle, daub, and brick.

I remember cracking the ice in the little sink in my room in order to splash my face with water on many a freezing winter morning. We lived in woolly sweaters, and the river Beult would burst its banks and flood the house at least once every two years, until the council put in a magic pump across the road. But the world of Bilbo and Frodo Baggins wasn't far from the world of my childhood—climbing trees and setting off bombs on Guy Fawkes night to scare Margery Philpot as she wobbled home on her bicycle after too many Biddenden ciders at the local tavern.

I liked the sense of community that revolved around our church, which had Norman architecture and boasted the widest unpillared nave in southern England. In church, we always sat on the same pew. I can still recall the patterns of grain in the wood— I remember the knot that looked like an eye staring at me. I remember the smell of the polish—"Mrs. Drury's elbow grease," we used to call it. I remember it all because I spent hours studying those lines and smelling the beeswax as the vicar chortled on, as hymns were sung and prayers were whispered from bowed heads. My father told me that if I looked behind me, my head would be bitten off by a crocodile. Naturally I believed him, although I couldn't understand where the crocodile lived at night. I presumed it feasted on all the little children who couldn't resist peeking back, because the congregation was clearly shrinking week by week. It never occurred to me that it might be due to changing times.

Of course, I never actually saw the crocodile, because I didn't want to lose my head. Instead, I would sit studying the framework of the roof, which I imagined to be an upturned ship, and fantasized about turning it upright and sailing away on a great adventure, then returning years later as a wiser man. I became obsessed with those dreams.

And now here I was, 30 years later, taking part in a real-life adventure in a foreign land, listening to a powerful man who saved lives by using violence against violence, talking about a cat with three paws. I sometimes wonder whether I should have peeked back to see if the crocodile was really there.

I drifted away from religion as I grew up. I loved the psalms, the rituals, and Mrs. Randolf's soprano performances, which were the same every week. But I couldn't buy into the fact that Jesus was the Son of God—literally—born from a virgin. It just didn't make any sense to me, whichever way it was spun. I couldn't bear the lie about Father Christmas. The truth of that was a great disappointment in my life.

What I loved was the music, and the feeling of being able to breathe when the service was over as I stepped out into a blustery morning and ran along the river to find a tree I hadn't yet climbed, while my parents sipped sherry with the Browns and talked about the good old days and how life would never be the same again.

I liked the way my childhood, my church, and my community taught me to think of others and gave me a code, a structure upon which I could hang my life when things got wobbly at the knees. I liked the lesson of loyalty and how that can give you strength, knowing that there are people out there somewhere who have as much compassion as I was taught to have. Can you teach compassion? Damn right you can.

So when Mr. Gill would steal us away from police headquarters, drill sergeants, tea, biscuits, and talk of terrorism and take us to places of worship, I found myself remembering and feeling some of those same sensations I'd experienced as a child. It was a different beast. There was no smell of beeswax and Mrs. Drury's elbow grease. There were new delights—of ritual, of space, of chanting and incense—that would hit you in the heart.

I'll never forget the temple of Chandri Hasni in Ratanpur. It was one of the most important in the country—certainly in Chhattisgarh. I attended Sandhya-Aarti, a daily service to give thanks to God for a good day, ask for a good sleep, and pray for a good tomorrow. The priest was young and busy. He chanted around the inner sanctum where the deities were housed, lighting incense and flitting about. The congregation answered his calls until the chanting became hypnotic and started to spin me away.

I noticed that half the worshippers were made up of the commandos, in stocking feet, their eyes glistening, automatic weapons slung over their backs to free their hands so they could pray or clap the rhythm. Strings of flowers were draped over their shoulders, plucked from the temple gardens. The colorful petals smelled fresh and sparkled in the light from naked flames.

And then the priest led a procession with candles held high. The chanting became more pronounced as he paraded us through the temple, making offerings with the flames to effigies of goddesses; Rama, Sita, and Lakshmana; and intricate paintings outside. The members of the congregation were as one—moving like a flock of birds, the mantra intoxicating, building in volume and rhythm until, after half an hour of singing, the prayer had been cast. Then the congregation broke up and the devoted went busily on their way, like we used to do back home, stepping between the gravestones in Smarden, wondering if it was going to rain.

"WHAT IS GOD, MR. GILL?" I asked over dinner that night.

"Well, I can't tell you what God is, but I can tell you that it's something I believe in."

"How can you believe in something when you don't know what it is?" I asked.

"When you think of God and put it into words that we can understand and with which we communicate with one another, we are then trying to describe God in human terms. And my feeling is that God is beyond any human term, any word, or any vocabulary that we can devise. So you cannot describe God."

"If you pray to Him and you believe in Him, but you can't describe what it is you are praying to, how is that ravine crossed?" I countered.

"That ravine is crossed through some internal experience. If you look at Sikhism, the religion to which I belong, the emphasis is on God being within you, and you have to find Him within yourself. If you follow certain paths, you will experience Him or get a glimpse of what He is all about, and that is about it!"

"Is God, therefore, a power?"

"The word *power* has so many implications. God is something I would say that *sustains* the universe—that permeates the universe and everything that is within the universe. And that sustaining power, if you want to call it such—the organizing power, the ordering power, the power that, shall we say, brings about a certain symmetry in the chaos we perceive the world to be in—is God."

THERE WAS SOMETHING IN THE AIR THE NEXT DAY. Mr. Gill wanted to introduce us to Maharaja Ram Chandra Singh, who lived in a massive palace in Korea (not the country, but a region of Chhattisgarh), and we were due to leave after breakfast.

Patrick had already almost met his maker before breakfast. I'd wanted to get shots of the police stables, which housed beautiful thoroughbreds that were exercised on the parade ground at dawn. So we'd commandeered an open police jeep from which to shoot, and a driver who drove like Speedy Gonzales. Above the entrance to the officers' mess was a concrete awning that kept out the hot sun. Patrick had been standing up in the back of the jeep, shooting the B camera as we returned to base. I remember looking up at him—and seeing that he was blissfully unaware of the fast-approaching concrete structure behind him. Suddenly everything went into slow motion . . . *"Duck! Duck!"* I screamed. Patrick slumped down into the jeep literally *seconds* before the concrete awning would have decapitated him.

"That was rather close," he said.

"I'm glad it was duck—not grouse," I quipped, although I was still shivering at the thought of what could have happened.

I mentioned the *near demise* of Patrick to Mr. Gill over breakfast. He stared at me from under those bushy eyebrows for a good few seconds. It was unnerving. When he finally spoke, his tone was the most serious I had ever heard him. "Life is full of moments that can change its direction when you least expect them," he said. "The lesson here is that we must all keep our eyes more open." How right he was. Patrick's close call was an omen of things to come.

We left after breakfast. We couldn't help noticing that our motorcade had increased yet again in size.

Snake country was how Chandi described it—and she wasn't referring to cobras. I used the time on the journey north to update my diary on my laptop, which is something of an acquired skill when you're driving on Indian roads. Thank God for spell-check.

We stopped for lunch at the guesthouse attached to a coal mine, where there was even more security. Mr. Gill disappeared for at least an hour with some very stern-looking senior police officers. Since we weren't invited, Chandi, Patrick, and I amused ourselves telling silly stories of past adventures, while sipping tea in the gardens, wondering what was going on.

Still more police vehicles arrived, and then off we went again. But instead of continuing north, we doubled back and headed in a southerly direction. Our convoy had now grown to at least 25 vehicles. It started to rain. Since Chandi was traveling in the white Ambassador, Patrick and I only had each other to answer our questions.

"What do you think is going on?" I asked.

"I have absolutely no idea," he shrugged.

WHEN YOU'RE ON THE ROAD BEHIND A CAMERA, there is a false sense of security, a foolish bravado that permeates your psyche, as if having the lens in front of you provides some kind of defense shield, like on the *Millennium Falcon* in *Star Wars*—which of course it is not. I call this *photojournalist syndrome*. I remember talking at length about it with my father, who had been in every theater of World War II (apart from the South Pacific) as a photojournalist for *Life* magazine.

"It's only luck that can save you, not the lens," he would say. In 1943 in Italy, when photographing the battles between the Germans and the Italians (who had just switched sides), my father had taken up a position in a cave in Mignano that he thought provided the safest vantage point overlooking a valley where he could safely shoot the action. Each morning, he'd get up before dawn to travel to the cave, where he'd spend the entire day waiting, only to return to camp in the relative safety of nightfall.

A week of this routine had already passed when one day he realized he'd forgotten his packed lunch. He spent several long minutes trying to work out whether he should risk the exposed daylight drive back to base to retrieve his lunch, or simply wait it out. His hunger got to him, so he had made the trip. When he returned to the cave, he found that it didn't exist anymore. A stray shell had scored a direct hit on his safe haven. I'd often thought about the fact that, without my father's insatiable appetite, I wouldn't be here.

A few years later, photojournalist syndrome, or bad luck, terminated the lives of his three best friends and colleagues.

In 1947 my father had founded the acclaimed photo agency Magnum Photos with Henri Cartier-Bresson, David (Chim) Seymour, and Robert Capa. It was to become the most important shift in photojournalism, when photographers, for the first time, were to control the copyright and marketing of their stories to the big newspapers and magazines—which at that time, pretelevision, were the main source of news. They were heady days in a new postwar world and the crème de la crème of photographers flocked to join their ranks to build what would become the most respected photo agency in the world—and one that is still around today.

But Magnum's legacy wasn't without sweat, pain, and death: Robert Capa stepped on a land mine in Indochina in 1954; acclaimed photojournalist Werner Bischof's car ran off a mountain road in the Andes in the same year; and David (Chim) Seymour was killed by Egyptian machine-gun fire while covering the armistice of the Suez War in 1956.

Of course, the young Magnum photographers had always known they were putting themselves at great risk, but at the same time there also was a feeling of invincibility among them. It was very hard on my father; the loss of his three best friends had exposed the unequivocal truth that we are not indestructible.

EARLIER THAT MORNING AS WE HAD BEEN TRAVELING north to Korea, not far from the coal mine where we would later stop for lunch, a little boy had remarked to his father that he'd seen some strange activity in a nearby ditch. The father had talked about it in his village, and because Mr. Gill's intelligence network had tentacles right across the state, this information wasn't missed. A police officer had been dispatched to investigate, and they had uncovered a complex Naxalite plot to assassinate Mr. Gill and everyone traveling with him—including Chandi, the commandos, Patrick, and me! Twenty-three roadside IEDs had been planted along our route with the intention of blowing our entire motorcade away. This was why we had made a 200-mile detour to get to Korea.

Patrick and I didn't discover this until a couple of years later. People often ask me if we were in any kind of danger while making this film. My answer is simple: *Yes, all the time.* But we were never aware of it—the bliss of ignorance.

The seriousness of the situation was further emphasized while I was writing this very book. On April 6, 2010, 76 members of the CRPF (Central Reserve Police Force) were massacred by IEDs and gunfire in the thick forests of Mukrana in the Dantewada district of Chhattisgarh. It was the greatest loss of life sustained by the Indian security forces in recent history.

We were meant to have been in Korea by late afternoon, but by the time we arrived at Ram Chandra Singh's rambling palace, it was almost dark. We entered the grounds through rusty old gates and drove down an overgrown lane.

Small and gopher-like, the Maharaja spoke impeccable English and bubbled with energy. His lineage stretched back generations. In 1926, his father had been the first person in India to introduce a minimum wage. The legislation hadn't stuck, but the man had kept up political pressure until he successfully had it reintroduced in 1946.

Owing to the light, the crumbling palace looked like Sleeping Beauty's "forgotten" castle in the fairy tale. It was massive, with more than 100 rooms, but it was in a very poor state of repair, having been built in 1930. I suspected nothing had been done to it since. Ram Chandra Singh lived in just two rooms on the ground floor; the rest of the palace was locked up.

I chuckle thinking of the sight we must have made weaving across the overgrown grass that was once a lawn, in an effort to find a suitable angle and at the same time avoid snakes. (We had just learned that we were in fact in cobra country, and 68 people had already died that year from snakebites in this state alone.)

Ram Chandra Singh had been trying for years to get Heritage Hotels to take over his palace and make it into a luxury golf-swinging destination for the wealthy, but with the nearest landing strip 75 kilometers (46 miles) away, it was far off the beaten track, and therefore too risky an investment.

As I set up the camera, it started to rain again. We continued nonetheless.

"I'm a Hindu, so we believe in many gods," Ram Chandra Singh said. "There's a god of wealth, a god of education, a god who protects you, a god who destroys you, a god that is the creator of the universe; and there is a supreme power. I believe that all religions are good, but unfortunately man twists them and tries to make people believe his religion is better than another. But the true way to worship God is to be good to other people."

Then he added something quite contradictory: "Evolution is a scientifically accepted fact. So sometimes you feel that if a religion has not told you anything about what has happened over millions of years through evolution, then one could feel that there may not be a God at all."

After the interview the staff opened up the palace, and I explored. I ventured into the massive structure, with its once-elegant courtyard and seemingly never-ending corridors, leading to rooms inhabited only by monkeys and cobras. I would have loved to have spent some time there exploring in daylight. I stumbled across trophy rooms filled with endless stuffed heads of giraffes and caribou—evidence of the present Maharaja's ancestors' privileged hunting trips to Africa. Two stuffed tigers were mounted on the wall as if they were jumping out from times past. It was very sad.

STILL IGNORANT OF THE FACT that we were the focus of a thwarted assassination attempt, Mr. Chou nevertheless thumped against the wall of my insides (perhaps he knew the dangers we'd been in). The fact was, apart from a personal enjoyment of the trip up north, there was nothing I'd filmed in the last few days that was particularly relevant and driving my story forward. There wasn't a lot I could use.

"It is what it is," said Patrick. "If you had the best interview so far, you wouldn't be complaining."

It didn't make me feel any better. The reality was that I knew I had an awfully long way to go, and I was tormented by the fact that I still felt I'd loaded far too much on my plate.

CHAPTER 7

Delhi and the Punjab

●

"It's when you put the load down that you
actually feel the weight."

— NAPKIN #7

A couple of days after returning to Raipur from the north of Chhattisgarh, we flew back to Delhi.

Flying with Mr. Gill was an experience in itself—half of Indira Gandhi International Airport was closed off for his arrival. As before, our bags appeared extremely quickly; and so used to the efficiency of Mr. Gill's police force had I become that I only gave a cursory check of our equipment, knowing that if it wasn't all there, it very soon would be, or someone would be facing a demotion.

Another city, another motorcade, and a new group of commandos. . . . We careened across the wide boulevards and through red lights in bulletproof Tata Safaris.

IN DELHI, MR. GILL CALLED IN HIS SIKH WARRIORS. These were the same soldiers who had been helping him wage war against the fundamentalists in the Punjab for years. They turned up looking magnificent in traditional dress.

As Patrick and I were the sum total of our film crew, my companion was often a little thinly spread. As the line producer (the person responsible for organizing the nuts and bolts of a shoot), he spent a lot of time on the phone; as soundman, he was always draped with a boom mike and a digital mixing desk. And as he was responsible for securing people's permission to be filmed, he also didn't dare go anywhere without his folder of release forms. On top of that, Patrick did duty as the grip (which meant carrying the tripod everywhere) and the B-camera operator—who gets to take all the behind-the-scenes material, as well as shoot me in my role as narrator. So I guess you could say that Patrick was somewhat overburdened at times.

Since capturing his attention at short notice with a peremptory shout of "B cam, Patrick!" seemed a bit offensive, and because the mere mention of the word *camera* would usually draw people's attention, we had adopted a similar ruse to the one used by Robert De Niro in *Meet the Fockers*. In the movie, De Niro's character and his wife mutter the code word "muskrat" as a verbal kick under the table whenever one of them is about to make a faux pas. Anytime something cropped up that was worth capturing on the B camera, I would shout out *"Mirchi!"* (the Indian word for "chili"), which, to us, sounded less rude.

So, when Mr. Gill's warriors turned up in all their finery, complete with huge orange, blue, and green turbans that looked to be at least three feet tall, I immediately shouted "Mirchi! Mirchi, Patrick, mirchi!" As usual, poor Patrick looked somewhat harried: with the permissions folder clamped between his teeth, boom mike swinging crazily across his shoulders, he attempted to wrestle the tripod, while at the same time divesting himself of the digital mixing desk.

In a quintessential British moment, without missing a beat, Patrick patiently replied, "Would that be before I extend the tripod, wire up the lavaliers, transfer the camera bags to you, and book our flight to Ladakh? Or—should I take care of the tripod *and* do the mirchi, while I'm on the phone? Or maybe I should set up the tripod, do the mirchi, *and* film you getting pissy because you have nowhere to put the A camera! What would be the best sequence, do you think?"

It was such a funny scene that Mr. Gill, Chandi, all the warriors, and I simply cracked up.

"Patrick—I think you need to grow some more arms." Chandi laughed.

"I think we have a new name for you, Patrick," chimed in Mr. Gill. "From now on we shall call you *Vishnu!*" In the Hindu pantheon, Vishnu is the master of the past, present, and future—the one who supports, sustains, and governs the universe—and is depicted in sculptures and paintings as a god with eight arms.

A nickname was born.

GOING SHOPPING WITH MR. GILL AND CHANDI was always inter-esting. Because of security, streets had to be closed down and all establishments thoroughly inspected before our arrival. In an amazing jewelry store in Delhi, I was introduced to the owner, Chhote Bharany, who was resplendent in white shirt and tie, sil-ver hair, and aviator glasses. Mr. Bharany conversed in a rapid-fire fashion. Mr. Gill had tipped me off that he would be well worth interviewing. I had minimal equipment with me that day, but just enough. No tripod, I propped the camera on the back of a chair and asked Mr. Bharany, "What is God?"

I didn't realize that my subject was a published philosopher.

"I have no opinion whatsoever. He may be there, but He may not be," said Mr. Bharany.

"Did God create man, or did man create God?" I asked.

"Both created each other," he replied with conviction.

"How is that possible?"

"If He's there, well and good. If He isn't, we shall have to *create* Him," he answered immediately.

"Why?" I asked.

"Because there is some greater power above us. This thought makes a man humble. It saves him from the ego, the pitfalls of life—the greatest enemy of man is the ego. If you know that God is there, you can get humble in life, and that is very important. Man conceived of the benevolent existence of God in order to protect himself from the enemy within, in the form of ego, to maintain humility and equanimity in life."

"So what about all the prophets: from Moses to Mohammed, from Krishna to Jesus? Didn't they claim to hear the voice of God?" I challenged.

"It was their *own* voice," Mr. Bharany fired back. "Let me ask you this—how many gods were they referring to?"

"I would have to say that it would be rational to assume they were referring to one god," I replied.

"In that case—how can that one God have so many different

voices contradicting each other?" He paused and leaned forward. "These gods are real and unreal at the same time. Unreal in the physical sense, but very real in the form of *philosophy*. Man gives form to that formless being, and those forms are all symbolic. The Hindus, for example, have always seen Vishnu, Shiva, Krishna. Buddhists see only Buddha. Christians only see Christ and the Mother Mary. Muslims see only Allah, and Mohammed as His prophet. All these are the reflections of their own inner consciousness—the image of their own divine thoughts conditioned by the society they were born into."

"Does that make God exist or not?" I challenged.

"In my view God exists and also does not."

"How's that?"

"If you think He's something that's apart from you, then He does not exist; but if you think He is in you, and you are in Him, then He exists. The mantras in the world remain the same; but the sentiments, philosophies, substance, and the gestures change. Man has to realize that man himself is the creator, the sustainer, the destroyer, and the seeker."

He paused, and then asked me a question: "What happens when you turn on a light switch?"

"The light comes on?"

"Ah, so you know about electricity?"

"Yes."

"Have you actually *seen* electricity, Peter?"

"Not electricity itself . . . it can't be seen."

"Exactly! But you know it's there when the bulb lights up, because if it wasn't there, it would still be dark, right?"

"Right."

"All the saints, sages, prophets—they derive power from the electricity, from the power station. They are only *big bulbs;* they are not the electricity itself. Great bulbs for the benefit of mankind, they all draw power from the big power station that is itself totality.

"There are no adjectives that can describe God. Nobody can say 'He is *this*.' Anytime anyone says He is *something,* they deceive themselves. It's like a drop saying, *I know the ocean.* The ocean can see the drop, but the drop is insignificant in the ocean. And this is where the problem starts. So in the case of religions that say 'He is *this,*' then God must be a criminal to create so many religions that fight with each other."

I let the camera roll, and Mr. Bharany rolled on.

"We are fighting for the same reason, because we have been conditioned, imprisoned by priests and the politicians; they are the criminals in my eyes, because they are the ones who are dividing instead of uniting. I burn inside when I see all these fights. 'He is only Allah,' 'He is only Krishna,' 'He is only Christ,' 'He is only this,' 'He is only that.' How do you know? You are limiting the limitless.

"From all of the scriptures, I can give you only two significant sentences: 'Helping others is a virtue. Harming others is a sin.' You don't really need the rest. If a man learns only these two sentences, he doesn't have to go to a church, a temple, a synagogue, a mosque. I'm not saying you shouldn't; they are good paths to take you to being a better human being. But none of them are the destination. What I am saying is, if you remember those two sentences, *you don't have to.*

"Learn from the past, live in the present, and brighten your future. Let's be *we* instead of *you and I.* The saints and prophets never fight; it is the followers who fight. Learn from Buddha, learn from Christ, learn from Krishna, learn from Mohammed, learn from everybody. But let it be from your own heart."

For some reason, after filming these scenes with Mr. Bharany, I felt compelled to go outside into the deserted street, which was still cordoned off because of our presence. I found a little step to sit on, and then I did something I hadn't done for years . . . I wept. I really couldn't put a finger on why, but I did.

A police officer came up to me and asked if I was okay. I was embarrassed. I wiped my tears away and said, "I'm fine, but thank you for asking." He left me alone.

A little later, I plucked up my courage, sniffed a bit, and then walked back to join the others as if nothing had happened.

What happened? To this day I still do not know.

WE WERE ON THE MOVE AGAIN, driving north through the night into the Punjab—a journey of endless roads, as well as endless sirens.

In India, drivers don't pay any attention to the police; they're too intent on keeping their eyes on the road in front of them. I'm not really sure driving schools exist there, as it seems to be a learn-as-you-go process. It's not uncommon to find vehicles on the wrong side of a two-lane road. This is when Mr. Gill's motorcade helps. Those poor police jeeps leading the way bear the brunt of vehicular abuse; the officers literally have to lean out and whack the sides of trucks with their sticks (called *latis*), until the oblivious drivers realize that there's a VIP approaching and move over to let the convoy pass.

Hour after hour we drove, through Kundi, Panipat, and Karnal, where we stayed overnight at the police HQ. Then on again the next day to Shahabad Markanda, Ambala, Khanna, and Ludhiana, until eventually we reached Mr. Gill's hometown of Jalandhar, where we left Mr. Gill behind so he could attend to some business, while Chandi, Vishnu, and I continued on to Amritsar and the Golden Temple.

Completed in 1604, the Golden Temple, which is really called Harmandir Sahib, earned its name because most of the exterior is literally covered in gold plate. It is the holiest shrine of Sikhism and was designed to encourage worship from men and women of all walks of life, belief systems, and religions—worshipping God, equally. Sitting in a large man-made lake called the "Lake of Holy Water," the temple boasts entrances on all four sides, signifying acceptance and openness. Its function today, apart from being one of India's most popular tourist attractions and holy sites, is to open its doors as a sanctuary for those who need to worship, as well as those in need of a good, wholesome meal.

By the time we arrived, dusk had fallen. With glittery lights strung everywhere, the temple was quite the most spectacular place I had seen, and lived up to its name. The manager gave us a private tour. Since filming in and around the building was usually forbidden, I felt very privileged to be allowed to strut around, getting angle after angle and trying not to get blinded by visual fatigue. Soothing Sikh chanting created an intoxicating atmosphere.

In keeping with their tolerant manifesto, the Sikhs don't close their doors to anyone, whoever you are, whatever color or creed—all are welcome. There is *no discrimination*. It was a refreshing experience; and I made a mental note that if everything went belly-up one day and I found myself in a strange town without a passport or money, I would seek out the Sikhs, where I knew I would be welcomed, fed, and provided with a roof over my head.

In huge halls, there were endless volunteers washing up plates that had been used to feed the poor, who, with their bellies full and their thirst quenched, now sat looking out in awe across the lake at the jewel of the temple glistening in the half-light. Chandi rolled up her sleeves and helped wash up, amid a large din of clashing stainless steel and mounds of bubbles. All walks of life were happy to be together in a place of peace and worship. It all seemed so civilized, so in tune with what every scripture preached, and no one asked me to convert into a Sikh in order to have the right to be there.

THAT NIGHT, BACK IN JALANDHAR, Mr. Gill had organized a private concert—a famous Punjabi Sufi musician and singer called Hans Raj Hans had been invited to the officers' mess to perform for us. Hans Raj Hans had not a hair out of place or a single crease in his immaculate outfit. He would toss his long, highlighted locks back as he sang. To look at, he was a cross between George Michael and Liberace, but when he opened his mouth, his singing was like a prayer. For two hours he sang the night away.

Having spent so much time with Mr. Gill, I was beginning to understand how much fun he was and what a privilege it was to be in his presence. I enjoyed his wisdom and his humor, and the four of us had become very close. Gone was the feeling of intimidation. Mr. Gill had become more a father figure and friend molded into one. Late that night, over single malt, I quizzed my host.

"Why do so many religions fight each other, Mr. Gill?"

"Why do religions fight?" His expression was very serious.

"Again, for someone who is deeply religious, it is very difficult to explain. But the fact is that religions do fight. There have been wars over religions. People have killed each other. But if you ask them, 'Why did you fight?' I don't think they'd be able to answer that question. I don't think it is religion. Religion is against violence within a human being.

"Interestingly, I remember asking a leading Sikh terrorist: 'Can you quote me any verse from the scriptures?' He thought long and hard. I then said, 'Can you tell me what Sikhism is?'

"So he thought about that for an even longer time, and he couldn't find an answer. Ultimately, he said, 'Sikhism means brotherhood.'

"'Then why are you killing people?' I asked. He had no answer to that. He could not quote a single line, or even half a line, of the scripture he was supposedly spreading about with the gun. The greatest misrepresentation of religion is created by the very people who profess to be the most devoted followers of that religion. Every single religion does it."

Fascinated, I continued to delve deeper. "What in your opinion produces a religious-fanatic terrorist, then?"

"I think that is the easiest thing to grasp. It's the easiest thing to be convinced that you, by virtue of your religion, are superior to others. It is so easy to be convinced that if you commit any act whatsoever and say that you are doing that act in the name of religion, it gets sanctified and no sin gets attached to it; and there is no guilt, and there is no feeling of having wronged somebody. And that being the case, you can kill, you can do anything in the name of religion, and get away with it. Religious terrorism is the easiest thing to cultivate in others, and in yourself."

"So what drives you, Mr. Gill?"

He paused. The swooshing of the fan became louder. The Sufi music from Hans Raj Hans still seemed to linger in the mess quarters where we sat. It must have been 3 A.M., but there was not one ounce of fatigue apparent in Mr. Gill's eyes, which flickered as he began to speak, so quietly that he was barely audible, but with a conviction that was palpable.

"At the time of independence, violence spread across India. In the Punjab we referred to it as 'partition.' I remember that incident vividly. We were a small family living on the outskirts of a township near Lahore, right next to a Muslim village. Suddenly, communities that had been friendly and had lived together for decades and centuries were at each other's throats.

"I remember my mother coming to me one evening with two swords in her hand, saying: 'You will sleep with these under your pillow. And your younger sister' (who was about five at that time) 'will sleep on the next bed. And if you're attacked by Muslims, you kill as many as you can, and if you find you are being overpowered, kill your sister and then kill yourself.'"

Mr. Gill paused, and then, with just a hint of emotion and determination showing on his heavily bearded face, continued with his story:

"At that age, it did not strike me as something out of the ordinary, but later on, many a time I have thought about it. I have thought about fear. I have thought about desperation. I have thought about the failure of the state. I have thought about the failure and the breakdown of civil society, and I have taken a pledge within myself that if I have the power, I will not allow *anyone* to be subjected to such a choice."

We listened in silence to the fan as the full weight of Mr. Gill's words hit home.

Vishnu broke the silence. "Well, I'm off to bed. Damned glad I don't have to sleep with a sword tonight. I might cut the wrong thing off!"

We said our good-nights and hit the hay.

AFTER ARRIVING BACK IN DELHI, Mr. Gill dispatched a police car to pick me up at the hotel where Vishnu and I were staying. Vishnu wasn't coming; he was far too busy photocopying the release forms—a wise precaution, I thought, but since this was India, it wasn't necessarily an easy task.

Mr. Gill's home was guarded like a fortress. With its sentry post and firing range, it looked more like a military compound than a regular house. Each night, his chief bodyguard would routinely fire off some rounds to check that his gun was working.

I was led through manicured gardens, past the main house, to a small single-story building situated at the other side of the lawn. My uniformed escort clicked his heels and knocked. There was a muffled "Come in." The police officer motioned me to enter and disappeared.

The door creaked as I slowly opened it to reveal a very comfortable-looking study lined with books. There, seated in a leather chair, looking very regal, dressed completely in white, was Mr. Gill. On the coffee table in front of him were mounds—and I mean *mounds*—of bottles and boxes of single-malt whisky.

Mr. Gill's eyes twinkled. "I've been collecting for some time. And as we are embarking on a journey to Vrindaban, where alcohol is strictly forbidden, I thought it would be wise for you to choose a couple of bottles to accompany us." He grinned mischievously.

Late that night, Vishnu and I joined Chandi and Mr. Gill in the Tata Safari, on a journey headed south. Mr. Gill reached into one of the vehicle's pockets and pulled out one of my choices— a 25-year-old Glenlivet—and three glasses. "We have much talking to do!" he said.

"Oh gosh," said Chandi, "I can see how interesting this ride is going to be!"

Despite sharing many a good tipple, we never overdrank with Mr. Gill. We enjoyed a couple of glasses together, and there would be a slight loosening of the tongue, which enabled me to quiz him on some of the usually taboo, party-pooper topics such as politics and religion, but never more than that.

"Cheers!" We clinked glasses and took a savoring sip.

"What irks you, Mr. Gill? What annoys you? What gets under your skin?"

"Bad scotch!" He snickered. "But as I don't drink bad scotch, I suppose it doesn't irk me." He paused, weighing up my question. "What gets under my skin the most is when those people that profess to be highly religious, who have done pilgrimages and are looked upon as symbols of religion, tell lies and deceive—when they internally propagate hatred and externally talk about peace and brotherhood, and are hypocritical. When those who are the worst of humanity are looked favorably upon, and are respected as the pillars of that particular religion—that's what irks me. That irks me a lot. And it has caused us an enormous amount of time, resources, and lives to combat."

"If I could take your words now and transport them into millions of people's houses across the world, what would you say?"

Mr. Gill answered without hesitation: "I would tell them: Try to access your scriptures by yourself. Let no priest stand between you and the scripture, and if you can be eclectic in your choice, and if you can empower yourself and try to read all the great scriptures of all the great religions of the world, you will see the unity within; and it is better that you find it by yourself than attend to the disunity, which is being created by the propagators of different religions today."

Mr. Gill had a way with words. The rest of that three-hour drive sped by, with Vishnu and me telling silly stories and sharing our adventures across the world. We chuckled our way south as Chandi fell asleep with a resigned *I knew this would happen* look on her face.

CHAPTER 8
Vrindaban

"Words are only valuable if you have the courage to act on them."

— NAPKIN #8

Vrindaban is a holy city that has an ancient past, and is located less than ten miles from Krishna's birthplace, Mathura, near the Delhi–Agra highway. It is an important Hindu place of pilgrimage and boasts more than 5,000 temples.

Situated in a poverty-stricken region, it is also the center of operations for the Chandi Duke Heffner International Foundation—Chandi's private trust—nicknamed *Project Balaram* (after Krishna's brother Balaram, who as a young man was a cowherd). Chandi provides free medical care for humans and animals, hospitalization and surgery, emergency food distribution, and thousands of blankets for the winter, serving more than 275,000 villagers. Assistance is given without regard to ethnicity, gender, and political or religious affiliation. In a nutshell, Chandi *saves lives*. Mr. Gill, as a trustee of the organization, and Chandi both work tirelessly day in, day out, improving conditions in the rural areas and combating more than a hundred horrendous diseases.

I wanted to portray Chandi's work saving lives and understand her view of God—since, without being sensationalist, one could say she was, in a sense, playing God. Her decisions, her actions, and her philanthropy would determine, in certain cases, who was to live and who was to die.

Vishnu and I stayed in a very basic but clean ashram down the road from Chandi's center of operations, which at that time was a pleasant apartment within a guarded "community" in town. The problem was that the other residents of the community were mainly white Hare Krishnas dressed in local attire. They would be chanting in Hindi at the top of their voices one minute, and then beating monkeys with sticks the next. They would scoff at Chandi and Mr. Gill because of all the commandos with weapons who would materialize to guard her apartment whenever the two of them were in town. The Hare Krishnas would write letters of complaint to the management about the guns and the fact that Chandi would *feed* the monkeys.

Mostly lost souls from France, the U.K., and other European countries, they had "escape" figuratively embossed on their foreheads, as it seemed obvious they were running away from something and hadn't yet realized it was *themselves*. They would cast judgmental glances at Vishnu and me as they scuffed by in their sandals with holier-than-thou eyes, probably because we dressed in Western attire and were constantly surrounded by cameras. Contradiction was etched into their faces—they weren't rolling up their sleeves and helping villagers, dressing wounds, and carrying the sick to the hospital; they were in India to *get something*, not to *give something.*

I was to learn that there is a great difference between those who embrace a culture because they feel they don't fit into their own anymore and those who do so because they respect its values and wish to contribute something. I nicknamed the Hare Krishnas—locally dressed, glazed-eyed Westerners—the *pseudo-sadhus.*

THE FIRST DAY, WE WENT OFF INTO THE WILD so Chandi and Mr. Gill could inspect one of her teams of doctors and veterinarians who traveled from village to village, treating sick people and animals, and educating the villagers about how to prevent malaria and other diseases.

Chandi's philosophy was that you couldn't just treat humans without also tending to their animals, as there were so many local diseases affecting both, such as actinomycosis, cowpox, giardia, scabies, tuberculosis, and *Yersinia pestis*—otherwise known as the plague. In fact, there were more than 70 such "zoonotic" diseases, and Chandi's philanthropy and methodology has not only stamped out some of these in certain areas, but also freed up manpower and resources to combat other diseases that were best avoided by preventive education. Chandi's warehouse was stacked with modern medicine, which she imported at great expense from the U.S., as anything that was available locally often proved to be more dangerous than the disease it was designed to cure.

The villagers were fabulous. I felt truly happy among them, because *they* were truly happy. Children running around playing; mothers preparing basic food over open fires; Grandma repairing Grandson's shoe, made out of an old tire; the men chatting in the shade, playing games with small stones . . . there was a vibe of immense peace, of spirit, of community. No one had cars, mortgage payments, careers, or money, yet even when food was a challenge, there was always a buzz in the air, a song to sing.

It wasn't difficult to understand why Chandi would turn her back on Rodeo Drive and the Kentucky Derby to be out here, where life is real and based on simple needs, despite severe problems.

Chandi showed off her impressive mobile clinic, and we met the doctors who were in the process of testing for malaria. I learned about the scourge of the mosquito—how it not only spread malaria, which was killing tens of thousands, but also myriad other nasty diseases as well, including chikungunya and dengue fever.

Malaria had all but disappeared following the introduction of DDT in the '70s, but the insecticide had been administered too randomly and had filtered into the water table, causing other problems, which had resulted in it being banned. Now malaria was rampant once more. Drugs couldn't catch up, were way too expensive, and were harmful to the liver, so the only way to combat the disease was through prevention, which primarily meant mosquito nets at night and bug spray. Don't get bitten!

Chandi escorted us around the village. "If they need hospital or surgery," she explained, "we take them to the best hospital in the area and pay for all their medical care. There's such a great need. The project goes out into the villages 362 or 363 days a year."

"Do some of them pretend they are sick?" I asked.

"All the time. We try to talk to the local people and see that these people are truly poor and they're not trying to pull a fast one on us."

"Do you get frustrated with your rich friends who aren't doing what you do?"

"I think if everybody in my position would give just a very, very small amount and make sure that all the money actually gets to the people and isn't wasted on advertising or administration costs, it would make a huge change in the world."

There were throngs of people lining up, waiting patiently to meet the doctors.

"We never give up," Chandi said. "With every case, every child, every adult, we do the best we can. Even when other doctors say, 'It's a lost cause; this person will never live,' we don't give up.

"The doctors write prescriptions, which are filled by the pharmacist. In case they don't read Hindi or English, each medicine is put in a different envelope so they can see that this one is taken one time a day, this is two times a day, this is three times a day. This ensures a lot of success.

"When we find patients that need to go to the hospital, we take them and admit them for surgery or further care. Otherwise everybody is treated here."

A young woman came up to us and presented Chandi with a flower. Her name was Mira. "About a year ago we were in a village, and the villagers carried a string bed to us. And there was Mira. She weighed 22 kilograms [49 pounds]. She has two children. We admitted her to the hospital and didn't really think she'd make it. Now she's cured and she looks great."

"What was wrong with her?"

"She had tuberculosis."

Mira's father appeared, bent down, and kissed Chandi's feet, muttering.

Chandi added, "Mira's father was wonderful. The whole time she was in the hospital her father stayed with her and took care of her. He's a wonderful father."

I turned to Mr. Gill and asked what the man was saying.

"He says she is like a god to him. The face of God," he replied.

THE VILLAGE WAS CLEAN AND PICTURESQUE, with little painted houses as colorful as the smiling faces. This was a Sapera village. The Sapera are snake catchers. For years they had been charming cobras in bazaars all across the country until animal-rights legislation made it illegal in 1972. Devoid of income, and with no support from the government, the Sapera ended up poor and dispossessed in villages such as this one. But off the beaten track, away from the prying eyes of the government, they did what they knew best—charmed snakes.

Out they came from little bags, until cobras and serpents of all shapes and sizes were slithering everywhere. Trying to film them without stepping on them became increasingly difficult. Now, I have to admit that like Indiana Jones, I am scared stiff of snakes. But oddly enough, the combination of the music and "photojournalist syndrome" must have worked its magic on me, because even as the cobras were passing between my feet, I managed to remain strangely calm behind my camera lens.

That is, until a couple of large bags containing two very angry pythons were opened up right in front of me. Although they weren't venomous, these reptiles were very *pissed!* The largest lunged forward, straight at me, fangs bared. Without even thinking I suddenly found myself 12 feet back. How I got there I don't know; it felt like I had teleported myself. Instinct had propelled me, I guess.

The snake handlers roared with laughter—they had the tails of the pythons firmly gripped in their hands like Dobermans on a chain . . . but *I* hadn't known that! Then, to my horror, more cobras started appearing out of nowhere, along with a host of menacing black scorpions. Within seconds I was completely surrounded.

Mr. Gill and Chandi laughed themselves almost out of their chairs as they watched me dance around like I was doing hopscotch, to the melancholic wailing of the snake charmers' pipes. Even Mr. Gill had cried out, "Mirchi, Vishnu. Mirchi!" But it had all happened so quickly, and Vishnu only had eight arms.

As the sun went down, the snakes were coiled into their baskets and carried off somewhere. The villagers closed around us, the pipers began to play a wonderful melody, and everybody began to sing. Young boys came out and started to dance.

The best dancer among them was missing an eye. He had contracted a nasty disease the year before that had caused the whole left side of his face to become infected. Chandi had found him and taken him to the hospital, where he'd sat at death's door for several days until the right antibiotics had been administered. His life had been saved, but it had cost him an eye. To help with his coordination, he'd thrown himself into dancing, and now he was jiving up a storm in front of us.

I observed Chandi, sitting with Mr. Gill in her pristine sari, and wondered how she felt, knowing that if it wasn't for her, this dance wouldn't be taking place. If it wasn't for her, there would be a shallow grave out there in the bush, and there wouldn't be that little glint of freedom and joy, bouncing around in front of us, and there wouldn't be that look of gratitude on the faces of the dancer's parents behind him.

I wondered what *that* had to do with God, my mission, and the film. I wondered what I was learning as the music filled my senses. I think I was beginning to learn how to breathe. And for the first time in several weeks, I was aware that even Mr. Chou seemed to be at peace.

It was a wonderful interlude. But Chandi was here on a mission, and the night was still young and there were lives to be saved.

THERE WAS AN ANNUAL PILGRIMAGE TAKING PLACE, called Yatra of Ramesh Baba, in which 7,000 Hindus—usually the poorest families—take part in a march that lasts for 40 days. Little attention had been devoted to the practicalities and organization of such an undertaking. Charities, supported by donations from the U.S., were good at providing basic nutrition and vast tents to house the pilgrims, but they weren't able to provide much medical help. With tuberculosis and malaria rife in the area and thousands of exhausted pilgrims sharing such close proximity, the tents where they slept at night were a breeding ground for disaster. Every night there were at least five or six deaths. Chandi had been sending her teams in to treat the sick and prevent any more casualties; and now that she was back in town, her top priority was to roll up her sleeves, go find those who seemed to be the closest to death that night, and save their lives.

It was a daunting and exhausting task. The encampment of tents seemed endless—miles of large, interlinked canvas caverns littered with bodies on little mats. A sea of people: families—the old, the sick, and the young—stretched out as far as the eye could see. Like an angel, Chandi would crisscross the tents, looking for those who appeared to be facing death most imminently. The sound of incessant coughing filled our ears. It was estimated that at least 30 to 40 percent of those in the tents had some form of tuberculosis. But many of them would hack harder in order to accentuate their condition in the hopes that it would draw attention, bringing them better food and a bed in the hospital instead of a night on stony ground and a ten-mile trek the following day. So Chandi would inquire and interrogate, and her doctors would take pulses and temperatures, in an effort to diagnose the worst-case scenarios so that precious beds wouldn't get wasted on those who would survive. Those with diarrhea, dysentery, cholera, and dehydration were priorities.

The conditions were very difficult for shooting. It was fascinating to see Chandi at work. She was adamant that she could not, *would* not, miss anybody who was in dire need or in danger. If there was a life to be saved that night, she would make sure that it would be saved, regardless of how long it might take. We traversed all the tents, asking many questions, with Chandi explaining things as we went.

"She's feeling as if she's got a fever. She's shaking. She feels very cold. We've arranged for the stretcher to come and pick her up because I don't think she can walk, so we're going to take her to our doctors, and if she needs to be admitted, we'll take her to Maheshwari Hospital."

After four hours, we had identified six people who were right at the very edge of life, and we escorted them to the hospital in the police vehicles.

"Why do you spend your life going around disease-ridden tents?" I asked Chandi.

"Because there's so much suffering that isn't being addressed, and people aren't being taken care of. I try to take care of the people who are suffering where there isn't another option for them."

"Have you always felt this way?"

"When I was very young, I grew up Catholic; and I think the influence of the nuns, charity, and good qualities were emphasized. What I have seen is that, whatever religion you are, there are many God-conscious people, and I feel that God is the same to everyone. It's just the leaders who seem to lose sight of the true God consciousness. Through gaining power, they often get lost."

With the sick loaded into the vehicles, we drove over to Maheshwari Hospital. On the way, Chandi reached forward and pulled out a travel pack of medicated hand towels.

"You might want to give your hands a wipe," she said. It was the only protection she, or we, had.

At the hospital, we were greeted by the doctor in charge. Overworked and overwhelmed in an understaffed establishment, he possessed every quality you would hope to see in a developing-world provincial hospital. Full of energy and compassion, he took us around, describing the conditions of the patients Chandi had brought in.

We hovered over a boy with a fractured skull and brain fluid leaking from his nose who was in dire need of endoscopic surgery, which would have to be performed in Delhi. Running a high fever, the boy was at risk of contracting meningitis. As if that wasn't enough, he had fallen off a train and had multiple fractures in his leg, and he needed a muscle flap created, as bone was exposed on his upper tibia. The boy cupped his hands and stared up at Chandi with wide, beautiful eyes.

"He can't have the leg operation until his temperature goes down," she explained. The doctor remarked that the boy had a fever of 103, and it wouldn't go down until the endoscopic surgery had been performed. Chandi agreed to send the boy to Delhi the following day so that he could get the care he desperately needed.

Another young boy had hydrocephalus (water on the brain), tuberculosis, and a broken arm. When Chandi first had him admitted, his head had been so enlarged with fluid that it was the size of a watermelon and had required immediate draining. They had inserted a tube with a valve into his brain that allowed the excess to drip down into his abdomen, because the tuberculosis had blocked his body's natural channel for this. Despite his discomfort, the boy was overjoyed to see us.

An old man was propped up on his bed. He had contracted a staph infection in his foot, and the doctor had been forced to amputate his leg below the knee. But the infection had spread, so they'd had to remove the rest of his leg. The man was now suffering from intense "phantom limb" pain. He moaned incessantly. Time was the only cure.

We spent about four hours at the hospital, inspecting more than a hundred patients. I will never forget the intensity of that visit, and the joy in the patients' eyes. There are no nurses or porters at these rural hospitals. The patients have to rely on their attendants—usually a relative—to be with them and to wash, feed, and support them. Chandi made sure that the attendants were well looked after, and that nutritious food was served to all.

In the hallway of the hospital stood a display case containing hundreds of jars of formaldehyde; and suspended inside them, with a variety of disturbing expressions etched into their faces, were dead human fetuses. It was a macabre site. Beside the display case, a sign announced: *Determination of sex of the fetus is punishable under the law. Not practiced here.* In India, boys are far more popular than girls, so a law had been passed in an effort to stamp out the termination of pregnancies based on gender.

On the way home, Chandi shared more about how she felt.

"I feel that people are being taken advantage of by power-intoxicated leaders. The people are so wonderful, so devout, so dedicated, so God-conscious, trying to do what's best, trying to do what's right. The leaders of religion could empower people to do so much good in the world, even if they would just tell them to each do just one kind act to another person each day. If we all helped each other, the world would be a different place."

"What is God, Chandi?" I asked.

"It's difficult to define God, but the evidence of His existence is right here. Evidence of God, to me, would be one thing—and that is the existence of everything. Humans can destroy, but we can't create. We can destroy life. We can kill, but we cannot even create a blade of grass."

VISHNU AND I GOT BACK TO THE ASHRAM at about 3 A.M. I was just opening my door when I heard, "Oh, bugger!" coming from Vishnu's room.

I walked over to see him staring, eyes wide in horror.

"Bloody hell!" I exclaimed. There must have been 3,000 to 5,000 mosquitoes in his room, all buzzing around the bare lightbulb. "You left your light on, didn't you?" I remarked unnecessarily.

"Hmm. And the window open!"

"Oh, deary me. Deary, deary me," I muttered in my best rendition of a Hindi accent. "How many diseases did that doc say were—?"

"Yes," Vishnu interrupted.

"Artillery time?"

"Yep. Let's bring it out."

We had picked up the weird spray cans in Delhi. They were labeled *Gone* and had a picture of a mosquito on its back, legs in the air, looking quite dead. The shopkeeper had warned us that they were only to be used in an emergency, because they were *very* effective. The product was banned in 136 countries, but it was "very good to make mosquitoes *gone*." He'd pointed to the illustration and muttered, "Very rigor mortis, this one, isn't it?" He also mentioned, as an afterthought, that it was extremely carcinogenic, so best not to use it too often.

As Vishnu was a professional 50-a-day smoker, he wasn't too concerned about those kinds of things, so we both started spraying with great gusto at the clouds of bugs. "I'd rather die from 'Gone' than one of those diseases." He coughed. Bodies fell from the air and collected on the bed and floor, until there was no more buzzing to be heard.

"Wow, that really is good stuff," I remarked approvingly, as Vishnu cranked on the powerful ceiling fan. A vortex of air and dead mosquito bodies formed in the room like tornado alley, until there was just a tiny patch directly beneath the fan that was devoid of the little black beasts.

"'Night," Vishnu muttered as he fell into the mosquito-free zone on the bed.

I noticed the window was still open. By the time I had closed it, Vishnu was snoring. I kept the fan on full and left him to his dreams.

Chandi's words resonated in my head: *We can kill, but we cannot even create a blade of grass.* I thought of Mr. Patel, a Jain I'd interviewed in Jalandhar a few days before, who had said, "We don't disturb anything in nature; we don't kill anything in nature. Not to harm anything in nature is the main belief of our religion, Jainism. God is in everyone's mind, in everyone's heart; God is everywhere, so we don't disturb nature." I suddenly felt very guilty about the thousands of dead mosquitoes next door, and wondered if the law of karma would have me returning to life as a maggot. I realized that I was extremely overtired.

THE NEXT MORNING, VISHNU must have been picking up on my *I don't really want to be here* vibe, as I could hear him muttering the words "Icy calm, icy calm," beneath his breath. It was a phrase he often used in an effort to keep me from falling into one of my silent, irritated moods, which are usually brought on by fatigue and frustration. But today, it was the pseudo-sadhus that were bothering me.

We were in the market opposite the "community," trying to get some Christmas shopping done for our families back home, and it was *teeming* with them. At a stall, we were attempting to bargain with a huge redheaded man (well, he would have been redheaded if he hadn't shaved his head) from Birmingham, England. He was dressed in a skirt and wore little round John Lennon–style glasses, behind which sat pudgy, glazed eyes.

"No. I'm not like the locals, you know. It's 800 rupees, just like it's labeled," he said belligerently. I was holding a relatively pretty necklace that was vastly overpriced.

"Yes, I can see you're not like the locals," I commented.

Chandi had just told us that when she first started her project, the pseudo-sadhus would try to stop her from helping the local people. They said relieving the suffering of humans and animals was wrong—that they all had a certain amount of suffering they would need to endure before leaving this earth, and by relieving it, she would be interfering with their karma and they'd have to be reborn again. Therefore, any help to poor people, the sick, or animals in need had to cease.

That story had really bothered me, especially after seeing what Chandi was doing for the local impoverished villagers. I think it had affected me more than I cared to admit, because if there's one thing I can't tolerate, it's hypocrisy. The pseudo-sadhus' double standards were beginning to get under my skin.

"What?" asked Burly Bill from Birmingham (as I was beginning to think of him).

"I can see you're not like the locals," I repeated. "You don't resemble them in any shape, form, or manner, despite attempting to dress like them; and you don't have even 10 percent of their politeness, or any care for their well-being."

"You're the jerks over there with that bloke with all the soldiers, aren't you?" he accused.

"Excuse me?"

"Whisking in, whisking out of here with those big fancy cameras, acting like you own the bloody place, thinking you're getting a piece of India, so you can go back to your fancy homes and sell what you took from here?"

"And what am I taking?"

"People, souls . . . everyone's been talking about you two," he almost spat.

"And what are *you* doing here?" I inquired with exaggerated politeness. "What are you running away from?"

"Icy calm, icy calm," Vishnu murmured.

"I'm not running away!" he said defensively.

It was too late. I was already on a roll. "Trying to be like them, in your sandals and your oh-so-holy robes. . . . What on earth are you trying to do? You don't even have the respect to involve the local population in your market here, do you? You bought this piece from the vendor down the street this morning, and now you're selling it for ten times as much." I continued on, like a runaway train. "You're putting the locals out of business with all your pseudo-sadhu, play-holy friends, spending Grandma's Christmas gifts discovering themselves." *There, you've done it!* I told myself. I'd finally called a pseudo-sadhu, a pseudo-sadhu.

"Excuse me, I'm *studying* their culture—that's why I'm here. I'm *studying!*"

"But what are you doing for *them?*" I continued relentlessly. "I've heard the stories about you types . . . coming here 'cause you can't face reality back home . . . taking over the town, intermingling, and upsetting people who are kind and loving and teach you their mantras, while you've got some cousin back in Birmingham picking up your social-security check that the British taxpayers fund, just so you can *discover* yourself! Only the more you discover, the more you despise, and the more you run away."

"Icy calm," breathed Vishnu behind me.

"You Westerners are all the same, with your money and your cargo pants!" Burly Bill shouted. "The only reason you're not running away is because you've never belonged. You'll never belong. You'll never be enlightened!" he spat, breaking into a chant that gradually grew in volume. *"Hare, Hare, Hare, Hare, Hare Krishna, Krishna Hare . . ."*

"Well, mate, as soon as you get enlightened, why don't you come with us and spend some of your meditation time squeezing the pus out of some young villager's infected neck so it doesn't cause him septicemia . . . or is that just too real for you?"

"Hare, Hare, Hare, Krishna Hare . . ." The chant accompanied us as Vishnu frog-marched me out of the market.

I started to feel guilty. The reality was, Burly Bill was probably a gentle chap underneath it all, who had likely never caused any distress to the locals and therefore didn't deserve my vitriol. "Perhaps I should go back and buy his necklace," I said.

"Oh, *puh*-lease!" Vishnu rolled his eyes.

THAT NIGHT WAS OUR LAST SUPPER WITH OUR HOSTS. Mr. Gill produced the second bottle of single malt, a 16-year-old Lagavulin, and we sipped it and talked. We were very sad to leave. The following morning Vishnu and I would be continuing north into the Himalayas without our friends, without the commandos, without the guns, without the conversation, and without the ability to film anywhere we wanted.

"I'm sorry I will not be with you up in Ladakh," said Mr. Gill. "I have friends there. I will ask them to keep an eye out."

"We're very sorry you and Chandi won't be there, too," I said sadly.

"Before you go—I was wondering . . . have you got a title for this film you are making?"

I said I did not. Titles were very hard things to come up with.

"You should call it *Oh My God.*" Mr. Gill smiled.

CHAPTER 9

North to "Little Tibet"

*"You might be the one who wants to move the rock,
but be prepared for the rock to move you."*

— NAPKIN #9

We were driven back up to Delhi early the next morning by one of Chandi's drivers. The journey took a lot longer without Mr. Gill's police escort—we had to stop at traffic lights!

We then flew north to Ladakh. The view from the plane over the Himalayas was spectacular; snowy mountain peaks stretched for eternity. An hour and a half after leaving Delhi, we touched down at Leh, the capital of Ladakh. It's easy to see why the region, home to devout Buddhists and nestled between mountain ranges that could be right out of *The Lord of the Rings,* is also known as Little Tibet. Situated at around 12,000 feet, with a temperature of −5 degrees Celsius (23 degrees Fahrenheit), it was a completely different world. The air was thin, and it was very quiet. Sound travels at a different pace through the atmosphere there, and falls off fast from lack of suspension, like planes in those scratchy films of man's first attempts to fly. So sounds that would normally linger died quickly, leaving a tremendous sense of tranquility.

We were met by our guide, Dorjay, who was small, smart, sweet, funny, and spoke very good English.

Dorjay first took us to get settled in our hotel, which was more of a guesthouse, and had no running water. We went up onto the roof and sipped Nescafé in the sun, desperately trying to keep our thin blood warm. Looking around at the majestic mountains, I experienced a great feeling of peace and calmness. Mr. Chou was blessedly silent. I liked this place.

Since we had to acclimate to the altitude, Vishnu and I took it pretty easy that first day.

Everything was basic there. Just like the sound waves, heat waves also fell short of reaching any destination in the poorly insulated rooms. What heat there was came from gas stoves that smelled awful and had to be moved dangerously close in order to be effective. I quickly learned that the only way to sleep was to upend the sofa against the wall to block the freezing air from whistling through the ill-fitted window frames, put on every single stitch of clothing I had, and create a cocoon out of the sparse bedcovers to bury myself in.

THE BRIGHT MOUNTAIN SUN BLASTED ME AWAKE the next morning. I watched my breath cloud forth in double gusts. There was still no water from the dormant taps, the buckets had iced over, and breakfast was pretty bad.

We were the only people staying at the hotel. I wanted to switch to the best one in town, but apparently it had been taken over by some rich American.

Dorjay managed to secure us a couple of rooms in the second-best hotel. There was no running water there either, but it did have other guests, which made it a little less depressing. All services were carried out by a very enthusiastic young chap called Dudst, whom we'd had the foresight to tip heavily on our arrival so that buckets of hot water would automatically arrive in our rooms within a few minutes of our return after each day's filming. Those buckets of water became a huge source of comfort throughout our stay there.

The only people who knew we had changed hotels were Dorjay, Vishnu, Dudst, and the hotel receptionist. So I was surprised when the ancient Bakelite phone began to vibrate the moment I walked into my room. All resonance had long since deserted the bell mechanism, but it still announced a call.

I picked it up. "Hello?" I said.

"Ahh, I just wanted to check and make sure everything was okay for you," announced a very familiar voice.

"Mr. Gill!" I exclaimed. A pause. "Sir, how do you know I am wherever I am?" Silence. "Silly question . . ." I chuckled, before continuing: "I'm better for hearing from you—thank you, sir."

Mr. Gill and I talked for several minutes about the altitude, the need to drink vast amounts of water, and his assurance that if we needed anything or got into any trouble, we were to mention his name and we would be fine. It was nice to know we were being watched over.

CAMERAS ASSEMBLED, WE DROVE OFF to the Thikse Gompa Buddhist monastery. It belonged to the Geluk (Yellow Hat) school of Buddhism founded by Tsongkhapa (A.D. 1357–1419), a Tibetan religious leader and philosopher. Built in the mid-15th century on a sacred hill above the ancient village of Thikse, the monastery comprises 12 stories of beautiful Tibetan architecture. Our timing was perfect: the annual Cham dance was being performed that very day.

A lively ceremony, accompanied by traditional Tibetan music, the Cham dance was performed by monks wearing heavily ornamented costumes, with their heads obscured by intricate, colorful representations of demons and characters from ancient folklore.

There was not a cloud in the deep blue sky. We huffed and puffed our way up endless steps with our camera equipment (which is not an easy task at 12,000 feet). Throngs of locals in traditional dress swarmed the turrets, walkways, and even the roof, jostling for the perfect viewpoint.

In a festive mood, the monks joked around mischievously. The musicians had two 20-foot-long horns, through which they blew, with cheeks puffed out—a sound so deep and resonating that it traveled for miles across the Indus Valley. A battle of good and evil was enacted, and little boys dressed in scary devil outfits taunted the audience. They pranced about, stealing hats and coats and making the locals guffaw to the *crash-boom-boom* of symbols from poker-faced monks, almost in a trance, playing out ancient, disjointed rhythms. The little devils even stole the wind guard off my on-camera microphone and threw it high in the thin air, to the delight of the onlookers. It was a buffet of sight, color, sound, and intense stimulation.

After shooting much colorful footage, we went down to the entrance for a late lunch and then off to film the exteriors. We headed back to the hotel as the sun was sinking behind the large, looming Tolkienesque peaks that surrounded the valley.

Dinners at the hotel were good. Although alcohol was not strictly legal, we would send Dudst out with a fistful of rupees, and he would return with cold beers.

There were four other guests at the hotel—all foreign, all male, and all looking very tired. In the middle of dinner, one of the men began to sing in Hebrew. There was a moment of silence, and then another of his group invited us to join them in celebrating Shabbat with a glass of kosher wine. Desperate for some new blood, we moved over to their table. Their names were David, Uri, Boaz, and Frank; and they were from Israel. Uri asked us what we were doing there.

"Shooting," I told him.

"Shooting? You're shooting here?"

"Yes."

"We're, er, shooting a lot, too," he said, with a meaningful look at the others. "What caliber?"

"Caliber?" I echoed, wondering if we were having a translation problem. "Um, HD."

"What?" Uri looked blank. "Is that small arms?"

"We're shooting a movie," I explained. "Are you making one as well?"

Uri looked at the others, and they all started to chuckle. Soon they were laughing so much that they almost toppled off their chairs.

"I wish!" Uri chortled, as another burst of hysterical giggling overtook the others.

Vishnu and I exchanged a baffled look. *Was what I said really* _that_ *funny?* I motioned. *Beats me!* he motioned back, with a bemused shrug.

"Certainly feels like we're in a movie!" chimed in David.

Vishnu and I continued to stare at one another, eyes growing wider by the minute, as we tried to work out whether it was the altitude, the kosher wine, or a bad case of cabin fever that was causing such loopy behavior in our new Israeli friends.

"A movie! This is so much better than a movie!" cackled Boaz.

The bout of hysteria began to subside, and then one of them would giggle again, setting the others off.

"Yep! Gotta be cabin fever . . ." I quietly proclaimed to Vishnu.

"Sorry. Sorry." Uri, with a muffled splutter, tried to explain: "You see, we *are* shooting here, but not a movie, and we've been here for *months!*" He paused briefly to catch his breath, then . . . "We're shooting a gun," he said. Another pause. "Or at least we're trying to!"

And with that, all four immediately broke out into another round of hysterics.

It took a while, but we eventually discovered that they were arms engineers. The Israeli company they worked for had developed a state-of-the-art artillery cannon that was linked up to satellite navigation and had an enormous, and very deadly, range. The Indian army had agreed to pay more than a billion dollars to purchase the cannons as protection against Pakistan. The prototype had been shipped over for trials in Rajasthan several months prior. The Indian Ministry of Defense was delighted . . . until they moved the testing phase to Leh, and found out that the high altitude affected the hydraulic system. The result was that the gun didn't work in the mountains. Our new friends had been at the Hotel Lasermo for six months trying to troubleshoot the problem. If they didn't figure it out by the end of the year, the Indian government was going to cancel the billion-dollar contract.

We refilled our glasses and raised a toast to the success of our shooting—one with a cannon and the other with a camera.

Later that night, burrowed beneath the blankets, I couldn't help analyzing our differences.

Our fellow guests were developing a weapon that killed people, but because it was a defense weapon, they were convinced it would save lives. Vishnu and I, on the other hand, were shooting a camera—not a gun—capturing images that, when cut together into a film, would hopefully promote tolerance, understanding, and even peace. But just like the defense engineers, I had to get *my* "hydraulics" right. Despite the altitude, I had to get footage that would work; otherwise, we too would be the butt of jokes back home. I decided we were more alike than I cared to admit.

WE ROSE AT 4 THE NEXT MORNING, had a very early breakfast, and climbed into our jeep to drive to Pangong Lake on the India/China border. I was excited about shooting the amazing landscapes around Ladakh, as I desperately wanted to pay homage to this visual paradise by cementing my film with the best shots possible.

The weather was definitely on our side. We were halfway through our climb up the second-highest road in the world when dawn broke, illuminating the most incredible sun-kissed peaks and deep shadows in the valleys below that had been patiently awaiting God's caresses. We were stunned by the glorious sight of layer upon layer of spiky terrain, moving through the entire spectrum, as the progression of the dawn brushed the scenery with an ever-changing kaleidoscope of hues. For the first time, I found myself grasping the concept of the "consistency of time."

In this ancient place, untouched by man, the same view had unfolded every day for millennia. It brought home to me how insignificant we really are . . . just an inconsequential blast of energy, like a spurt from an aerosol can, or Uri's cannon. I could understand why the Buddhists chose to build their monasteries here, within the folds of these soaring towers of rocks, at such lofty heights, so that they could become grounded to the earth in such searching shapes, ever reaching upward into incandescent skies. I could understand how we, and our lives, are just minuscule blips of something far greater than anything that can be described.

The rocks were still here just as they were when they were born, albeit eroded by winds, rain, and snow that whistled south from China's rugged brow. I found myself thinking that we still have so much to learn about our connection to nature and our reason for being here on Earth. There is so much more to life and living than the harried lives we are leading. What would it take for us all to shut off our e-mail and the Internet, and walk free from the imprisonment of our modern-day lifestyles in a ruthless, competitive world? How difficult is it, really, to stop, sit back, and just *appreciate* the beauty that surrounds us? What do we have to do to get to that place? Is it selfishness or survival that keeps us shackled to the self-created treadmills that we call "life in the West"? If only we could relax and *be*—then perhaps we would feel that we *belonged,* instead of dreaming of somewhere we *long to be.*

Is this what the Buddhists are preaching? I asked myself. Is this why they're here?

By the time we had climbed to 17,820 feet, I was sure I'd left my hands back down below. Operating the cameras with gloves proved impossible, as did operating it without them. There was little doubt the elements were in control here.

Altitude affects the brain, making you stupid and slow. Lack of concentration meant I had to reshoot some scenes several times. Actions that were normally automatic had to be thought through with great care. Consequently, we spent a lot of time at the summit, capturing the souls of the rocks, the snow, the light, the peaks, and everything else that gave these mountains their something-to-write-home-about air. Judging by the number of prayer flags flapping colorfully in the biting breeze, the locals considered this place to be much closer to God than their homes down below.

Driving was treacherous. There were no roads to speak of on the high mountain passes, just simple tracks that were hangovers from the Silk Routes of the past. Looking out from time to time, I'd flinch to see that in some places there was as little as six inches' space between a 1,000-foot drop and the wheel of the jeep. Down below in the valley, the carcasses of past victims lay rusting—sober reminders of the hostility of this terrain. The Border Roads Organisation had signs posted at intervals along the route, with such homilies as: *"Better to be Mister Late than a Late Mister,"* and *"If you're married—get a divorce from Speed."* There were many "Late Misters" down there.

The last sign before we spotted our destination had English on one side and Hindi on the other. Big bright yellow and black letters pronounced grandly: WAYS OF WORSHIP MAY BE DIFFERENT, BUT GOD IS ONE. *How profound,* I thought—especially as it was paid for by the government.

After eight hours of driving, the cobalt blue waters of Pongong Lake looked absolutely magical. The highest saltwater lake in the world, it bordered India and Tibet. It was beautiful, and extremely remote. I too felt remote, and I felt privileged to be so; I had earned it. Vibrant, billowy clouds cast black shadows over rusty-red hills bordering the lake. The sound of the water was so intoxicating that I stole it by recording it, knowing that when I got back home, playing that sound for a few hours would always instantly transport me back to this magical, untouched place.

Energized and invigorated by the sheer beauty and integrity of Pongong Lake, we flung ourselves around, shooting angle after angle for as long as the sun was willing to light up the scene.

With shooting completed, it was time to eat the packed lunch the hotel had prepared for us. I opened the plastic box to reveal a soggy sandwich, a hard-boiled egg whose yolk was so blue it looked black, and a wrinkly clementine with a skin as thick as that of the inhabitants' faces of the Indus Valley, and as dry as a bone inside. Vishnu was chuckling to himself.

"What's so funny?" I asked.

"The look on your face when you opened your lunch box."

"I'm extremely hungry."

"I know you are. You've gone all quiet and evil."

"Hmm." I sniffed the sandwich. It smelled awful.

"I wouldn't if I were you," Vishnu warned, grinning from ear to ear. "One bite of that and you'd be very loose on the way home!"

"What are you looking so smug about?" I asked.

"Loving the view."

"No. Not buying it. Something's up."

I could hear Dorjay sniggering behind Vishnu's back.

"You two have been up to something," I accused.

Vishnu got to his feet and, rubbing two of his eight hands together, went to the back of the jeep and, to my astonishment, just like a stage magician, pulled out with a flourish . . . a bottle of Dom Pérignon, a tin of beluga caviar, and a roasted duck.

"I'm afraid we'll have to eat the caviar with chapatis. Just pretend they're blinis," he said smoothly.

To this day, I still have no idea where Vishnu had acquired the victuals . . . but it was the best picnic I've ever had.

I went to bed that night with the sound of the wind in my ears, breathing the thin air into my lungs, feeling completely at peace.

"GOD IS PARTICULAR TO EACH INDIVIDUAL. Belief is very difficult to understand."

We were back at Thikse monastery. Dorjay had arranged for us to speak with Lobsang Chodak, the Lama, who was standing by a gold statue of Buddha, looking somewhat incongruous in his fine red Buddhist robes and aviator sunglasses—"to filter out the harsh ultraviolet rays," he said. We filmed him in a room that had the most incredible eagle's view across the barren Indus Valley. It was mesmerizingly peaceful. He finally condescended to remove his fake Ray-Bans, revealing a pair of merry, smiling eyes. Passionate, frank, and sincere, he spoke with a refreshing lack of pretense and really enjoyed being in front of the lens.

"God has given understanding to everyone. For every religion, God has shown different paths—for Muslims, Hindus, and Christians. That's why they have all labeled God as their own. The Buddha has shown many paths, and he has taught us not to harm anything. We don't have any reason to fight, and anyway, it is not allowed."

It was very tough, interviewing someone who not only didn't speak English, but whose own language referenced metaphors instead of concrete adjectives, so I take my hat off to Dorjay, who at the end of the shoot sat down with Vishnu and me and translated hours of footage, line by line.

"Fighting happens when people are too full of pride. In Buddhism, we work for peace. Buddha treated all religions the same, according to what he taught in his books. As Buddhists, we pray for the salvation of all. In the world there are many gods and goddesses, and it's very difficult to say that this or that god is more powerful. Claiming that power of God conditions the way people think; we need to ignore the voices of those who pontificate for selfish reasons and their own gain."

The Lama explained in great detail about how there were three gods in Buddhism—Buddha God, Prayer God, and Man God. *Conchuksum* literally means "Three Gods." Then he embarked upon several lengthy explanations involving history and the path to enlightenment. It was enough to make my head spin. I had to remind myself that this film was about what God meant to individuals, not about religion.

The Lama concluded, "*Conchuk* [God] is very difficult to explain as a common human being. As Buddhists, we worship Buddha, who was born a common man like us. He faced many struggles and left everything behind to find enlightenment. After death we think that life is over, but it isn't until, like Buddha, we reach enlightenment. There should be no fear of death."

UP A MOUNTAIN IN THE HIMALAYAS, surrounded by kind people, and enveloped in a sense of absolute peace, I found that it all made sense to me. But as we were driving around the bumpy mountain roads, Mr. Chou's presence would constantly force me to analyze my discoveries. *Was I really going down the road of explaining God?* I hoped not. I never wanted that burden and would make many enemies if I did. I think I just wanted people to see life without corruption.

Does man taint the beauty of purity? Human beings are very good at littering roads with plastic bottles. Are some religious pundits doing just that in the name of God? I wondered. There can be toxicity in such actions, and some religious leaders know it. And some are full of grace and goodwill. Others are just ill informed, and many throw detritus out the window and expect the common person to pick it up. If I believed in the devil, then surely he dwells in that no-man's-land—in the misinterpretation of the power of God and goodness, in the misinterpretation of love.

We came across an amazing suspension bridge adorned with prayer flags. It provided such a striking visual that we pulled over, and Vishnu and I set up to shoot. The sound of the water tumbling over rocks transported me back into the past, to Scotland, and to one of my earliest memories up the river Ettrick in the lowlands. I was there with my family. I must have been around three or four years old and was fascinated by the round, smooth boulders, and the clean water rushing by with such energy and efficiency. We had seen salmon jumping earlier that day. I'd spotted a large round rock. I can still feel its texture deep in the folds of my memory. I'd picked it up and it was very heavy. I'd swung it with all my might into the river, but somehow the rock had stayed where it was, and *I* had ended up in the freezing water instead. I'd howled, and my family had howled with laughter at the sight of me.

As I stared down at the Ettrick's counterpart in the Himalayas, thinking back on that day in Scotland years before, I saw again my late father's face smiling at me as I was picked up and my wet clothes changed. The memory was still so vivid; I could almost feel the Scottish air caressing my innocent skin. I was hugged and loved and wrapped in the picnic blanket. My father had made a "nest" for me in the back of the station wagon. I'd lain there, listening to "Scarborough Fair" on the radio, watching the trees whisk by the window, as we'd made our way to Bonchester Bridge, where we'd sat, sipping hot cocoa by an open fire.

I pulled myself together and climbed back up to the bridge, where I spotted a young boy of about eight walking across toward me. He was from a Tibetan refugee camp. His mouth curved in the sweetest smile, and snot was all over his nose and face. I asked Dorjay to get the boy to repeat the journey a couple of times so I could film him. Then I asked him, "What is God?"

"Conchuk, Conchuk," he replied.

"God is God."

CHILDREN WERE AN INTEGRAL PART OF THIS JOURNEY. We visited the monastery of Hemis, which is also a school for monks. It was a 17th-century building and one of the largest monasteries in Ladakh, hidden right back in a gorge of spectacular terrain displaying curiously lopsided strata. It looked as if the hand of God Himself had skewed the earth at a 45-degree angle.

The monastery was full of children. I interviewed one of the teaching monks with his flock of kids. The conditions were basic, and the kids were a lot of fun. We soon had them singing songs and turning prayer wheels. Then Vishnu put on his headmaster voice and had them racing each other up and down the courtyard. We climbed to the top of the monastery and filmed the children blowing shells, calling the monks to prayer. It was an amazing shot, with crisp mountains behind and eerie sounds that bounced, echoing off the rocks. The children were so invigorating that they inspired me to write some words on our journey back to Leh. I later used this as a voice-over in the film:

> Perhaps God has something to do with the excitement of the unknown. When we are children, there are so many unanswered questions. Every day is an adventure, full of powerful, swinging emotions. As we grow up, we miss these intense reactions to our everyday world. Life can become mundane. Many of us try to compensate, to live life with the intensity we felt as a child. Alcohol, drugs, sex, and religion are some of the tools we use in an attempt to fill that vacuum. Maybe that's why so many people's lives are governed by the search for something greater than the sum of all their parts.

THE ISRAELI ARMS ENGINEERS were in great form that night. There had been a major breakthrough with the cannon. Dudst had provided an obscene amount of beer, and we joined in the celebrations. Since the problem appeared to be caused by the viscosity of the oil in the hydraulic mechanism, the engineers had concocted a new synthetic that gave much better consistency and resistance to the cold, as well as the pressure changes. Maybe the contract wouldn't die now, they laughed. Maybe the gun would work. Maybe their lives were saved. Maybe their kids would be going to college after all.

A thought occurred to me. "Why don't you just build a pressurized box around the mechanism, like a plane; then you could control both the atmosphere and the temperature and be done with it," I suggested.

There was a deathly silence.

Oops! I hope I haven't insulted anyone, I thought, as I watched the four guys amble quietly off to bed.

"Did I say something wrong?" I asked Vishnu.

"You shouldn't tell your grandmother how to suck eggs," was all he said.

WE WERE ON OUR WAY TO CHOKLAMSAR, a Tibetan refugee village. It was very early in the morning. When we arrived and took in our surroundings, it was as if we'd stepped back in time, with the settlement's traditional squat houses; the smell of wood smoke; and the hint of snow in the scent of the clean, thin air. Mammoth mountains loomed impossibly tall, their vastness fooling the eye, for they were much farther away than they seemed. Hardened women wrestled with buckets of icy-cold water. Mules shuffled by, hauling logs for the upcoming winter nights. There was the odd sound of a dog barking—which was immediately followed by the distinctive opening bars of "Money" by Pink Floyd.

"*Duh-duh-duh-duh-duh-duh-duh-duuuuh-duh.*" For a moment I was stunned, and then I remembered it was the ring tone of my long-forgotten U.S. cell phone. My local Lexus dealer back in California was calling to remind me to schedule my car for a service. "Not right now. Please call back in a couple of months." I stared at the phone, marveling at the smallness of the earth.

OUR FLIGHT BACK TO DELHI HAD BEEN CANCELLED, leaving us in a tricky leave-a-day-early-or-stay-another-week situation. Since I had all the footage I needed, we opted to leave early. Once aboard our early-morning flight, we discovered the identity of the rich American who had commandeered all the rooms at the best hotel in town. It was Brad Pitt. Vishnu spotted him boarding the plane at the last minute with his entourage and settling down quietly and discreetly at the pointy end. It wasn't difficult to piece the story together: Angelina Jolie was currently shooting the movie *A Mighty Heart* in Maharashtra. Brad Pitt was one of the producers, and Leh was the perfect place for a weeklong getaway.

Mr. Gill had invited us to join him for dinner that night; he was eager to hear all about our adventures in the north. So it was no surprise to find ourselves once again being greeted with VIP treatment when we landed. As had happened at Raipur, our names were announced, our escort appeared, and we exited via the rear of the aircraft onto the baking tarmac. Officers with whom we were now well acquainted had collected our bags for us. We just couldn't help ourselves—as we marched past Mr. Pitt and his people, waiting patiently for their luggage to come off the conveyor belt, Vishnu and I exchanged a smug smile of one-upmanship. Brad Pitt might be a Hollywood superstar, but here in Delhi, it was Mr. Gill who held all the cards.

We soon learned, however, that having friends in high places didn't solve everything. The city was packed, and since we'd arrived back ahead of our reservation, finding a hotel room for under $1,200 a night was a formidable task. After much frantic phoning, Vishnu finally managed to get us into the only place he could find.

"At least it isn't going to cost a fortune, and it's a roof over our heads," he reassured me.

The hotel was situated on a large roundabout, a short distance from the airport. The staff had an attitude, particularly the manager, who, when he wasn't hiding himself away in the little office behind the reception area, would look down his nose at us as if we were objects so far beneath him that we belonged on the bottom of his shoes. We nicknamed him *Beaver.*

"I suspect it has something to do with British imperialism; they certainly don't like Englishmen," Vishnu remarked as he handed over our U.K. passports. We were given the worst rooms, situated either side of the reception on the ground floor (no doubt so Beaver could keep an eye on us). No sooner had the bellboy ushered me into my room than the phone rang.

"Hello, sir! Yes. We've arrived." It was Mr. Gill, calling to say that he would pick us up at 8 P.M.

At 7:50, Vishnu and I were waiting in the reception area, dressed for dinner, clutching a couple of bottles of scotch for Mr. Gill's collection, which we'd had the good fortune to find in town, when the familiar sounds of police sirens rent the air. They seemed to be coming from everywhere.

"Here we go again," said Vishnu, as police jeeps careened into the roundabout outside the hotel, spilling out commandos, who immediately leapt into action, locking down the traffic with loud whistles. The sound of motors was soon submerged beneath a cacophony of horns blaring from the mass of cars and motor rickshaws that were now stacking up impatiently behind uniformed lines.

The din went on for several minutes; and then at precisely 8 P.M., Mr. Gill's personal motorcade arrived, disgorging a long line of commandos that literally reached all the way to the hotel's doors. The Delhi chief of police alighted. We'd had the pleasure of enjoying his company the last time we'd been in town. He marched up the hotel steps and, in front of an incredulous Beaver and his extremely bewildered staff, snapped to attention in front of us and said, "Mr. Peter, Mr. Vishnu . . . Mr. Gill is ready, sirs."

As we were escorted down the steps to our awaiting car, I couldn't resist taking a backward glance at Beaver, whose lower jaw seemed to be doing a very good job of polishing the floor.

"I can see it's going to take me a while to shake off being called Vishnu," remarked Vishnu.

We snaked our way through New Delhi to Mr. Gill's compound, where, after an excellent dinner, we talked late into the night about security, God, religion, fanatics, 9/11, Ladakh, Buddhists, our dingy hotel, and scotch.

It was a wonderful evening, made bittersweet by the knowledge that an important chapter in our story was coming to an end. It was to be our last night with our friends. Vishnu had secured us flights out early the next morning, heading southwest across the Indian Ocean, to Africa.

I knew we had to come back to India again soon. Mr. Gill said we'd better; otherwise he would have to rent a warehouse to store all the single malt he'd acquired.

At about 2:30 A.M. Mr. Gill personally accompanied us back to "Beaver Palace" with the same massive police escort. Once again, he warned me to be careful. I was meddling with forces that could possibly do me harm, he said, and ignorance, naïveté, and lack of common sense were futile forms of protection. If ever I needed any help, anywhere in the world, all I had to do was call. He made me read out the numbers of all six of his personal mobile phones to make sure I'd recorded them correctly.

I shook him by the hand and said we would be back, and then headed into the hotel. The police stayed until they knew we were safe. As we walked to our rooms, Beaver suddenly appeared from the back office, with a smile like a scar running from ear to ear.

"Good evening, gentlemen. How very nice to see you home safe and sound. I wanted to personally make sure you had everything you needed," he said, unctuously.

With studied indifference, I turned my back and, ignoring him completely, waved at the convoy that had just started to move off.

As the sound of sirens died away, Vishnu and I scuttled off to our rooms for 85 minutes of sleep.

CHAPTER 10

Africa

"The truth about truth is that it is not the potency of truth itself that is important, but the execution of truth."

— Napkin #10

Poor Vishnu. Another airport, another encounter with his nemesis: *the dreaded porter.* At international airports in the developing world, the baggage handlers (whom we British call porters) all seemed to be the same. Invariably dressed in gray uniforms, they would materialize before the car had even stopped at the drop-off zone, ready to unload your bags, put them on carts, and escort you through the bedlam of other travelers—for a tip. Competition was fierce, and in certain countries, like India, they could descend upon you like a plague of locusts. For some reason Vishnu despised them. Since he was meticulous about the organization and handling of our baggage and equipment, it never failed that the sharklike "feeding frenzy" of the porters would upset his equilibrium, riling him into a completely different personality.

A long scotch-infused evening followed by too little sleep was not the best way to prepare for our early-morning appointment at Delhi International Airport. It was uncanny how this usually calm friend of mine would change at the mere sight of these poor underpaid, overworked human beings. It started the moment we got in the taxi—a low-pitched, almost animalistic growl that slowly became more audible the closer we got to our drop-off point. By the time we alighted from the taxi, he was in full throttle.

"Get away! Get away from me! I don't want you. Go away!" he yelled.

His mood did not improve when he discovered that our flight to Nairobi had been delayed by nine hours.

WE WERE ON OUR WAY TO KENYA, and I was very excited. I'd been there many years before with my father and had fond memories of it. I wanted to find out, from the members of a tradition that hadn't changed for thousands of years, what their thoughts on God were. Indigenous populations were as important to the film as those within organized religions, and I felt their opinions were essential in order to gain as much variety as possible.

It was overcast and stormy when we arrived early the next day in Nairobi. We were met by a driver who led us out to a white safari Land Rover and drove us, smiling all the way, to a district called Karen, where we were surprised to see an enclave of beautiful, ranch-style houses that, to our eyes, spoke more of Beverly Hills or the upper-middle-class estates of Surrey in England than they did of Africa.

Our tired eyes drank in the sights like a thirsty man gulps down water. The rough red-earth roads with women walking, baskets of washing perched comfortably upon their heads, provided a startling contrast to the deserted asphalt drives dividing perfectly tended, freshly watered green lawns behind high walls.

Elizabeth Warner was an old family friend. Soumaya and I had first met her when she had been an international fashion model based out of Los Angeles. After a few years of the rat race, she'd decided to go back to live in Kenya, which, she confided, was the one place in the world where she was truly happy.

Elizabeth and her business partner, Anthony Russell, had just built a luxury lodge in Shompole, southern Kenya, which was right in the middle of Maasai country, close to the Tanzania border. A true pioneer, Anthony was the first white man to construct a hotel that was actually owned and run by the Maasai themselves, thereby guaranteeing that the profits would go straight back into the community for education, health, and water programs. He had raised the financing in Europe and had built an amazing complex out in the wilds, situated on a hilltop overlooking the plains. I'd decided it would be the perfect base from which to film tribal Africa.

Set amid ten acres of paradise, Elizabeth's residence, which was going to be our first port of call, wouldn't have been out of place in a book of fairy tales. Elizabeth had designed it herself. She'd done such an amazing job that many architectural and fashion magazines, from *Elle Decoration* to *Vanity Fair,* had shared her talent with the world. The "house" comprised a series of buildings, set among mature tropical grounds surrounding an Italianate stone courtyard. Guest suites were dotted about the gardens.

Vishnu and I thought we had died and gone to heaven as we emerged from the Land Rover and were greeted by my old friend.

We entered the main living area, which boasted a huge vaulted ceiling and many doors so that the cooler mountain air and hypnotic birdsong could drift in, along with the scent of plumeria, roses, and honeysuckle. A mile above sea level, here the climate was much different from the rest of the country; hence it had attracted many British settlers who wanted to be reminded a little of home. A large fireplace surrounded by massive cushions was evidence of cold evenings. We were served a lavish breakfast: a feast of eggs, pancakes, papaya, and Lapsang Souchong tea in exquisite blue and white china. I felt as if I were on the set of the movie *White Mischief.*

An American who had been educated in Britain, Elizabeth was graced with an impeccable English accent and a sense of humor to match. She had organized everything: Today we would rest, tomorrow we would set out on our adventure, and the following week was Thanksgiving. We simply had to be back for that, as she was throwing a formal bash for 80 people, and the British and American ambassadors were coming. In Kenya, everyone knew everyone else, so the prospect of new "meat" in the form of Vishnu and myself was already creating quite a stir among the locals, Elizabeth enlightened us. We weren't quite sure what to make of that.

Elizabeth's new beau, Mark, came over for lunch. He looked like me, laughed like me, and spoke like me; he was my doppelgänger. It wasn't long before we were calling each other "brother."

There was a terrific thunderstorm in the afternoon, so we built a roaring fire until the sun reappeared, then went out riding. Elizabeth had ten horses, and I ended up on a frisky little lady called Fairchild who wanted to gallop all the time; and since I hadn't ridden for a few years, I rediscovered all sorts of muscles in interesting places that I'd forgotten about.

In the evening we ate roast lamb, washed down with excellent Kenyan red wine, and shared stories. That night I stumbled into my beautifully designed guest suite and was asleep before my head hit the pillow.

THE NEXT DAY, WE TOOK OFF on the five-hour drive to Shompole. Elizabeth and Mark were accompanying us halfway for a picnic, and then the hotel staff would take us the rest of the journey.

We stocked up with Parma ham, fresh bread, coffee from Mark's own plantation, smoked salmon, Italian sausages, chocolate, and grappa for the hardy. I sat on the roof of Mark's Land Cruiser, shooting our drive through the Rift mountains, feeling the air getting warmer and muggier as we meandered down from the Kenyan highlands onto the plains, where the weather changed to the African *hot* that I remembered from my last visit many years before.

We found a peaceful spot by a river and sat down on cushions to enjoy our gourmet picnic.

"*Jambo, Jambo,*" a voice startled us from behind. It was John Langoi, a Maasai warrior and member of the Shompole lodge who was going to be our guide. Attired in Maasai traditional dress, known as *Shúkà*—bright red robes of practical, light cotton—John cut a dashing figure. He was so calm, peaceful, and balanced; he made me realize just how much we miss when we live our confined, modern lives, without the freedom that seems to exist under African skies.

They say everyone has a big house on the plains of Africa, including the termites—because the *house* is the land. Certainly, history has proven how difficult it is to carve it up, segment it off, and call it names.

Gazing across the savanna—at the distant mountains and the spectacular cumulonimbus clouds gathering above the thermals in preparation for the dramatic storms that occur most afternoons—I could easily see why so many people have developed such an intense passion for this land. It was my father's experience of humanity in its rawest and purest state, on the plains of this very continent, that had persuaded him to abandon photographing the worst aspects of man—the degradation, inhumanity, and cruelty of war. And here I was, many years later, seeing the same landscape and smelling the same fragrances. I felt strangely as if I had returned home.

We transferred the gear to John's safari Land Cruiser and headed off across the plains toward the mountain of Shompole that graced the horizon. After about an hour, we climbed into the hills and made our way to the lodge itself.

Anthony's dream was to build the most opulent African experience possible, catering to the European and American elite. Seventy miles from the nearest town, the lodge truly was in the center of unspoiled Africa. Designed by Elizabeth, each guest "house" was organic—which is to say, open-air—with a thatched roof, no walls, and its own swimming pool that snaked about in curves and waterfalls. The bathroom, which was completely exposed to the elements but was actually very private, offered beautiful far-reaching views. The only eyes that could penetrate one's solitude were those belonging to the giraffes, lions, and elephants that lived on the plain below. *What a contrast,* I thought. *Only last week I was freezing in the Hotel Lasermo with a group of Israeli arms engineers.*

As there were no walls or doors to each house, requests for privacy were indicated by planting a spear in the pathway leading to it so the staff knew not to bother you. There was no need for concern about security. Money, traveler's checks, passports, and equipment were completely safe, as we were miles away from any turmoil or crime. I sighed as I sat down on crisp white sheets and gazed off into infinity.

I was glad I hadn't touched any of the grappa at lunch, as I was aching to shoot. Vast thunderclouds could be seen amassing on the horizon, creating dramatic shapes that somehow merged with the mountainous skyline. It was an archetypal African scene, so John drove us to the top of a nearby hill, where I filmed the landscape to the sounds of birds chirping as the horizon gradually grew more and more dramatic.

We watched as a massive sandstorm etched its way across the savanna below, driven by an approaching storm. Distant thunder and the odd flash of lightning excited the air. I managed to get back to my "house" just in time. As the rains came down, I sat in a chair and watched the dusk fill with dark blue tendrils falling from the ominous storm clouds, while I listened to sounds of water hitting the reeds above my head. The smells of electrically charged precipitation on dry land wafted up and surrounded me.

That night after dinner, I retired to my huge bed with the 180-degree view, and reflected that the only downside to staying in such glorious places as this was that Soumaya wasn't here to share it with me. I went to sleep listening to the rain.

THE MAASAI ARE A SEMINOMADIC PEOPLE who originated in the lower Nile Valley north of Lake Turkana, which is situated in northwest Kenya. Unlike many other tribes, the Maasai never practiced slavery and coexisted with the wild animals of the savanna, with an aversion to eating game and birds; they were essentially shepherds and herdsmen. A Maasai myth relates that God gave them all the cattle on Earth, which probably explained why they had no compunction about rustling cattle from other tribes, since they were simply taking back what was rightfully theirs—although I hasten to add that rustling is rarely practiced in Kenya these days.

The Tanzanian and Kenyan governments had both tried to make the Maasai adopt a more settled lifestyle, but ironically, their centuries-old seminomadic way of life has proven the perfect antidote to localized drought and other unfortunate conditions caused by climate changes—if their water runs out, the Maasai simply move to another place. Consequently, they have demanded and received grazing rights to many of the national parks in both Kenya and Tanzania.

I was in a good mood the next morning and anxious to explore. John and our driver, Simon, drove us to Tanzania. It didn't take long to arrive there, and we didn't experience any problems getting through customs, for the simple reason that if it wasn't for the five-foot obelisk sticking up from the grass like an afterthought, we wouldn't have even known that we were crossing an important line that officially separated one country from the other.

We had some fun shooting silly footage here of me getting out my passport and looking for a midget border-control officer hiding somewhere at the base of the obelisk, then getting disappointed because I couldn't find someone to stamp my passport. Of course, it was far too slapstick to include in the final cut of the movie, but we did use the location to prove a point.

"So, John, you want to go to Tanzania?"

"Yeah."

"Okay, let's go to Tanzania." We walked a few steps to the other side of the obelisk. "Now here we are in Tanzania."

"Actually, I've just thought of something," I remarked. "This is illustrative of something I'm doing in the film, which is that boundaries are drawn by man and not by God—because a minute ago we were in Kenya, and it feels exactly the same as being in Tanzania. So, who's to say where we are, apart from man?"

We continued on into the bush, until we stumbled across an incredibly picturesque village. The star-shaped or circular *Inkajijik* houses were built by the able-bodied women of the village, who constructed them out of a latticework of interwoven branches plastered with a mix of mud, sticks, grass, cow dung, ash, and human urine. Surrounding the cluster of huts was a defensive wall of sticks and felled thorn trees, designed to keep out hyenas, lions, and any other African predator.

John rounded up a village elder and a couple of young warriors for me to interview. As we sat beneath the shade of an acacia tree, the sounds of nature all around us were intoxicating: baby lambs bleating, birds chirping, children laughing in the distance. . . . I recorded as many as I could, capturing and preserving the moment by stealing the sounds of now so that I could return to them later, whenever I felt the need for a reminder of what peace and the natural world sound like and feel like.

The village elder looked resplendent in his red tartanlike robe. Speaking only the native Maa language, he was incredibly relaxed. John translated for us both:

"What is God?" I asked.

"God is in heaven," he replied.

"Is God a spirit?"

"God is a spirit. God gives a human the ability to live his life. God gives the rains from the sky, but also brings bad things, like drought."

"Why does God bring bad things?"

"God brings good things and bad things by His own will. We can't do anything to God because He is above us, so whatever He does is His own wish."

"So bad things don't come from the action of the villagers? They just happen?"

"It has nothing to do with people. . . . It has nothing to do with our strength or goodness or weakness or badness—it's just His wish."

"Is your God the same as every other religion's God?" I asked.

The elder rocked back and forth with gentle laughter. "God is one. No matter whether you are white or black, it's the style people use to pray to God that is different. We Maasai sacrifice goats and cows, and we go to the fig trees wearing skins and pray; and maybe God listens to the Maasai at that time. Other tribes use their own style to pray, but God remains the same God, and we don't have to oppose the method of praying from anyone else."

"Then why do religions fight with each other?"

"I don't understand why people are bothered by the style of someone else's prayers. The Maasai don't discriminate, whether you're another tribe, Kikuyu, white man. All we know is that we pray to our God by sacrificing, and going to the bushes and mountains and fig trees, which are sacred. I have no idea why people fight over this."

"What do you think happens when you die?"

"I have no idea. That is a very difficult question, because in all the history of the Maasai, there is no record of ever talking to someone who has died and then come back to life!" He erupted into a huge guffaw. "We just die, but we are aware of the human spirit. We pray to our ancestors, knowing that they are dead, but we also know that their spirits can do something good for us."

"Is there anything you would like to say to the rest of the world?"

"It is meaningless for people to fight over religion. God is the only one to decide who is correct. So the best thing is for people to stay together, and don't tell anyone else how to pray. Remain who you are; pray to who you think God is. Stay aware of where you come from, but leave everyone else alone."

I was astounded by the elder's wisdom. What he said made so much sense. He spoke in such a simple way. With his twinkling eyes and ready laughter, he seemed to be a very balanced and contented man.

I moved over to one of the young warriors who had just been through the traditional (and very painful) Maasai rite of passage of being circumcised without an anesthetic. The ceremony, which was called *emorata,* marked the passage from boyhood to junior warrior. The ritual is carried out by the elders, who use a sharpened knife and cattle-hide bandages for the procedure. During the operation, the boy must remain absolutely silent and still, as exclamations of pain would bring dishonor to him and his family, while flinching could result in disturbing consequences of another kind. It takes around three to four months to heal from these procedures, and urination is often a challenge. During this time, the young warrior has to wear black clothes and live in a separate hut called a *manyatta,* which is specially built by his mother.

When I was a young child in the '70s, my father had been the first photojournalist to document an authentic circumcision ceremony. It had been considered quite a scoop at the time. I remember wincing when I looked at the photographs.

The Maasai are a very handsome race, with high cheekbones and wide eyes. Our warrior's name was Orkando. He was 19 years old. Dressed in purple cotton and adorned with beads, he had a striking presence.

"What is God?" I asked Orkando.

"God is a spirit. I believe God is in the blue sky."

"Do you pray to God?"

"Recently," he said, "I have learned from the Catholics to pray to Jesus Christ." He crossed himself. "Jesus Christ is the face of God."

His response was so unexpected that it took me several seconds to recover from the surprise. At the same time, there was something eerily familiar about Orkando's answer. For a moment, I wondered if I was having a déjà vu experience. Then I remembered the three Marys in Tuba City—members of another indigenous people with remarkably similar belief systems. Despite living thousands of miles away from Orkando, they too saw God through Jesus Christ.

So I asked him: "Is the God in the blue sky that you refer to, the same God that the Maasai worship, the same as the face of Jesus Christ?"

He shook his head. "No. It is a different God. The only face of God is Jesus Christ."

I was astounded. I couldn't believe that two such disparate answers had been given to me by members of the same village, and in such a relaxed and confident manner.

Over a picnic lunch I quizzed John about this. He said it had become very complicated. The traditional Maasai culture would soon be a thing of the past. The tribe was losing its way, and losing its God. Both the Catholics and the Pentecostals were actively converting the Maasai to their way of thinking. The government was trying slowly to eradicate the tribal ways. There was a lot of controversy over female circumcision, which was still being practiced.

"One of the ways the Maasai pray is by sacrifice. The Catholics try to get this banned—they don't believe in sacrificing animals in this way," John said.

I could see how complicated the situation was: the tribe was being torn apart by two different belief systems. While I believe that female circumcision is abhorrent, I also recognized the pain that John's people were suffering, as thousands of years of identity, rituals, and practices were slowly being eroded. Right here, on these peaceful plains of Africa, I was witnessing a microcosm of the conflict of modern thinking versus tradition that was dividing the world at large. It was unbearably sad to see these balanced, cultured people destroyed by a difference of opinion—just as sad as hearing of yet another young girl's life being ruined by a traditional female rite of passage.

I asked John if he could introduce me to the priest who was converting these young people to Christianity. I wanted to know what he had to say.

WE DROVE BACK TO KENYA. John was taking us to a traditional Maasai dance at the foot of Shompole mountain. It was part of a coming-of-age ceremony for one of the warriors of the tribe, known as an *Eunoto*.

We arrived early. Vishnu and I were in good spirits, and we cracked jokes as we set up. Then we heard them. . . .

From somewhere far off in the distance came the sound of rhythmic grunting. It was the most bizarre sound I'd ever heard, yet it fit in so organically with the other sounds of the savanna. The noise gradually grew louder. Then we spotted a long line of Maasai, traveling in single-file formation, outlined against the backdrop of the huge Shompole mountain. But instead of walking, they were executing an elaborate skipping form of locomotion. What's more, every warrior's step was completely in sync with everyone else's; it was like one enormous organism, undulating its way toward us like some giant anaconda. One warrior carried a twisted horn, which emitted a strong primal sound.

When they got closer, they formed a circle, which then split into a figure eight, before they doubled back and stopped right in front of the mountain in a perfectly straight, clean line. The girls sang out and were answered by the warriors. They bobbed their heads, necks adorned by multiple rings of brightly colored beads, below pretty, smooth-skinned, smiling faces, and started jiving off beat to the rhythm. To the girls' accompanying cackles and high-pitched cries, like that of hyenas, the warriors alternated running forward and jumping higher and higher, as if to see who could be best at touching the sky. The jumping dance, I learned, is known as *adamu*. Competitive, the other members of the tribe—especially the girls—raise their voices, encouraging their favorite warrior to jump the highest.

By the time it was all over, I was exhausted and soaked in sweat, reeling from the physicality of sprinting around with a heavy camera, combined with the intense concentration required to capture sounds and images . . . which, when cut together, would show off this incredible ritual in all its glory.

I understood, then, why my father had fallen so in love with Africa.

—⊘—

CHAPTER 11

White Mischief

"When you think you are right, there's usually someone who will think you are wrong. But if you are wrong, it doesn't mean to say they are right."

— NAPKIN #11

John took us to a village to witness a ritual that goes on every day in Maasai country: A warrior bent down on one knee, raised a bow and arrow, and fired it into the jugular vein of a cow. The animal mooed loudly as a tide of crimson blood gushed from the wound into a gourd held by another warrior. As soon as the gourd was full, a hand was placed on the wound, while another scooped up a handful of earth from the ground and massaged a mixture of dust and ash into the skin until the bleeding stopped.

The cow was released, and it went on its merry way as the gourd was passed on to an old lady who sat on a mat, cross-legged, back straight as an arrow. She smiled a toothless grin as she used a stick to stir the blood around and around in the gourd. A young boy of about six sat beside her, eyes wide with anticipation, like a kid in a candy store. After a good whisking, the old woman pulled the stick out of the gourd to reveal a large, wobbling mass of coagulated blood. She held the stick high, and the boy moved forward, hungrily claiming the red clot and sucking it greedily into his mouth, as if it were a Popsicle. With an ecstatic smile, he gulped it down and ran his tongue around his blood-smeared mouth, in the same way that a child back home would lick melted chocolate. He looked just like a young vampire in training.

As gross as it might seem to us, however, the magnificent ritual I had filmed was a completely normal, natural part of Maasai culture. The mixture of cow's blood and milk is their staple diet, along with maize meal. To the Maasai, there are no religious undertones to the extraction of the blood; it's just something that happens every day in the preparation of their food. To us, it was something indicative of a tradition that had been going on for thousands of years.

The old woman poured milk into the gourd, mixed it with the rest of the blood inside, and divided it between tin mugs lined up in front of several other hungry children, all of whom were now salivating at the prospect of the drink. They gobbled it down like Charlie in Roald Dahl's *Charlie and the Chocolate Factory.*

THAT AFTERNOON, SIMON DROVE JOHN, VISHNU, AND ME back across the border into Tanzania, to another beautiful village.

We were ushered into the inner circle of the collection of huts. A corral ringed with thornbushes held the village goats. A *moran* warrior entered, surveyed the goats, and immediately lunged to grab one by its hind leg, causing it to bleat profoundly. He led the goat to the center of the village and laid it down on fronds cut from a sacred fig tree, and without hesitation, started to choke the animal to death.

That morning's bloodletting ritual from the cows was nothing compared to this serious traditional sacrifice. The goat swallowed audibly with a disturbing gurgle, until it lay still and succumbed to sacrifice. A fire was built; the goat was drained of its blood and expertly butchered in front of us. Strips of its meat were cut up and suspended above the fire to cook. When it was ready, the elders—all men—sat in a circle and ate their offering. Life given over to death, ritual, and prayer, every morsel of the goat's body was either consumed or used for something.

A living being had died in front of my lens. I'd seen it suffocated to death, hacked to pieces, its blood drained and flesh sucked from its warm bones by hungry mouths. Right before my very eyes, the goat had been transformed, until it was a goat no longer.

It was a graphic, heady experience. Deep within me, there was a primal understanding of the intensity of the ritual—the transformation, the relationship between death and spirituality, and the way the sacrifice empowered those who carried it out. It was real, and it was ancient. I knew that back home I would be criticized for filming such a ritual, by people who, after expressing their distaste, would probably think nothing of eating a piece of chicken, or buying their kids a burger at McDonald's.

The world really is a bizarre melting pot of contradictions and differences of opinion. *How colorful,* I thought. *How balanced we really are, despite the terrible conflicts that surround us and will continue to do so.* The law of the jungle, the law of the savanna, the law of the universe . . . we ought to rejoice in all of them, to accept their bad points, their good points, and all of their contradictions. There was something about the experience I'd just filmed that made me feel remarkably whole. Perhaps there is a way to *let go*—to allow ourselves to just be, and to simply accept the paradise surrounding us for what it is. Of course, this is much easier to contemplate on the plains of Tanzania than it is on a wet November Monday afternoon in Des Moines or Newcastle.

Months later, musician, songwriter, and political activist Sir Bob Geldof articulated to me the difference between us, our culture, and our ways of thinking. In our interview, I had just brought up Live Aid, which was arguably the biggest and most ambitious fund-raising concert of its day back in 1985. I was one of an estimated 400 million viewers in more than 60 countries who had watched it. I remember seeing Bob Geldof on television thumping his hand on a desk saying something like: "Just don't have that pint tonight and send that money in." He had raised $283 million (in 1985 dollars) for famine relief in Ethiopia and had become quite an authority on Africa as a whole.

"We live in a world of surplus. That's one of the great benefits of civilization," he said. "Certainly in the '80s the argument was about food surplus—paying money to grow unnecessary food that nobody could eat; paying more taxes to store it; and, more obscenely, paying even more taxes to destroy that food, while eight miles south of our continent [Europe] lay the poorest continent on the planet, where 30 million people were starving.

"This was ridiculous—to die of want in a world of surplus. It's not only intellectually absurd, it is morally repulsive; and you don't require God to impose a reality.

"We need each other to exist. It's wired into our DNA. Assisting others is a part of the survival mechanism, and culture stems from that. And how it works is this: I would not exist by myself on this planet; I would die. So I need others to help me to thrive, so I must contribute to the group in order to help them survive. And you still see it functioning in groups in Africa, where it's particularly true. Collectivism really is necessary where there is so little to go around that you need to share each piece in order to make the group grow and protect the individual.

"We've developed in the West this very successful construct of individualism stemming from Greco-Roman and then religious ideas—Judeo-Christian—which holds that the individual is in the image of God. So religion picked up on these philosophical ideas and enshrined them. If that's true—that we're the very image of God, that God so specifically likes this species, we are a reflection of God—it follows that we have rights. If we are so special to God that each individual is uniquely sacred—or as Monty Python would have it, 'Every sperm is sacred'—and if we have inalienable rights, then we have points of view that must be expressed.

"Now this worked very well for us. It gave rise to the end of massive coercive religion into the Enlightenment. From the Enlightenment came ideas of democracy, where we would band together of our own choice and elect people, and from that came a hugely successful type of running the economy. Now that works for us. It doesn't really work for Africans, who have a completely separate, but nonetheless coherent, way of living—collectivism—and for very obvious reasons, it works there.

"So when we try and impose our ideas of how things work on other cultures, generally it won't work. We can't bomb them into it. We can't coerce them into it. We can't blackmail them into it, because we're running against the cultural grain. So it's very hard for other cultures to adopt the things that we say are universal values, but they may just turn out to be parochial concerns."

On hearing Bob Geldof say these words, my mind immediately replayed the image of the little Maasai boy licking the congealed blood. That conjured up thoughts of the Eucharist and gave significance to the idea of drinking the blood of Christ, just as the image of the Maasai elders eating the sacrificed goat reminded me of little white slivers dissolving on my tongue as I knelt in Communion as a child, smelling Mrs. Drury's polish on the railing that separated the congregation from the altar.

It made me realize that, despite the many cultural divides on this planet, our similarities are staring us all in the face. Isn't it obvious? Are we blinded by our own addiction to history and the attitudes toward ritual that get instilled in us as we grow? Is this not the reason there is so much conflict in the world today—the "My God is greater than your God" syndrome that inspired me to travel and make this film in the first place? It began to dawn on me that life is actually very simple—it's just humankind that likes to complicate it.

THE FOLLOWING AFTERNOON WAS SCORCHING HOT as we drove into the compound belonging to the Reverend Peter Ole Kasingi, the Pentecostal priest with whom I'd asked John Langoi to set up an interview. Actually, it was hardly a compound—more like a single-room hut constructed from baked mud and sticks, behind which loomed a massive black water tank that seemed to dominate the area. I soon deduced that it was the presence of the water tank that earned the property the right to be called a "compound." It signified power—no one else for miles around had his or her *own water tank*.

John knocked on the rough hut door. Despite the heat, the Reverend appeared in a thick black cotton shirt and "dog collar." An earnest and extremely polite man, he seemed a little nervous. Like all Maasai, his two lower central incisors had been removed according to tradition. I couldn't help thinking that this mark of heritage also provided a constant visual reminder of his past and the conflict he had chosen.

John quietly confided to me that since the Reverend had betrayed his culture, he really should get fitted with dentures. I'm sure if the man could have afforded the trip to Nairobi and the dental fees, he probably would have.

Our interview started with the same question as most of the others: "Reverend, what is God?"

"God is a spirit, and God is living everywhere."

"What is your denomination?" I asked.

"I am Hope Restoration, which is a Pentecostal denomination. I'm born here, I live here, I serve God here."

"When did you convert to Christianity?"

"I was at Shompole primary school, about 30 kilometers westward. I was converted when missionaries came and passed our school and preached there so that I might receive Christianity."

"Do you believe that the God you pray to as a Christian is the same God that the Maasai pray to in their traditional beliefs?"

He shook his head, shocked by my question. "No, no, no, no, not at all," he rattled off like a machine gun. "The God we are praying to as a Christian—that is a sovereign God, the God that created heaven and Earth. The Maasai are praying in a different way—indirect. They pray through trees, through mountains, through stones, but now as Christians, we are praying to God direct, without the medium of a stone or a tree." He sat up defiantly, victorious after his statement.

"But do you think it's the same God?"

"No, no, no, no. It's a different god. Maasai are praying to idols." He looked at me as if I were really stupid. "A tree is an idol, created by God; but we Christians, we are praying direct to God."

"But what about other major religions? Is the Christian God you pray to the same God as Allah? Is that the same God that the Hindus pray to, the same God other religions pray to?"

"No, no, no!" he said, even more defiantly. "The God Allah and the God of the Hindus—that is not God. Hindus have many gods. Also, like Maasai, they are praying to idols. Allah is not God either. Muslims pray to Allah, and Allah himself is not God, so the prophet Mohammed is the prophet of a nongod, the prophet of an idol; but Jesus Christ, as I believe, is the Son of the living God."

"Obviously you grew up Maasai," I continued. "There are a lot of traditions associated with the Maasai, like piercing of the ears, male circumcision, female circumcision, and the initiation of warriors. Do you accept the Maasai keeping those values, or would you like that to change?"

"These values need to be changed as far as Christianity is concerned, like the circumcision of women. In the Bible there is nothing like that, but in the Old Testament, Abraham was circumcised. Also, Jesus was circumcised, so men must be circumcised. And other things like the initiation of warriors—those are traditional things, and we don't believe in tradition. So we are preaching for people to change those cultures that have no benefit."

"But the Maasai have had these traditions longer than Christianity. What right do you think you have to change traditions that have been in existence for so long?"

"Since the beginning, Christianity has been there. As I read in the Bible, Jesus was the creator of this world; he was with God since the beginning. Christianity is not a new thing. Tradition is a new thing, because men, like Maasai men, are created by God, so they came later. Christianity is the earlier thing."

"Don't you think there is a danger in undermining the status quo of this part of Kenya by confusing traditional people with new sets of values from Christianity?" I ventured.

"There's no danger, because I believe Christianity is a movement that will change the mind of people, direct to God."

"What happens when you die, Reverend?"

"When I die as a Christian, I believe with my own heart that my spirit will go direct to heaven where God is. Because the Bible tells me man is created from the dust, my body will go to the dust, but my spirit will go to God."

"So you think you'll meet Him one day?"

"Yes, I believe. I believe the Bible tells me there's a day of resurrection; and when Christ comes with all his glory and might, when the trumpet is blown, every dead person will arise and meet Jesus— those believers. And those nonbelievers will go straight to hell."

"Do you believe that a Maasai traditional villager, if he has not converted to Christianity, is a nonbeliever, and therefore when he dies, will go to hell?"

The priest nodded fervently. "Yes, I believe. My worry is this: if Jesus came today, all these people who are not converted to Christianity will go to hell."

"So you believe it's your mission to save the people you came from, the traditional Maasai people, to avoid them having to go to hell?"

"Yes," he answered with utter conviction. "That's why I am here in Maasai. I'm born here. I'm serving God here, trying to convert them to Christianity so that when they die, they will go to heaven. I am following the footsteps of Jesus Christ to show the way to heaven." He sat back like a Hindu idol and added, "Prevent them from perishing in hell!"

So here's the rub: I'm certain no one would deny that the abolition of female circumcision would be a healthy, progressive, and compassionate move. So many young women and girls have been horribly scarred and have died horrendous deaths as a result of this practice. That is a matter for careful handling, for gentle government intervention and education. But here in Shompole, Reverend Kasingi had made it his life's mission to convert his own people to Christianity in such a way that they were expected to abolish their entire culture and all their traditions, not just those that modern understanding and thinking deem cruel and dangerous.

But that isn't the real rub—it's the *methods* of this well-intentioned but sadly misinformed man that are causing the damage. He is coercing the Maasai to convert out of fear: *if you don't convert—you will go to hell*. The only education available in the area is run by Christians. Consequently, there is an ongoing mass transference to Christianity . . . and the death of a culture that has existed in that part of the world for thousands of years.

This is what was frustrating John Langoi. He told us that he felt his people had become dispossessed. He was worried about the divisions this created in villages between those who remained loyal to traditional ways and those who had converted. And this was—still is—happening in the name of God. Moreover, those who had converted were receiving a distorted understanding of what Christianity is really about.

Here was a microcosm of the complexities of the human existence right alongside the elephants, hyenas, cattle, and goats. No wonder Africa seems to be collapsing like a house of cards, with corruption, ethnic cleansing, and conflicts erupting all over the continent. With such misguided, fear-induced influences, the people are becoming utterly confused; and the very foundations of their culture, which have supported them for generations, are being uprooted so rapidly that very soon there will be nothing left for them to hold on to.

In light of this, it's not hard to understand why so many members of indigenous cultures, like the Maasai, are becoming addicted to money and alcohol, neither of which mix well with their genetics, or their culture of collectivism.

What makes this situation even creepier, to my mind, is the fact that people like Reverend Peter Ole Kasingi actually have good intentions; they may be misguided, but they are far from malicious or evil.

"Whoever tries to force another the way of worshipping God is a liar," John added. I had to admit, I agreed with him.

THAT EVENING AS I STARED OUT AT THE SAVANNA from my opulent cliff-top aerie, a full rainbow appeared right in front of me. It touched the ground twice—once on the left and once on the right. I realized I had found my two pots of gold in Africa . . . one was the heart of the people, which was more precious than any metal; the other, despite the politics of the continent, was nothing less than paradise itself.

WE HITCHED A PLANE RIDE BACK TO NAIROBI. It was a magnificent flight. We flew low over lakes speckled with pink flamingos, and dodged thunderclouds as we traveled back to green vegetation and another world that belonged somewhere in the middle of the last century.

We arrived back at Elizabeth's house to a scene of absolute bedlam. Houseboys, maids, waiters, and cooks rushed around carrying trays of glasses, wine bottles, champagne buckets, suckling pigs, stuffed turkeys—there was even a whole sheep—in preparation for that evening's Thanksgiving party.

It was going to be a black-tie affair, and Elizabeth had kindly procured a couple of tuxedos for us. The problem was, there were no bow ties to be found. I rummaged around in the grip case and pulled out our last remaining roll of black gaffer tape. *Perfect.* It took a bit of designing, but by the time we joined the ball, Vishnu and I looked very fetching in our improvised 1920s-style black bow ties.

The main room of the house had been set with ten impeccably adorned round tables, each of which seated eight people. It was a who's who of Kenya. Everyone knew everyone else in the community, and Vishnu and I soon understood what Elizabeth had meant about our being "fresh meat." The ladies were dressed to the hilt in ball gowns, tiaras, and enough jewelry to pay off the national debt of several banana republics. There was a swish of exquisite silks, a chorus of oohs, ahhs, and "How-delightful-to-meet-you's"; and before we knew it, Vishnu and I were lost in a sea of ladies of all different shapes, sizes, ages, and intellects.

Unbeknownst to us, Elizabeth's chef—a long-haired Londoner with a frightfully posh accent—had gotten so drunk that he'd forgotten to put the pig, sheep, and lamb into the ovens on time. With dinner running late, Elizabeth was out in the garden, taking the only sensible action under the circumstances: arranging to serve more drinks to keep her hungry guests happy.

Inside the house, I was backed up against a wall by a delightful young lady in a fluffy pink gown—to whom I was explaining how sad it was that my *wife* couldn't be here, as she was back home *with the children,* in an attempt to deflect any advances—when an aristocratic nose materialized in front of me and butted in with a determined: "I say, is that satin?"

The owner of the nose reminded me of my old headmistress at prep school in England, Mrs. Tingly. "Your bow tie . . . it looks like satin. So very Edwardian," the voice continued.

To my absolute horror, I realized that this lady, who must have been at least a generation my senior, was probably—actually definitely—trying to pick me up.

"No, madam. It's gaffer tape," I said, noting her wince at being referred to as "madam."

"Gaffer tape?"

"Yes, madam. Gaffer tape . . . the Americans refer to it as duct tape. It's the same stuff that George W. Bush told the citizens to stock up on after 9/11."

"And why, pray, do you have a black tie made out of gaffer tape?" she inquired, fluttering her eyelashes flirtatiously.

"Because I'm making a film, and when you make a film, gaffer tape is always on hand, and I am Elizabeth's houseguest, and I didn't bring a bow tie with—"

"Oh my God!" she exclaimed, before I could finish. "You're the *Oh My God* chappie, aren't you?!"

"O-M-G!" chirped the young lady in pink.

"I say, well done!" the elder lady simpered. "I could have absolutely sworn it was satin. You could make a business out of this, you know, if it all goes to pot!" She started to guffaw, emitting peal after peal of braying laughter. But thankfully, rescue was at hand.

"Deirdre . . ." a voice called out. "Ah, there you are!" A stocky, energetic-looking man materialized in front of us. "Oh—you must be the fresh meat Elizabeth was talking about." He beamed at me.

"Yes, Harold. We were just talking about his gorgeous bow tie made out of, er . . . gammy tape."

"Gaffer tape," I corrected.

"Gaffer tape," she amended.

"Oh dear . . ." He peered at me with a concerned expression. "Jolly good to meet you. . . . She didn't choke you, did she?"

"No, no, I'm still intact!" I took a deep breath. "Airways open."

"Low blood sugar, you know," he offered by way of explanation, as he started to lead Deirdre away by the hand. Then he turned, and in a lower voice, whispered, "If she bothers you again, just shout out 'Zanzibar!' and I'll be there in a jiff . . . spit spot!" As he waltzed off, I heard him saying, "More champagne, darling? I'm sure we'll be eating soon."

Vishnu had the perfect solution in order to head off any advances at the pass. Obviously inspired by the Reverend Peter Ole Kasingi, he removed his gaffer-tape bow tie and detachable collar and stood up straight. From that moment on, he was respectfully referred to as "Father Vishnu," and mercifully (for him), he was left alone.

"Okay, *now!*" shouted my doppelgänger, Mark. I ran down the hill, my feet pulverizing the intense red Kenyan earth until, suddenly, they were pumping air. Young boys ran about waving below as we soared skyward. I was strapped beneath Mark as we flew in tandem, harnessed beneath a bright orange paraglider.

It was exhilarating. We sailed the constant rift currents that caressed the hillside. Mark spotted an eagle, and to our delight, it glided over and flew beside us as we navigated the currents to keep altitude. It was our last day in Africa, and I'd left my camera back at the house. I had taken a day off, one of the first in more than 75 days of traveling and working, and I'll never forget it.

Up high and silent like this, it was suddenly easy to get perspective on the deep red and green earth below me. Cattle were like specks, mountains loomed tall far away across the savanna, the air was warm and fragrant . . . the continent of Africa—with all her problems, her wealth, her famine, and her smiles—was spread below like a carpet full of intricate stitches, a mosaic that begged to be unraveled, but somehow would always remain the same.

I did what my father had done years before: I promised myself I would return. I had fallen in love with this part of the world. No matter what craziness might be going on inside me, no matter how good Mr. Chou might have become at trapeze work, I knew that when in this part of the world, I would wake up with a smile on my face and embrace the day with excitement and tranquility all wrapped up in one.

"If you wanna know what I think God is, bro," Mark shouted, ". . . this is God!"

CHAPTER 12

The Holy Land

"Doors are only a problem when you think they are locked."

— NAPKIN #12

After a surprisingly easy passage from Nairobi, via Addis Ababa, we reached the Holy Land, the boiling pot of monotheistic religions—a land of corralled Palestinians and frightened faces; the land of God's chosen; a land of soldiers, Mossad, terrorists, broken dreams, and headaches . . . the Promised Land. Vishnu and I walked through customs and breathed sighs of relief. We were here to ask people "What is God?" with cameras, but sans permissions, permits, or any official authority . . . and they had allowed us entry. *Phew!*

I didn't want to make a political film, but I also realized that I couldn't very well make a documentary about what people think God is without coming to the Holy Land. It was a delicate matter, so I'd decided that rather than hunting down the clichés, I would allow circumstance and fate to take me in the right direction.

Uri Fruchtmann, a friend from London, had hooked us up with a local "fixer" named Rina Shatil. A serious young lady, she had been briefed by Vishnu to come up with an eclectic group of individuals for us to interview, while allowing us sufficient time to explore the Palestinian Territories and get perspectives from all angles. I knew it would be a difficult task to accomplish without getting sucked into the obvious. I was also fiercely committed to ensuring that the film would be equally appreciated by Israelis and Palestinians. I had no idea how I was going to pull *that* off. Mr. Chou, who had been relatively quiet the last couple of weeks, had started to make his presence known somewhere over southern Ethiopia. I hoped it wasn't a sign of trouble brewing.

We hit the ground running. I hadn't planned it that way, but owing to a communication error, we somehow managed to lose a day. Apart from our last day in Africa, we had been either traveling or shooting nonstop for two and a half months. I desperately needed a break. We had been to three continents and had logged more than 12,350 miles by car. We had visited the highest (and hottest) places in the world. When filming, we'd been shooting 14 hours a day, followed by two hours of data downloading. In addition to functioning as a cameraman and sound mixer, I'd had to conceptualize on the fly; write in my head; and meet, communicate with, and "light" a host of people. Plus, I was frequently required to be in front of the camera myself.

Then there was the rest of my life: my business, my family, things to take care of back home that you can't simply shove under a carpet (like invoices); tax issues; jobs to be quoted, negotiated, and wrapped so I could earn a living—all of which were now having to be accomplished via Internet connections that rarely worked properly.

By far the greatest stress factor, aside from the fatigue, was money itself. *Will this film work? Will I get my money back? Will people want to see it? Will people pay to see it? Will I get a distribution deal? How will I be able to live while I edit it? Should I invest in an editor now? If so, how? Am I mad? What have I done? . . . What am I doing, funding it on credit cards? If it doesn't work, I'm going to go bankrupt. Help!* Add fatigue into that mix and you can get a pretty accurate picture of how I was beginning to feel.

But I had no choice but to carry on.

I LIKE THE ISRAELIS IMMENSELY; despite the many anxieties and difficulties that constantly beset them, they choose to express their feelings with witty jokes and wry humor. Perhaps it's a result of the volatility of their surroundings, knowing that just 993 miles to the east, Mahmoud Ahmadinejad is spouting rhetoric implying he wants to wipe their country off the map. And of course he's not the only one.

We interviewed many different people—from a Buddhist yoga teacher and a Muslim who was teaching Islam to Israelis, to a Holocaust-history teacher, to a traditional Hasidic rabbi—and I was beginning to get extremely frustrated. They were all saying the same thing. They were all tolerant, and understanding of the issues of faith; their God was the same as every other religion's God; they had great empathy for the Palestinians. . . . Wait a minute—where was the vitriol? Where was the conflict? This couldn't be reality—this wasn't what we were constantly hearing on the news.

After two days of interviews in and around Tel Aviv, we piled into a rental car and crossed over into the Palestinian Territories . . . and into another world.

Our first port of call was the Jewish settlement of Tekoa, where we would be interviewing an Ashkenazi Orthodox rabbi by the name of Menachem Froman. The Jewish settlement looked like something you would expect to see in California or Texas, rather than the Middle East. With its neat little trees and shrubs and squeaky-clean roadways, it felt like it was trying too hard to make the terrain look like something it was not.

Rabbi Froman was a well-known peacemaker and negotiator who had close ties to Palestinian leaders from the PLO and Hamas. And what a colorful character he was, too. Dressed in traditional black, he had Gandalf's long white hair and beard, and eyes that crinkled when he smiled. Strapped to his forehead was a black *tefillin*—a box made from kosher leather, containing scrolls from the Torah written in kosher black ink.

A charismatic and passionately spoken man, Rabbi Froman had me in stitches with his wonderful sense of humor. I liked him a lot. We conducted our interview on a hilltop overlooking Bethlehem. Gazing across at the fabled town, I couldn't help comparing the scene to the visions I'd conjured up as a child. The skyline of modern-day Bethlehem was a far cry from the image I'd had in mind when mouthing the words to "We Three Kings of Orient Are" beneath the upturned ship of Smarden Church. As if to punctuate those thoughts, there was a constant *chop, chop, chop* of Israeli helicopters flying watchfully overhead. Rabbi Froman sat on a rock with his wife beside him, cracking jokes while we waited for the helicopters to go away.

When he was finally able to speak, the rabbi said, "Well, I was informed that you are making a very important film on God, and you are interviewing many important personalities to speak about God. Now I suggest you interview God Himself." He pointed upward with his finger and said again, "God Himself!"

He continued: "God, from the Jewish point of view, as much as I understand it, exists between us. God doesn't reveal Himself in any creature, in any part of creation, but in the relations *between* the parts of creation—in the relations between me and my wife, me and my neighbor, me and heaven." He pointed to the sky again. "Between me and the earth. So I suggest you focus your camera toward God Himself—to the open space between us." He motioned to the space between him and his wife. "Between us," he repeated for emphasis.

"God is in the space between my people and the Palestinians," Rabbi Froman went on. "Every Jewish child is supposed to know the famous story about one of our masters who was asked to summarize Judaism in one sentence, and he answered by quoting the verse from Leviticus, from the Torah, 'Love thy neighbor.'" He pointed over his shoulder. "The Palestinians are our neighbors, and God exists between us and them. God exists between the Jewish people and the Arabs, between the Western civilization and the great Arab culture, the great Muslim culture. I think it's enough for you, no?" He laughed.

I got straight to the point. "There is so much conflict here. Do you think there will ever be any reconciliation? Everyone wants a piece of this land. Who should walk these hills?" I asked.

"There are conflicts between me and my wife. There are conflicts between the Jews and the Palestinians, but this is exactly our problem. Our challenge is to reveal God, to reveal peace. In Hebrew and in Arabic, *Shalom, Salaam*—'peace'—is the very name of God. There is the possibility of war, but there is also the possibility of the revelation of God, of peace, between us—with God's help, with the help of Shalom, with the help of Salaam."

I was about to ask another question when Rabbi Froman spoke up again. "Perhaps my wife will speak a little, huh? You got the impression she is a sad, obedient wife, but that is not the reality, so you had better hear the truth!"

"I would be delighted."

"So what would you like to ask my wife? How many times a day I beat her? Yes? No?" He chuckled.

The rabbi's wife started talking in Hebrew, and when she finished, Rabbi Froman said, "If you had understood what my wife said, then you would see that she doesn't agree with me. Who is right? Which one of us expressed the word of God? Neither of us. Not she, not me. The truth, the word of God, exists between us."

"I look forward to having her words translated," I said.

"I'll give you a short summary: She said the British are a nasty people. Most of them will have to be killed, but some of them can be corrected with years of reeducation!" Then he threw his head back and started laughing loudly, while his wife, who had clearly understood everything he'd said, went beet red.

I asked the rabbi how he knew that God existed. His answer was immediate: "You know better than I—you've just spent the last half hour filming Him! No? Don't you see Him? He's right here!"

"I see a rock."

"Your camera is pointing right at Him. He's right here—between me and my wife. The freedom . . . can't you see it? The freedom that I have to not agree with her—is that not the revelation of God Himself? God is freedom, Peter. The freedom I have to not obey my wife is the very word of God."

At that moment, I was startled by the sudden strains of "Row, row, row your boat gently down the stream" echoing out from the school across the valley. "Merrily, merrily, merrily, merrily, life is but a dream . . ."

It was surreal; I couldn't help wondering if there was a deeper significance to the lyrics. When I looked them up, I learned that the song is a metaphor for life's difficult choices, and thus the boat is often interpreted as a reference to oneself.

I HAD MIXED FEELINGS ABOUT THE ISRAELI-PALESTINIAN conflict. I felt that it was one of the most misunderstood political conundrums in recent history, and there certainly seemed to be no hope of any kind of resolution. Clearly, it wasn't a conflict over God—it was a conflict over land; money; and, more significantly, *emotion.*

I don't think the British handled it very well after they pulled out of what used to be called Palestine, just as they didn't handle pulling out of the Sudan very well, or India and what was to become Pakistan. There was too much hurt, guilt, and violence and too many politics in a land that had been fought over for thousands of years. The distaste of Jews and Arabs for one another was like a family feud—the very worst type of conflict—stemming right back to Ishmael and Isaac, the two sons of Abraham.

It was Arthur J. Balfour, the architect of the Balfour Declaration, who stated in 1917:

> His Majesty's Government views with favor the establishment in Palestine of a national home for the Jewish people and will use their best endeavors to facilitate the achievement of that object, it being clearly understood that nothing shall be done which may prejudice the civil and religious rights of existing non-Jewish communities in Palestine.

In 1948, modern Israel was born, but many Palestinians felt dispossessed. They felt they'd been turned out of their homes, lost their businesses, and been corralled into different sections of what now constituted the Palestinian Territories—with no rights, no freedom, and no ability to travel freely from one sector to the next.

Some Palestinians cite global sympathy for the ghastly fate of the Jewish community in Europe during World War II as a contributing factor that tipped the balance out of their favor. The U.S. has brokered many reconciliation attempts, but the terms for a peaceful Palestinian state seem to be as elusive today as they were in 1948. And violent terrorist activity on the part of militant Palestinians and the sweeping Israeli reprisals that inevitably follow have only served to compound the problems.

So where does that leave us? We live in a polarized world, with the Israeli-Palestinian conflict always at the center, providing a convenient political excuse for economic-based activities, warfare, global terrorism, and even 9/11. Throw in biblical revelations that prophesy things like "The last great battle will pit Israel against the rest of the Middle East and its allies," and it is no wonder the situation is not only delicate but also incendiary.

I was acutely aware that I must make it my utmost responsibility to be unbiased in my material. I was making a film about what people think God is—not a political statement.

I questioned philosophy professor Meir Bozolo from the Hebrew University in Jerusalem about conflict and the role of God. I loved his answer:

"There cannot be two true believers in God that fight each other and hate each other. To believe in God means to be close to God. That's why you are close to any other believer, because if two of you are close to something, then you must be close to each other. If there is a fight between religions, then surely one of them, at least, has no relation to God. *At least*—or maybe both of them have no relation to God.

"The fact that there is evil in the world, and the fact that you believe in God, is an indication that you know only part of the picture. God, or the idea of God, is perhaps one of the ideas that are mostly abused by human beings. People have abused this idea to make all of the ugly things that you can imagine in this world. You can make God not someone you are aspiring to, but someone that you are *using* to do something; and you can use God to empower your anger or your jealousy. But the devil, perhaps, is one indication of the existence of God, because in secular terms, there is no notion of the devil or evil. So if you use the word *devil,* you are using religious language. Once you use religious language, you are very close to God."

RABBI FROMAN AND PROFESSOR BOZOLO ASIDE, I was frustrated with the material I was getting in Israel. When I expressed my concerns to Rina, she suggested we drive to Jenin, in the Palestinian Territories, the next day and see if we could track down a Hamas leader she had heard of. That was more like it.

The reality was that no Palestinian in his right mind was going to speak his heart for fear of Israeli recriminations. Only politically committed Palestinians, like a Hamas member, would say what they thought, because they *wanted* to get their opinions across—to hell with any reprisals. Israelis, on the other hand, chose their words very carefully as well so as not to make any waves. Hence, anyone who was likely to have any really interesting opinions about the situation probably wouldn't be found in Israel or the Palestinian Territories at all.

As we made our way northeast from Tel Aviv the next morning, I couldn't shake off the feeling that I might never get the footage I had hoped for, which I believed would be so crucial to the film.

As things transpired, it became impossible to get to Jenin. The first two checkpoints were closed, forcing us to loop around south and then north again in an effort to approach the city from another direction. After the 17th checkpoint, we finally accepted that we were never going to make it in time to shoot anything; we'd been driving for eight hours, and as it was winter, the light was going.

There is no clear demarcation line between the Palestinian Territories and Israel. However, there are pockets of territories—*lots of them*. First there are "A" pockets, which are pure Palestinian areas, run by the Palestinian Authority. Then there are "B" pockets, which comprise Palestinian land with Jewish settlements on them. And then there is Israel itself. Between each pocket is a checkpoint, and while you might be allowed into a B area at one checkpoint, you could easily be stopped entering an A area from another. Consequently, travel between pockets required trying several different checkpoints and hoping for the best.

Worse yet, news had spread that we had cameras but no permit, so it didn't take long before we found ourselves being turned away by angry Israeli soldiers . . . before we even reached the checkpoint.

I was not pleased. Neither was Mr. Chou, who seemed to be attempting to deep-fry falafels in my stomach.

When we stopped at a crossing near the city of Nablus, I decided to explain on camera that travel in the Holy Land is much more complicated than one can possibly imagine. However, each time I started to speak, a car horn would blast out.

"Turn around and go away is the motto of the—" I would start to say, then be abruptly cut off by a very long and loud *bee-eee-eee-pppp!*

"Turn around and go away," I'd start again . . . *bee-eee-eee-pppp!*

Without fail, every time I said the word *Turn*, another horn would go off—and from a different vehicle. We did take after take. Finally, after about eight tries, I said in frustration to the camera: "Every time I say 'Turn,' someone f**king hoots." Right on cue, just as I emitted the expletive, a horn went off and censored my line.

It was such a fitting portrayal of the frustration I was feeling, as well as the frustration of that part of the world, with all its failed peace talks, that we decided to cut the sequence into the film, just as we recorded it—complete with the fluffs.

THE NEXT DAY, WE DROVE TO BETHLEHEM to meet up with a Palestinian guide called Mohammed, who was to show us the various places of interest—like the birthplace of Jesus Christ under the Church of the Nativity.

It took *forever* to get there. There's one thing about the Holy Land that people just don't understand until they've actually visited: It is *tiny*. The whole area could fit into a glove. It is the most bizarre fact—so much history; so many stories; so much upheaval, strife, legend, and spilt blood has all taken place in an area that could fit between Santa Monica and Hollywood, or between Richmond and Central London. And just like London and Hollywood, the traffic, especially during rush hour, is terrible. What should have taken an hour took three. We were concerned that Mohammed might have given up on us, but there he was, waiting patiently outside the Church of the Nativity, when we finally arrived.

Being late meant emergency work mode. I had a lot I wanted to cover here, and we met our first disappointment very quickly at the Greek Orthodox church.

The Church of the Nativity comprises three parts: Greek Orthodox, Franciscan Catholic, and Armenian Catholic. The best-looking interior is the old Greek Orthodox part—which houses the grotto of Jesus Christ, complete with a manger in a cave below the church. I wanted to interview the bishop inside the church, which we were told was possible if we bought a permit for $100. But every one of the Greek Orthodox monks we met en route to the bishop—who was in the monastery at the back—was rude, nasty, and confrontational.

We finally caught up with the boss, and I have to say, he was one of the most disgusting men I had come across so far on this journey. Fat and angry, he strutted around as if he owned the place. He was about as close to godliness as Pluto is from the sun. There was only one word he had in his vocabulary, and that was *No!* If I wanted to film, I had to go to Jerusalem to the central office by the Jaffa Gate and submit my application in writing . . . blah, blah, blah.

Between us, Vishnu and I had filmed in more than 90 countries, so we understood protocol, rules, permits, and legislation. It was all part of the filmmaking process. Had the Church of the Nativity been central to the plot of the film, and if we'd had the resources, we would have paid a location manager to set it up well in advance. As it wasn't central to the plot, we thought we would be able to obtain a day permit. Red tape can always get in the way, but what surprised me was the defensive manner of this supposed man of God. I appealed to his godliness and said I had come a long way, and it would be very fitting to pay a tribute to him and his church, as it was the most important in the whole of Christendom.

All he could say was "No." He called his monks and had us escorted off the property. What he didn't know was that I'd already sneaked in as a tourist beforehand and shot the whole place on the little B camera (an insurance policy Vishnu and I had taken out).

The grotto of Jesus Christ had been spiritually empty for me. I am sensitive to great sacred places, but I have felt more holiness, and more of a connection, on a mountaintop in Thailand, in a forest in Scotland, or gazing out at the crashing ocean in New Zealand than I felt down there in that cave. It just didn't ring true to me, and I don't know why. I wondered if it really was the birthplace of Jesus Christ, the Son of God, as Christians believe; and if it was so special a place, why was there such an ugly bunch of disgruntled human beings looming over it? I was deeply disappointed.

The adjoining Church of the Nativity, on the other hand, was run by Franciscan monks; and what a kind, loving bunch of humans they were—the complete antithesis of those next door. We made ourselves known to Father Amjad Sabarra, who was in charge of the church. Father Sabarra immediately dropped everything and agreed to be interviewed. He bubbled benevolence, and seemed very sincere in his life's mission.

A Palestinian Christian, he was a gentle, humble soul who spoke with a deep, calming voice that resonated beautifully in the acoustics of the cloisters. As pastor of the oldest Catholic parish in the world, he'd been in the basilica when it had been under siege from April 2 to May 11, 2002, in the famous standoff between Palestinian members of Fatah, Hamas, and the Palestinian Islamic Jihad, who had sought refuge in the church, and the IDF (Israeli Defense Forces), who had surrounded it outside. It had been an international incident that many had feared would result in a bloodbath. In the end, the peacemakers had managed to negotiate a successful resolution. Although eight Palestinians had died in the skirmishes, the number of casualties turned out to be far less than feared.

During that time, the Franciscan monks had cared for the wounded and looked after the 208 Palestinians who had sought sanctuary in the church, irrespective of their political motives. The monks were never hostages, Father Sabarra insisted, contrary to what the international media had reported; the Franciscans simply felt it was their duty to care for those who sought shelter in the holiest site in Christendom.

I positioned him so that his head was framed by three graphic stone arches, and fired my first question at him:

"We are standing at the birthplace of Jesus Christ. Can you explain what the relationship is between man and God?"

"In this place, the history of God interacts with the history of man. The word of God became flesh in this place because God wanted to be beside man, so as to give man a sense for his life, especially for the people who had been forgotten and were lost.

Also, if we sin, we find that His love gives us a new hope that we can continue our life straight to heaven and to God Himself."

"Is the God you pray to the same God all religions pray to?"

"We believe in one God. As Jesus said, who can speak about God is better than the one that comes from God. God is one. God is love."

"So it doesn't matter who you are or what religion you are—it's the same God?"

"Yes."

"It's so charged in this part of the world. Why do you think religions fight so much?"

"It's not religions that fight. It is man that fights. If we study all the books that have been revealed by God Himself—the Koran, the Old Testament, the New Testament—we find that God is the same to everybody, and whoever knows God should love the man beside him, so for this reason if we really believe in God, there would be no war."

"Is there anything you would like to do in your life to promote those words?"

"As Franciscans, we try to be like our founder, Saint Francis, the first peacemaker. He says everyone has to be the channel of peace in every place that we are, and we have to do it with humility and to live this every day and act it with love to each one that God put into our life."

"Do you think you will meet God?"

"I meet God every day because I am meeting man, and we know that God is revealed in man."

We filmed the service in the church. I loved the monks' singing. The tones, the architecture, and the location certainly lifted my spirits; and I could understand why places of worship can create a feeling of otherworldliness for followers of the faith.

MOHAMMED TOOK US TO A DELICIOUS PLACE for lunch, where I had the best hummus I have ever tasted. I liked Bethlehem; it was full of life and activity, a cauldron of a little bit of everything.

As darkness descends early at that time of year, I wanted

to shoot the famous city and the notorious wall that separates the Palestinians from Israel. It was a sad afternoon, and a sharp contrast to the touristy Manger Square—where the Church of the Nativity is situated, along with the Bethlehem Peace Center. The wall is ugly. With its vertical concrete slabs interspersed with gun turrets, it reminded me of a prison. Several miles long, it is adorned with graffiti such as "Israel Bullshit," "Occupation is a crime," "Free Palestine," "Open your heart," and "*All* beings want to be free."

I can't think of anywhere else in the world where groups of people are treated with such disrespect because of their heritage. If our guide, Mohammed, wanted to see his aunt in Ramallah, it would take him five hours to travel a distance of just 43 miles. It is virtually impossible for him, as a Palestinian, to go abroad. He has no identity, and no rights whatsoever. Whenever he goes through a checkpoint, he is subjected to abuse from the Israeli soldiers.

This disrespect breeds contempt. The contempt leads to anger; the anger leads to conflict, which in turn leads to acts of violence until Katyusha rockets are hurled over into Israel, killing innocent Israelis and causing the IDF to retaliate with their full military might, which inevitably leads to innocent Palestinians being killed in turn. It's a vicious cycle that just keeps causing more distress and resentment. But it isn't as simple as that. There is too much money, too much power, too many voices, and too much anger involved.

For some, religion is the link between man and God, but when I came across walls such as these, it became extremely clear to me that religion is sometimes much more of a barrier than a bridge.

I filmed Palestinian kids throwing rocks at the wall under a large blood-red graffiti statement spelling out: STOP THE RACIST WALL.

I wanted to throw more light on this, so later when I got back to Los Angeles, I sought an interview with Rabbi Yitzchok Adlerstein, Director of Interfaith Affairs at the Snider Social Action Institute. This is what he said:

"The trouble with religion today is that there's just enough of it for people to learn to hate each other, but not enough for them to learn to love each other. A God that can ask His followers in His name to murder and maim and commit acts of terror, I don't believe is really the same God. I fear that some people may have stepped over the border and may be worshipping something quite different.

"There must be some state for Palestinians. The vast majority of Israelis and Jews have no problem with that and would be quite relieved to wake up one morning and find a peaceful Palestinian state living next door to them. How we arrive at that is another matter. God built into the fabric of creation a final, utopian existence. In that existence, either there will be an independent Palestinian state or the Palestinians won't care about it anymore, but everybody will be holding hands and singing 'Kumbaya' in Yiddish.

"But ask your Muslim friends in the Middle East, if they had a Palestinian state, what rights would be given to Jews or Christians? How many Arab states today will allow a Jew to live there?"

Well, quite a few actually, including Morocco, where one of the chief advisors to King Mohammed VI, André Azoulay, whom I had the pleasure of interviewing a few weeks later, is Jewish. But then there were other places, such as Saudi Arabia and some of the Gulf states, where Rabbi Adlerstein's comment definitely had some relevance.

THE DAY AFTER VISHNU AND I LEFT BETHLEHEM, we drove to Ramallah, the capital of the Palestinian Territories. Ramallah is in an A sector (unlike Bethlehem, which is a B sector). It is literally right outside Jerusalem, but it could not be more different. Driving from Israel into Ramallah is like driving from San Diego to Tijuana in Mexico. Everything on the Israeli side of the wall is clean, well manicured, and modern. Conversely, the Palestinian side of the checkpoint is like a developing country, with potholes, ancient taxis, beeping horns, lively markets, and the raucous hubbub of life. Unlike our journey to Jenin, we had no trouble entering. Mohammed met us there, having spent almost five hours to cover the 43 miles and pass through seven checkpoints.

Muezzins cried out from the mosques, calling the faithful to prayer. Peeling posters of Arafat were everywhere, along with pictures of Hamas leaders and other politicians. The green Hamas flag flew from many rooftops. The Palestinians themselves conducted their day with fixed expressions and furrowed brows. We were welcomed everywhere with true Arab hospitality.

Although we were technically not allowed, no one stopped us from driving right into Ramallah in our Israeli rental car. I started by filming general shots downtown; then I interviewed a taxi driver. It soon became evident that I was not going to get any remotely truthful dialogue. Many people would say things to me off camera that were frightening. They wanted to speak their mind, but there was no way they were going to do so publicly. There was such hatred of and resentment toward the Israelis that most of the populace lived their lives in exasperated resignation. They felt like cattle, like subhumans. It was very sad.

I was worried that none of my footage from this part of the journey was going to be useful. After our failed attempt to reach the Hamas member in Jenin, I still felt we needed a politician—someone who wasn't afraid to say what he or she thought. So we drove to the parliament building, parked outside, and Vishnu literally walked straight in and went politician hunting. Twenty minutes later he emerged with a smug grin on his face. "I have your man. We can do the interview right now. He's waiting for us." Just like that.

We walked into the Palestinian Authority parliament building with our gear, without a glance from anyone. Our subject, Ayman Daraghmeh, was not only a politician, but also happened to be a member of the Hamas Palestinian Legislative Council. He was remarkably candid.

"What is God, sir?" I began.

"God is the creator, the mercy, the power, the supporter for his slaves on the ground. There is one God only."

I asked him if his God was the same God that other religions believed in.

"I feel that Muslims, Christians, and Jews believe in one God, in His Almighty. Hindus and Buddhists have their God, but they also worship many gods to reach His Almighty."

"Why do you think so many religions fight?"

Mr. Daraghmeh saw this question coming and snickered. "They should not fight; they should solve problems with peace.

I don't believe wars happen because of religion. If we understand religion, we would not fight each other."

"Do you think the conflict between Israel and the Palestinians is about religion, or about land and money?"

"We are here in Ramallah, but our capital is Jerusalem, which of course is occupied by the Israelis. The problem between the Palestinians and the Israelis is not about religion; it's a land conflict. We want to build an independent state, and this is a problem with the Israelis. The media doesn't show how it really is. It shows a conflict between Muslims and Jews, but of course we don't have a problem with Jews in America or in Europe. We are having problems with the occupiers."

"So how do you see an end to the crisis?"

"There are 10,000 Palestinians in Israeli jails. This crisis will not end until our refugees come back home. We should get our rights, including our independent state, with Jerusalem as its capital. Otherwise this conflict will continue."

Stalemate. It was becoming very clear just how difficult it was going to be to continue in this part of the world without getting sucked into politics.

We spent the rest of the day interviewing people on the street—a teacher, a market store owner, a restaurateur. There was no anxiety. Everyone was courteous and kind, and nobody gave us any grief when filming. The police were helpful and never asked for the permit we didn't have. It was a pleasant experience. But no one, apart from Ayman Daraghmeh, had said anything definitive. I still felt we were missing the piece that would bind this segment together, and our shooting time was rapidly running out.

It was Rabbi Froman who came up with the perfect solution. He called and invited us to meet him right then, in the old city of Jerusalem.

First, he took us to the Wailing Wall so we could see how his people prayed, but we were refused entrance because of the size of my camera. Rabbi Froman did what he could to secure us permission, but there was far too much red tape, so he took us into the Jewish quarter of old Jerusalem, to an amazing spot that looked out across the square to the wall. It was a wonderful vantage point.

He went off to worship, and using a very long lens, I caught him praying at the wall.

After the Wailing Wall, we jumped into the car and headed out of the old city to the Mount of Olives—another famous place we'd all heard so much about—but here again, the reality was so different from the stories. It was just a stark hill, covered in roads with bright yellow mercury lamps that emitted an eerie and modern, yet at the same time curiously dated, vibe. It was quite different from the pictures I'd formed in my head when I was a child—Jesus Christ, surrounded by disciples and olive trees, delivering the Sermon on the Mount. My feelings of disappointment and crushed preconceptions were accentuated by a group of teenagers smoking and drinking in the parking lot to the loud, distorted sounds of Britney Spears.

Rabbi Froman asked us to pull over. We walked across the lot to another amazing vantage point, which revealed the Dome of the Rock in all its golden glory across the valley in old Jerusalem. The Dome of the Rock is the oldest Islamic building in the world, and, ironically, also the holiest spot in Judaism, owing to the fact that it houses the Foundation Stone, toward which Jews all over the world pray every day. At the same time, because Muslims believe that the prophet Mohammed stepped upon this very same stone and rose to the heavens to receive guidance from the creator, Allah, the Foundation Rock is also the third-holiest place in the world for Muslims.

We were soon joined by Ibrahim Ahmed Abu El-Hawa, one of Rabbi Froman's closest friends and an active Palestinian peacemaker. The Rabbi introduced his friend as his brother, as a befitting reference to Ishmael and Isaac.

Vishnu politely asked the partying youths to turn off Britney. As they sped off with screeching tires, I framed a Muslim in long white robes and *keffiyeh* (Arab headdress) with an Orthodox rabbi in traditional black robes and *yarmulke* (skull cap), with the Dome of the Rock behind them.

Ibrahim spoke first. "My name is Ibrahim Ahmed El-Hawa. I am an Arab Palestinian Muslim. I was born here and have lived here my whole life. How can you love your neighbor if you don't know him? We have a problem with the wall. Not the wall the government built, but the wall we build between one another because we don't listen to one another."

He and Rabbi Froman then embraced. There were tears in their eyes.

"You see the open space?" Rabbi Froman asked me, as he wiped his tears with a handkerchief. "I don't represent God. Ibrahim doesn't represent God. The victorious formula is that nobody represents God. God is between us. There." He pointed between himself and Ibrahim. "There." He pointed to the Dome of the Rock. "There." He pointed to the sky.

Fate, aided by Rina, had brought this moment together. She had done a wonderful job of keeping politics away from my camera. Many people have wept when they've seen this footage of a Palestinian and a rabbi embracing in such a location, because you can't fake the message, and it exposes the school-yard mentality that surrounds this centuries-old (yet modern) conflict. Against this image, political rhetoric sounds hollow, futile, childish, and tiring; it's just fancy words that don't mean a thing, promises that will never be kept, and dreams that will never come true. The love between these two men, which was so starkly real and so evident in its truthfulness, can never be taken away.

The message was clear—our shoot in Israel was thus complete; it was time to move on.

CHAPTER 13

Morocco

"It never goes back, yet never stands still. It can fly, but doesn't have wings. It can be measured, yet never seen. It has no voice and is absent in our dreams. It's Time."

— NAPKIN #13

Getting into Israel was easy. Getting out was horrendous. Fortunately, Vishnu and I had both figured it could take a while, so we'd arrived at the airport super early. We were pulled over by security, split up, and interrogated.

They must have a casting agency for the security staff. I had three girls attending to me, and all were extremely attractive and very polite, but they asked an enormous amount of questions. They wanted to know about my past, my upbringing, my political views, my career, my school, and the color of the wallpaper of my grandmother's downstairs toilet. They went through the equipment and luggage about three times, carting off bags to different parts of the airport and scanning them in a variety of different high-tech machines, until they eventually decided to confiscate one of my portable lights. To this day, I have absolutely no idea why. The light arrived a couple of days later at my office in Los Angeles, and I'm just glad they didn't confiscate the A camera.

Finally they allowed us to get on the plane to Madrid.

We were on our way to Morocco and had to go via Spain, as there were no direct flights from Israel. When we finally touched down in Tangier, Mr. Chou was stirring up a storm—it was at this very airport months earlier that I'd stared at the black conveyor belt, waiting for the equipment that would never arrive. But these were different times, and soon all the bags appeared and Mr. Chou settled down.

Tangier was a town made famous—or infamous—by American writers from the beat generation such as William Burroughs, Jack Kerouac, Allen Ginsberg, Gregory Corso, and Paul Bowles. Core elements of "beat" culture included a rejection of materialism, drug and sexual experimentation, and an interest in music and Eastern religion. From the 1950s onward, Tangier would be molded into stories from these writers' minds. I'd been the last person to photograph Paul Bowles, back in November 1999, a few days before he died of heart failure. It was a very sad photograph of a legend, propped up in bed, childlike, with two straws poking out of plastic cups sitting on a tray and a bare lightbulb above his head.

Tangier was like a second home to me, as my wife, Soumaya, had grown up there. Her father, Abdesalam Akaaboune, lived in the Kasbah, the oldest part of the town, in a rambling *riad* (a large Moroccan house) called the *Palais de Ben Abou* that dated back 800 years. Coincidentally, Abdesalam had once held a position in Moroccan security similar to the one Mr. Gill held in India, but had long since retired from active service to become a businessman and property developer. The house was like the castle in Mervyn Peake's *Gormenghast,* with spiral staircases, secret rooms, and courtyards with fountains.

Abdesalam was a colorful local figure whom the family nicknamed the Pink Panther. Impeccably, and sometimes outrageously, dressed, he would swoosh around town in his signature Panama hat. Everyone knew Akaaboune. The Rolling Stones had recorded "Continental Drift" in his palace, and Bernardo Bertolucci and John Malkovich had stayed with him when shooting *The Sheltering Sky.* He used to own the trendiest jazz club in Africa, and when you stayed *chez* Akaaboune, the doorbell would constantly ring; guests, known and unknown, would appear; and musicians would play until the early hours, sitting in the courtyard under twinkling Mediterranean stars. His home was legendary. He was my father-in-law and my best friend all at the same time.

Abdesalam met us at the airport in his Panama hat. Tall and lithe, he danced rather than moved. He had bushy eyebrows, an Inspector Clouseau mustache, and a kind yet mischievous grin.

His face was dominated by the vulturelike Akaaboune nose, which accentuated his charisma.

It was a beautiful, crisp North African day, with not a cloud in the sky. We drove to Abdesalam's beach house for lunch and sat sipping beers as we talked about our recent ventures and watched the sun glint on the merge of the Atlantic Ocean and Mediterranean Sea. Abdesalam had organized a road trip that would take us to the Royal Palace in Rabat and on to Marrakech. We were in for another adventure.

That night my mother-in-law, Khadija, cooked a delicious dinner, and we sat upstairs in what I call the "room with a view," because it has arched windows that look out across the rooftops of Tangier toward the port in the distance. There are no cars in the Kasbah, as the streets are only six feet wide, so the sounds that waft up from the town below are of ancient times—laughter, crying, music, and drums—interspersed with the odd blast of a foghorn from the Strait of Gibraltar, the Gnawa musicians who paraded the streets with beats from Ghana, and the muezzin calling the faithful to prayer. We laughed and caught up.

As usual, the doorbell soon began to ring, and people came and went. A famous French singer appeared, sang an aria, and left. She was followed by a flutist who kicked himself for not arriving earlier, missing a chance to play with a diva. The flutist had arrived at the same time as a moody artist who said not a word, but sat in the corner and glowered at everyone. I tried to make conversation with him, but all I got was a grunt. I never did find out his name. A British aristocrat popped in to ask for Abdesalam's advice on a property he was about to buy, followed by some hilarious guys in a Moroccan rock band, who grabbed guitars and soon had the Brit performing the cha-cha backward to an upbeat version of "Auld Lang Syne." It was nice to be home.

OUR ADVENTURE STARTED EARLY THE NEXT MORNING in torrential rain. If there was one thing I had learned about my father-in-law, it was that when in his presence the best thing to do is just go with the flow. We had an appointment that afternoon with André Azoulay, who was *le Conseiller de Sa Majesté le Roi*, one of King

Mohammed VI of Morocco's most important advisors. It was especially interesting for the film, because the country is Muslim, and, as previously mentioned, André Azoulay is Jewish.

Abdesalam's French friend Didier had kindly lent us his Renault for the journey, but the problem was that one of the rear windows was broken. We managed to patch it up with trash bags and gaffer tape (the last of the roll after the bow-tie-manufacturing experience), but the rain was so relentless that the adhesive wouldn't stick. We had to spread towels all over the luggage stacked on the backseat to keep them dry. The wind in the gaping hole made a terrible racket the whole journey. To cap it all, Abdesalam had insisted on driving, which wouldn't have been a problem if his eyesight hadn't started deteriorating five years before and Didier had been in the habit of changing his wiper blades from time to time. It rarely rained in Tangier, so no one had noticed the state of the blades until that day. The rubber was so atrophied that it smeared the water rather than removed it, which reduced visibility to almost zero. Oh, and the heater was also broken, so de-misting was executed with toilet paper, which further compounded our problems by adding streaks to the interior of the glass.

I have never in my entire life experienced such a frightening drive. We had driven across mountains with 2,000-foot drops to one side and along roads made dangerous by terrorist threats, but this journey topped them all. Before we had even left Tangier, Abdesalam had managed to drive over a median, caused a cyclist to topple on the curb, and dinged the rear of the car on a post. (There were so many dings that we guessed Didier wouldn't notice another.) When he started driving in the wrong direction down a one-way street, I decided I had better say something.

"Er, Abdesalam . . ." I began nervously, as I glanced back at a decidedly pasty-faced Vishnu assuming the "brace" position, "I think we're on a one-way street."

Abdesalam started accelerating. "Yes," he agreed, in such a soft tone that I had to strain to hear him over the flapping racket from the broken window. "Silly people. They really ought to read the signs . . . just look at this idiot!" He shook his head as another car almost front-ended us, lights flashing, horn blazing, arms frantically waving.

"Abdesalam," I tried again, "I think it's *us* going the wrong way, not them."

"Nonsense," he whispered back.

By the time we reached the freeway to Rabat, I'd aged about ten years. I could feel my hair going white. What's more, the heavens had added a few more rain clouds, making visibility even worse. Abdesalam didn't seem in the least bit fazed, though; he simply slammed his foot on the gas and, to my horror, used the taillights of the vehicle in front to navigate. I guess he hadn't heard of the three-second rule. I glanced at the speedometer—we were doing 120 kilometers (75 miles) per hour. I winced.

"We need the rain. Tangier is suffering a terrible drought," he said cheerfully. "Good for all of us!"

I decided it probably wasn't the best idea to initiate conversation with Abdesalam while he was driving, as he would always look you in the eye when talking, which meant his eyes *weren't on the road.*

We stopped for lunch in a restaurant on the outskirts of Rabat. It was there I noticed that the rear lights on the car and one of the headlights didn't work.

Vishnu couldn't speak at lunch, only grunt, like the silent artist of the night before. I've never seen him so petrified. I too marveled at the fact that we had actually made it without a fatal accident.

Since we were about to visit the king's Royal Palace, we had to look respectable. But when we pulled our suits out of the luggage, they were soaking wet from the rain that had been pelting through the broken window for the past four hours. As we changed our clothes in the restaurant's bathroom, I got a fit of the giggles at the thought of us: here we were—me, my crazy father-in-law, and a friend who was so shocked that he'd lost all ability to talk—off to the Royal Palace in heavily creased, soaking-wet suits and socks that squelched in our shoes.

I tried to suppress my giggling, but I almost lost it when I walked out of the bathroom to find Abdesalam dressed in a purple velvet suit, with 1970s flares and wide lapels; a frilly pink shirt with no top button; and . . . a brown felt cloak—"to keep off the rain," he explained. I had a hard time keeping a straight face. Abdesalam looked like a cross between an aristocratic southern European superhero and a gay disco king. Without batting an eyelid, he plopped his Panama hat on his head and said, "Been a while. Let's go!" All I could think was, *Quentin Crisp would have approved.*

We got lost trying to find the palace. Abdesalam thought he knew where it was, but the building he'd had in mind turned out to be the local prison. Since we were now running late, he stepped on the gas. When a kind police officer indicated the walls to the palace up ahead, Abdesalam pointed the car in that direction and drove, blissfully oblivious to the local traffic laws. By the time we arrived, Vishnu (who had still not uttered a word) and I were both exhausted.

André Azoulay was wonderful. He welcomed us into his office, offered us tea, and accepted us for who we were. My father-in-law, despite his eccentricities, was a very well-respected member of the Moroccan community, and he and Mr. Azoulay chatted about old times.

But we had work to do, and the winter light was fading. So I set up the camera, and soon the interview was under way.

"God makes me a free man. I feel very rich in the way I was educated as a Jewish person in a small town in the south of Morocco, but more than anything else, I consider my religion as the best way to be an individual who is able to take care of his neighbor."

"Is Judaism a race or a religion?"

"It's more than a race. It's more than a religion; it's a philosophy. It's also a way for a person to find peace and live on this earth with mutual respect and with acceptance of all other believers. I don't feel Jewish by my blood; it's not a question of that. I feel Jewish by what I keep alive in my mind in terms of value and the etiquette of life . . . all the values we have in common with other believers—Muslim, Christian, Jewish, or any other religion. Those who have in mind the logic of confrontation are those who are spoiling the message of God," he added.

"In Morocco, a Muslim country, there seems to be harmony between Muslims and Jews. I've just come from Israel, where there is a distinct disharmony between the two religions. What is there that Israel can learn from Morocco?" I probed.

"First of all, we have to differentiate between Israel and Judaism. We cannot address Judaism issues and mix that with the political situation in Israel. I am more than 2,000 years old as a Jewish person. The Jews arrived in Morocco before Islam, so I feel I have no problem. I feel part of this country; part of the history; part of the memory; part of the air, the atmosphere . . . everything. I feel richer by adding my own identity and spirituality to my Muslim compatriots.

"The foundation of the Moroccan people was Jewish. After that came the Berbers, and after that the Arab and Muslim people, so Morocco is a mixture of those three civilizations. We are a melting pot of dimensions. So I consider it a privilege being an Arab Jew, and a privilege to tell the rest of the world the art of possibility. I don't see any deadlock between Jews and Muslims. On the contrary, I see the Moroccan reality; and Moroccan history shows that we can live together in mutual respect, in harmony, in peace. Until the Palestinian people can enjoy the same freedom, the same dignity, the same justice that I enjoy myself, I feel weak as a Jewish person, and I feel Judaism is in danger. I hope that the future of the young generations of Israelis is in finding, as quickly as possible, the best solution to the legitimate expectations of the Palestinian people so that they too can enjoy freedom and dignity."

"The word *Islam* seems to be a dirty word in the West, particularly the USA. Why do you think that is?" I pressed.

"Ignorance. I think that now it's time to retake over our God. It's time to retake over our values. It's time also to ask all the believers in the three religions of the Holy Book what it means to be Muslim, what it means to be Jewish, and what it means to be Christian—and what it means to live together." He paused and then continued: "I think that, for me as a Jewish person, if I call my God by saying 'Allah,' it's exactly what I want. I mean, I see no contradiction to pray or to express my faith by sharing with my Muslim compatriots the name of Allah. For me it's the same."

We shuffled out into the rain. I was very happy to have captured such an enlightened perspective on an incendiary situation.

As SOLDIERS WERE CHANGING GUARD in the palace square, Abdesalam went to pick up the Renault, which was parked across the courtyard, where it contrasted greatly with the nearby fleet of sleek black Mercedes that made up King Mohammed VI's motorcade.

"I don't think I'll be able to survive all the way to Marrakech," Vishnu commented dryly. "I think I will die from heart failure."

"Okay," I said.

"I'd gladly drive, but I'm not sure how to execute that. Perhaps you should drive," he added.

At that instant, Didier's car fired to life and, careening backward instead of forward, smashed straight into one of the king's Mercedes.

"O-kaayy," I said again.

Abdesalam got out of the Renault to see if there was any damage. One of the police officers rushed over to him. We watched in awe as, instead of arresting my father-in-law on the spot, the man first saluted him and then vigorously shook his hand. Abdesalam got back into the car and, with a loud grinding of gears, pulled up in front of us as if absolutely nothing had happened. "I remember that officer from when he was a kid. Small world," he said with a grin. "Let's go!"

"Abdesalam, I don't know if Soumaya has told you, but I suffer from extreme car sickness," I lied. "I think that was why I was so quiet on the drive down—and there's only one cure when it comes on . . ."

"You should drive!" he exclaimed. "They say if you watch the road, you won't get sick."

It had worked!

Abdesalam got out and moved around to the other side of the car. "Thank you," Vishnu mouthed from the backseat as Abdesalam climbed in. Before we moved on our way, however, we took the soaked towels off the baggage and squeezed them out. We only had 340 kilometers to go.

As I started the car, I was horrified to see that every possible warning light, apart from the gas gauge, was alight. I mentioned this to Abdesalam, who shrugged and said that ever since Didier had bought the car a couple of years before, he hadn't been able to work out how to open up the hood. Consequently, he had a feeling that some of the fluids down there might need filling up.

It was impossible to see out. I understood why Abdesalam had tailgated. I tried my best not to. The storm had worsened. Abdesalam sat back and regaled us with wonderful stories. He fished around in his bag and pulled out a bottle of scotch, a thermos of ice, and three glasses. It reminded me of someone.

"Would you like a drink?" he invited. "It's that time of day."

"No, it's okay. I'm driving," I said.

"It might make you see better in this rain," he encouraged.

"No. No, it's okay. It's probably not a good idea on top of the road sickness."

My main concern was that at 6 P.M. that day, I had to take part in a conference call relating to a Toyota advertising job that I had booked for our return. It was a creative call with about 12 different people dotted all over the United States. I'd just have to wing it as I drove.

In his old age, Abdesalam had become very partial to smoking a pipe of keef—marijuana grass—that he mixed with hashish. In the West this would be considered a serious offense, but although theoretically illegal in Morocco, hashish smoking was very much a part of the culture. So my father-in-law fired up his long pipe and filled the vehicle with billows of pungent, blue hashish smoke as he kept us amused with hilarious stories about the battles with his neighbor and the storm drain on the roof of the palace.

"Duh-duh-duh-duh-duh-duh-duh-duuuuh-duh." Pink Floyd! It was my conference call with Saatchi & Saatchi in Los Angeles. I propped the phone up to my ear. It was very dark, and having only one headlight working made driving even trickier as I commenced a lengthy discussion about the color of the models' bikini bottoms in the advertisement I was about to shoot for the agency. The call went on and on: *Green . . . no greens . . . I didn't want primary colors*

anyway. Muted colors, better—shapely and modern—what designer should we be using?

I was desperately trying to navigate through the streaky, misty glass; there were trucks and taillights, more rain, roadworks, an off-ramp. I used my free hand to wipe the interior with the soggy toilet tissue in an effort to see more. *I don't like brown. No one wears brown bikinis. We can use primary colors, but let's not go garish.* Abdesalam had just fired up another pipe, making visibility even worse. I opened the window to let out some of the smoke.

"Oh no!" Abdesalam suddenly cried out. "I think we had to go that way." He pointed at the off-ramp I had already passed. "Pull over there . . . pull up."

I should have ignored him, but I was trying to turn the client away from *patterned bikini tops,* so I pulled up to the spot that Abdesalam had pointed to . . . and the next thing I knew, I was staring up at a uniformed police officer brandishing a menacing submachine gun. He rattled off some words in Arabic.

"I'm sorry," I apologized to the police officer. "Just a second, everyone," I said down the phone.

The police officer sniffed, and peered in the car. "No lights! On phone?!" He sniffed again. "Alcohol?!" An even more pronounced sniff. "DRUGS?!" He reeled back and beckoned behind him. Suddenly six machine guns were pointed at me. Images of *Midnight Express* flashed inside my head.

"Get out of the car!"

"Just a second!" I replied to the officer. "Excuse me, everyone," I said into the phone. "I am on the road from Rabat to Marrakech in Morocco. I've just been pulled over, and I have six machine guns pointed at me. Can I possibly call you back?"

Abdesalam had been speaking throughout this, trying to get the attention of the officers.

"I have to call you back!" I announced abruptly into the phone.

"Get out of the car!"

"Agi, agi agi," Abdesalam was saying. Which is "Here, here, here" in English.

"I think my father-in-law has something to say, officers," I said in my best attempt at French.

The first cop leaned in and scrutinized the interior. His eyes fell on the open bottle of scotch, and the pot pipe. There were still clouds of smoke billowing everywhere. Vishnu was sitting very quietly in the back, so quietly that the silence was deafening.

Abdesalam pointed at himself, still looking like a gay aristocratic European disco-dancing superhero with a cloak—and a Panama hat—and uttered the word *Akaaboune.*

"Akaaboune?" The police officer leaned in farther. His jaw dropped. His eyes widened incredulously, and he repeated, "Akaaboune?!"

He pulled his head out of the car, pointed at Abdesalam, and announced triumphantly: "AKAABOUNE!"

Within minutes, we were surrounded by a fleet of police vehicles with their sirens blaring. They stopped the traffic on the main freeway, escorted us backward so we could exit the ramp in reverse, and gave us a police escort to the nearest town. I felt like I was back in India with Mr. Gill.

Abdesalam continued his story, and I managed to finish my conference call. "I'm glad they remembered my name," was all he said about the incident.

It was a stressful and exhausting drive. As we were going up a hill, Didier's car sputtered and finally died. I just managed to pull off the highway.

"I think it's lacking some liquids in there," I remarked. Vishnu and I pulled out a Maglite and tried to work out how to open the hood. We finally found a lever, but it wasn't connected; no wonder Didier couldn't open it.

There was a tea shop nearby, so we decided to go and sit it out. After a lot of hot, sweet Moroccan tea and cakes, Abdesalam declared that the car would be fine now, as it had had a rest. We piled back into it. I held my breath and turned the key. All the warning lights blinked on, and to our amazement, the engine spluttered back to life. Apart from having a terrible dislike of inclines, which the Renault could only cope with at a speed of about ten miles per hour, we actually made the next 100 kilometers in reasonable time, despite the terrible discomfort and humiliation of having traffic backed up miles behind us with horns blaring whenever we had to crawl over yet another hill.

When we pulled into the grounds of our friend Abel Damoussi's luxury hotel, the Kasbah Agafay, we were welcomed with open arms. Although the kitchen was closed, they whipped up a delicious meal for us as we sat warming our frozen, damp bones by a roaring fire.

"WE NEVER DIE," Abdesalam's barely audible voice announced. We were drinking scotch and unwinding after our ordeal. I'd switched on the B camera to record what he was saying.

Abdesalam was pure Berber—the name referring to the indigenous peoples of North Africa. Although as a Moroccan he'd been brought up Muslim, he was a self-confessed agnostic. He had little patience for those using God's name to manipulate and take advantage of disenfranchised groups of disillusioned youths—and this applied especially to those who preyed upon the uneducated. He was deeply concerned with the ramifications of the polarity between Islam and the rest of the world post-9/11, and felt that the situation would only deteriorate. What I liked the most about Abdesalam's mind was that he would think outside the box.

"Men with money are dangerous. Imagine the church, the mosques—all the religions—with all the money they have . . . they are a million times more dangerous. They are monsters. And you get men doing really bad things, thinking they are serving God, praying five times a day. Those are dangerous people, because they lead you into thinking they are good, honest people. Before you know it, *bang, bang.*

"In my education, it's more than that. God cannot be like me. He's much more powerful than that. God has no substitute and no army of angels. When someone goes to a church or a mosque or a holy place and asks for help, they probably think they are close to God, as throughout their lives they have worshipped, and been part of the community. And one day they might need something—their son is sick; they have just lost their job. They go to the holy place and ask God for special treatment—to sort out their problem. And at the end, what do they do? They put money in the box. Human beings are not perfection."

He continued: "I read that we all came from fungus originally; we came from spores. Evolution has made life what it is today—nature, animals, sex, and all of that. There is a great balance of nature; animals live on us, and we live off them. That's why we're here. But when we go away, when we finish what we call life, our brain continues and functions, and by doing so, leads us to another life. The real life—when you've reached that moment you've learned how to pilot, how to conduct—that's paradise.

"Let's say 24 hours is eternity. What about one second? Let's say that one second represents 100,000 years. Now dying—your body dies, your brain continues. Whatever blood is left in there can perhaps continue the brain activity for one hour. Imagine what you can do in that one hour when 24 hours is an eternity and each second is 100,000 years. It has nothing to do with the soul. It has everything to do with the little blood that remains in your brain. In the billionth of a second that the bullet hits your brain, you can live a billion lives. You could even be a small bird, a sparrow flying over the Himalayas to Everest, with its little wings rubbing against the summit of the mountain.

"Today, it would take you a whole day to get from Los Angeles to Tangier. You have to buy a ticket, get on a plane, go to the airport. At the moment of death, you can travel anywhere you want to go in a billionth of a second! What fun. I'm looking forward to that day!"

Abdesalam chuckled and repeated, "I'm looking forward to that."

THE FIRST THING WE DID IN MARRAKECH was to fix up Didier's car. There was no oil in the engine, let alone coolant, water, or window-washer fluid. New wiper blades made a great difference. A new window meant the end of the constant racket and we could actually *think* as we drove. Abel Damoussi invited us to his club in the center of Marrakech so that we could get better access to the town.

We filmed the markets, the people, the activity, the main square, and the shafts of light piercing through the slats in the maze of the medina.

We conducted many interviews in Morocco with people from all walks of life. It certainly changed my perspective. I'd visited the country on countless occasions, but this was the first time I had asked any questions or dug deep to understand its culture, its people, and its religion.

After 9/11, we were so conditioned in the West to be anti anything *Muslim*. I found that it had even affected me—someone who not only traveled constantly, but also had family who resided in a Muslim country. It seemed that every terrorist who cropped up in the news was—Muslim. Yet where were the voices of other Muslims condemning these people? I was baffled by the silence of 1.7 billion members of the same religion. So I have to admit I had my preconceptions, but once I learned what Islam is really about, I discovered that, as with any other religion, its avowed cornerstones are peace, tolerance, understanding, and love. The screams of the minority—the bigots and the hotheads who are using Islam to further their nefarious, evil agendas—are drowning out the voice of the majority of Muslims, a voice that probably will never be heard, as it isn't sensationalist . . . good news is no news.

This was definitely a thread that had to be explored—but where? I had to interview some Muslim militants and fanatics to get their perspective, and then counter those with the voice of the majority, just as I'd sought to do in Israel and the Palestinian Territories. I also knew that I wasn't going to find them in Morocco. Everyone thus far had been far too tolerant, intelligent, and understanding to shed any light on any fanatical way of thinking.

As we embarked on the long journey back home to the United States, I reflected on our Moroccan chapter. True, we'd gotten a couple of good interviews for the film, but more important, I'd gone on a road trip with my father-in-law and best friend. We'd chewed the fat and traveled across the country, been to the Royal Palace, and sat together drinking tea in the square of Marrakech. We had filmed the great Hassan II Mosque in Casablanca. We had talked about God, politics, death, and identity; about his daughter, my wife; and his grandson, my son; and about terrorism, injustice, fanaticism, and pain. We had laughed and shared stories about our fears, dreams, realities, family, and friends. We had almost been arrested by the police, and turned the situation around so that they'd provided us with an escort instead. We had talked about time, about life, about living, about dying, and about getting the most out of every day.

I will never forget the sight of Abdesalam, wearing his Panama hat, with his grandiose mustache and larger-than-life smile, waving me good-bye at Tangier airport.

He had just told me the following: "You are getting on a plane, my son, to fly back to America. Remember—they have the clock, but we have the time."

As we walked across the tarmac to the plane, I turned back for one last wave. His hand made the shape of a pistol. I watched him fire an imaginary bullet. His hands flicked up, as if to illustrate *Poof—gone away*. He was referring to the bullet that hits the brain in a billionth of a second—the moment of freedom.

That was the last time I saw my friend. One year, to the very day, after he had said those words to Vishnu and me in Marrakech, Abdesalam passed away. I often think of him flipping around the world in that billionth of a second, living many lives simultaneously and being as free as the "sparrow flying over the Himalayas to Everest, with its little wings rubbing against the summit of the mountain."

"You never die," he had said. "You never die."

PART II

HUMANITY AND INHUMANITY

CHAPTER 14

A Time of Contrasts

*"When you open your eyes, you believe you can see,
but you never really see until you believe."*

— NAPKIN #14

I flew back to Los Angeles, and Vishnu went home to Acapulco.

Forty-seven hours after waving good-bye to Abdesalam on the tarmac of Tangier airport, I found myself in a studio in Hollywood shooting 22 girls in bikinis who were draped over a yacht. I chuckled at the array of bikini bottoms, and the memory of my conversation about primary colors while facing the wrong end of a submachine gun in the rain on the road from Rabat to Marrakech. It was a wonderful contrast.

But the reality was, despite the Toyota job, I was in trouble. I realized that I'd bitten off far more than I could chew. I was running out of money, and the amount of ground that still had to be covered was daunting. The more I uncovered on this quest, the more I realized I *still* had to cover. At the same time, I felt I was a very lucky human being, so regardless of the problems, I just had to soldier on and have faith that everything would work out fine.

My first priority was to cut some of the footage into a teaser to encourage investors to come in so that I could finish the film. It took seven weeks to complete; there was so much footage that it took three weeks just to view and log it all. Thankfully, the reaction to the promo could not have been better. I put it on the Internet and almost instantly started receiving encouraging e-mails from people about the message of the film and what I was attempting to do. It felt good, and what felt even better was seeing some of the images edited together on the screen.

But then there was God—*God Himself.* I heard the echo of Rabbi Froman's thick accent churning in my head. What did I think of God now? Even to me it was such a charged question. Would people care what I thought? Did *I* care what I thought? Would what I thought help or hinder the film? I had no idea. I realized the whole concept of God was incredibly convoluted. The very word *God* referred to so many different things to different cultures and belief systems.

Ironically, it appeared that the three monotheistic religions were the most united in the foundation of their beliefs. For the Jews, in the Torah, there were the Ten Commandments, a wonderful code of practice for life. For the Christians, the Bible not only embraced the Ten Commandments in the Old Testament, but there was also Jesus Christ's wonderful Sermon on the Mount in the New Testament—again, a superb code of practice for life. And for the Muslims, there were the five pillars of Islam, which basically said the same thing as the other books.

So why were they so divided? Why were the Catholics at odds with the Protestants? What *was* the cause of all that upheaval in Northern Ireland when I was growing up? Why did the Shiites and the Sunnis blow up each other's mosques in Iraq? Wars were being fought and people were being killed because they didn't belong to the same *club.*

Clearly, it was more the word *God* than what *God stood for* that was causing all this conflict and pain. Human beings had lost sight of the truth of what they worshipped, and many had become pawns, being manipulated by people who had no qualms at all about using God's name to further their political agendas. And the majority of those perpetrators felt that they were acting in the best interests of humankind under the banner of the God *they* worshipped . . . and around and around we go.

Meanwhile, the only thing I had to do was remain as objective as possible, and perhaps somewhere in all of these answers, something would emerge to provide a basis for my audience of viewers to make up their own minds.

As for me, I am convinced that "God" is an invention of man—a word, a concept, a figurehead to give substance to something that cannot be seen, yet is probably the motor that drives our world. The scriptures of most religions are all metaphors for this, so I wasn't denying the existence of God, but was merely concluding that the word used to describe this motor (God) is overused, and it is *this* that complicates the entire subject.

So many people take comfort from an entity that doesn't answer back. Witness the number of bumper stickers we see declaring: "I love Jesus." By all accounts, Jesus died approximately 2,000 years ago; how could anyone have a relationship with such a silent ghost? I wondered what the attraction was to an entity with which a monologue is the only form of conversation one could ever have.

It's so convenient to put our problems in an imaginary box and send them away for God to deal with. And it's so comforting to do this in a nice church, with beautiful music and like-minded individuals lighting candles and burning incense, kneeling, and begging forgiveness for the nasty things they've done in their lives. God's silence is deafening. How can people use a God that preaches tolerance in such an *in*tolerant manner? If God is real, why doesn't He answer back, or intervene whenever His name is used in vain?

Is the entity of God somehow above communication with human beings? And if so, should we trust scriptures that were written thousands of years ago by men claiming that God had talked to them? Are human beings collectively delusional?

Many religious people had told me that God had spoken to them. How? How did that come about? How do we know that it was God? How do we *not* know that it was God? Did these individuals feel it? Did the words creep up from within their souls? Maybe it was just their inner selves talking to them, like Chhote Bharany believed. Maybe we're all collectively God.

So there I was, still a long way from the end of my journey, and the whole God concept wasn't stacking up; indeed, it made absolutely no sense whatsoever to me. Out of all the many reasons people justified their belief in God, four seemed to stick out:

1. They had no idea how we got here; therefore, God was the *creator.*

2. Good deeds bought us a place in heaven; therefore, God was the *policeman.*

3. One sure thing happened when we died—our bodies rotted—and the rest was speculation; therefore, God was the *giver of eternal life.*

4. When things went wrong, many dismissed horrendous outcomes by saying it was God's will; therefore, God was the *scapegoat.*

As I PREVIOUSLY MENTIONED, MY FATHER, George Rodger, was a photojournalist for *Life* magazine during World War II. He had photographed everything from the Blitz in London, to Montgomery's campaign in North Africa, to the invasion of Burma by the Japanese (from which he'd escaped by walking across the Naga Hills to India), to D-day, to the liberation of Brussels and Paris, and the flooding of Holland. He'd traveled farther than any other photojournalist and had become so well known that the magazine would often publish long essays about him. After five and a half years of constant travel and life-threatening adventures, he was the first photojournalist to enter Hitler's den of iniquity when the British army liberated the Bergen-Belsen concentration camp on April 15, 1945.

Nothing had prepared my father for what he found in that camp. Witnessing the evidence of man's inhumanity to man, he vowed never to photograph war again. From that moment on, he dedicated his work to documenting humankind in its ultimate form of existing purity—the rapidly diminishing tribes of Africa.

In the postwar early Magnum Photos days, the photographers divided the world between them, and Africa became my father's hunting ground. There, he discovered the Nuba in Kordofan, Sudan, and felt that, finally, he was witnessing humanity in its most basic, purest form. Decades later, the Nuba were a dispossessed people, victims of genocide and ethnic cleansing (just like the Jews in Europe in the last century), having been caught in the middle of one of the worst examples of man's inhumanity to man in recent history: the horror of the conflict in Darfur. The very people my father had found to balance his sense of despair had now become victims of the same heinous actions that had motivated him to discover them in the first place.

The word *Holocaust* was banned in our house when I was growing up. It was too painful for my father to bear. Even as an observer, it had made him question himself: How could he have been so numb as to find himself making a photographic composition out of mounds of dead bodies? What on earth had happened to him that he had sunk so far? The story he wrote on Bergen-Belsen had been published all over the world. It was the first real *proof* of the Holocaust—proof that, today, the president of Iran, Mahmoud Ahmadinejad, vehemently denies.

One of the most famous images in this series of photographs was of a small boy named Sieg Montag walking along a path with dead bodies piled up on either side. The expression of stoicism, submission, and horror was etched into the child's face. The power of the image was undeniable and had been printed all over the world.

Sieg had thought that his family had perished. The family thought *he* had perished. When the photograph came out, his aunt, who had escaped to New York before the war, saw it and recognized him. She immediately contacted her sister, Sieg's mother, who was still alive and recovering in a hospital in Amsterdam. She broke the news: Sieg was not dead—he was alive! A multicountry search was mounted for the tortured little boy. He was found just two weeks later in a recovery home one block away from his mother in Amsterdam, and they were reunited. It was probably just one small story out of hundreds of thousands from that tumultuous time, but it was a remarkably serendipitous moment for Sieg and his family, and it had come about as a result of the power of my father's eye.

The poignancy of the photographic essay wasn't just founded on the horror, however, but also on the portraits of the camp commandant and his prison guards—once *normal* people in a civilized world who had been reduced to carrying out horrific acts that, even today, our new generations have trouble understanding.

In a way, too, my father inflicted a lot of guilt and blame upon himself. It ran so deep; it took root in his subconscious like a snake, constantly slithering around, baring its fangs and making its presence known. It was his monster, and it grew bigger as he got older. He'd believed that having a family would banish the snake, but it was evident to me that it was still present, lurking menacingly beneath the surface right up until the day my father passed away in 1995.

It was a source of pain for all of us who grew up with him; melancholia and depression are contagious and difficult to deal with in family situations, a continuum of despair. It is an insidious virus: the guilt, the shame, the hurt, and the pain can jump from human to human without your knowledge, sometimes surfacing years later to affect you in a variety of subtle ways—an uncomfortable feeling, a weakness for drugs and alcohol, or simply just a sense of unfathomable melancholy when the sun disappears on an autumn night.

These feelings in my father elicited enormous compassion from the rest of the family, and an unspoken understanding, even from the time we were all very small children. My sister, Rana, and I called it *The Thing*. We could see it in my father's eyes even when he laughed. He would suffer from intolerable headaches, and it all went back to *The Thing*—the guilt; the horror; and the realization that not only was there unspeakable evil in the world, but he had seen it, lived it, and been part of it. He had even smelled it as the British trucks sped toward Bergen-Belsen that April morning—the stench of decay; of death; of the very worst of life in its most ugly, uncensored form. That's why we were forbidden to talk about it. That's why my father never talked about it—with us, or to the press—and shuddered at the sight of those images that still haunt and horrify us all today.

Once I was with my father at our family home. It was the mid-1980s, and there was a piece on the news: a documentary had been uncovered in someone's garage—a film edited by Alfred Hitchcock from the footage of the British military cameramen who had liberated Bergen-Belsen. The newscaster warned that the content was disturbing, and that anyone who felt they couldn't take it should leave the room or turn off the TV. They cut to a commercial break. My father and I stood in silence, staring at the screen as a Heineken advertisement played out: "The 'worta' in Majorca don't taste like what it 'oughta.' The water in Majorca doesn't taste quite like it should."

Then the news came back on. It opened with a shot of my father filmed on liberation day: April 15, 1945. He was standing, Rolleiflex in hand, in Bergen-Belsen, surrounded by mounds and mounds of dead bodies. The camera lingered on him as he clicked the shutter, stoically photographing what the world needed to see.

I sucked in my breath, unsure what to do. We had just been talking about compost and lettuces . . . and now *this?* I looked at my father. He started to shake. He had to sit down. His body convulsed. His eyes were fixated on the image of himself all those years earlier. The bogeyman was there all right, right in front of him, in front of us. Everything went into slow motion. I had never seen my father cry. He had never raised his voice. He was Mr. Cool, Mr. Calm, Mr. Collected. Yet here, right now, I was seeing him sob. He writhed in pain.

The footage was unrelenting as it moved to images of the horror. You could almost smell the stench. The man I had revered as a god all my life—the man who was always right, who was so wise, who had been around the world and always knew what to do . . . the man who had single-handedly built the house we were standing in, who was larger than life—was reduced to a sobbing, blubbering wreck from a pain too great to bear.

That was the moment when I realized that my father was not God, but a man—just like me. I had so much love for him that it was almost overwhelming, but there was nothing I could do to help alleviate the pain—nothing. I realized there are some memories in life that will never go away. Bergen-Belsen was one of those for my father, and he was just a witness, not an inmate. Although many of my father's Jewish friends had died in the war, none of our family members had been directly involved. But that didn't stop the emotions I witnessed that day. How godless I felt. How utterly godless.

TWO AND A HALF MONTHS AFTER RETURNING from Morocco, I found myself driving along the same road my father had taken that fateful morning in April 1945. It was almost 62 years to the day since he had made the journey he would later describe by its stench.

It was not like that for me. I was in a smooth, powerful Volvo with Andrea Jarach, who had commissioned me to write and direct a film he was funding. I'd been happy to get away from *Oh My God* for a while, to work on another project and earn some money. I purposely hadn't brought the *OMG* cameras with me. It was a field trip to learn about the Holocaust. My assignment was to write a story that featured Anne Frank in it somewhere, and get across the fact that people never learn . . . that "man's inhumanity to man" continues. The aim was to remind us what we are capable of, and hopefully increase awareness so that such atrocities don't repeat themselves. Anne Frank had died at Bergen-Belsen. I had been to the annex in Amsterdam, and I wanted to visit her grave . . . and the ghost of my father's pain.

It was an intense day. Hitler had always hidden his death camps amid the most beautiful surroundings. I wondered how much the sight of the bucolic woods, with their sounds of peaceful birdsong and the smell of damp pines, had tormented those poor inmates who had been stuck behind barbed fences, denied of food, their dignity, and, eventually, life itself. It was a barbaric contrast. The insidious stench of my intellectual understanding of evil must have permeated my cells, for I felt Mr. Chou's slow writhing, like the snake that had taken up residence in my father's soul.

There's a museum at the camp's entrance. Huge blowups of some of my father's pictures adorn the walls—a portrait of the camp commander Josef Kramer, the piles of dead bodies, the shot of Sieg Montag . . . they were all there. I was nervous and uncomfortable to be standing, safely looking at these pictures in exactly the same place where my father had entered years before to see emaciated inmates in dirty, striped uniforms. This was how he described it:

Under the pine trees the scattered dead were lying, not in their twos or threes or dozens, but in their thousands. The living tore ragged clothing from the corpses to build fires, over which they boiled pine needles and roots for soup. Little children rested their heads against the stinking corpses of their mothers, too nearly dead themselves to cry. An emaciated man approached me. 'Look, Englishman,' he said, 'this is German Culture,' and he fell down dead in front of me. Bodies with gaping wounds in the region of the kidneys, liver and heart testified to the cannibalism that had been resorted to, degradation begetting degradation.

(George Rodger, *Humanity and Inhumanity:*
The Photographic Journey of George Rodger)

It had been hell on Earth. There was absolutely no other way to describe it. Mr. Chou fluttered uncomfortably at the disparity. For me, standing in the same spot, it was one of the starkest examples of beautiful countryside you could imagine—in a word, paradisiacal. Hell and heaven separated by 62 years. I wondered what my father would think if he were standing beside me now.

I politely asked Andrea if I could be left alone, and I went out exploring. I wanted to find the exact spot where my father had taken the picture of Sieg Montag all those years before. I wanted to experience the precise location of the event that had taken my father's soul and bored a hole right through it. I've heard it said that there are pivotal moments in a person's life that forever change the nature of that human being. That day in Bergen-Belsen was a turning point for my father . . . and now that I was here, I was suddenly consumed with the need to understand—to see, smell, and *feel* for myself—the place where he had been infected by such a profound melancholia that it would remain with him for the rest of his life.

I breathed in the sweet Bergen-Belsen air. Fragrances of tranquility wafted across my path—of mushrooms and damp leaves, of sap and moss—and I watched the ferns moving gracefully in the breeze. How on earth could I be in the same place? I passed the mass graves. I recalled the shots my father had taken—of bulldozers shoveling corpses, the drivers with scarves wrapped around their faces to keep out the stench. In my head, I could hear the sound of the 1940s engines and even smell the diesel, but all I could see was a mound beneath which lay tens of thousands of human bones.

I sat on a bench and gazed around, trying to feel whether there was any energetic residue of the souls who had perished all around me—human beings, just like me, who had vanished in a despair of shattered dreams . . . human beings who had died when their faith had finally collapsed and starvation had taken their wretched, malnourished forms, all shreds of dignity long gone. Where was that energy? Where were these poor people now?

Where was God in all of this?

But I felt nothing but peace. An immense and palpable peace—and that disturbed me. It was such a paradox; it infused Mr. Chou with a shot of adrenaline. The irony was not lost on me. Outside all was peace; inside my body it was another story.

I continued on. Having conducted an enormous amount of research, I knew by looking at maps where the shot of Sieg Montag must have been taken. When I got there, I couldn't believe I was in the same place. First of all, the trees were now fully grown, so it was a little difficult to pinpoint the exact location, but when I found it, my skin crawled from head to toe.

I recalled the day I had watched that news feature with my father all those years before: "The 'worta' in Majorca . . ." The bogeyman who had stared my father in the face was here . . . I could feel him. I sat down on the edge of the path and just watched. I pulled out a copy of the picture and held it up, comparing yesteryear's hell with today's paradise. . . . I winced. I was roughly the same age my father had been when he was here, but what a difference. . . .

What am I to learn from this? I wondered. *What does this have to do with my quest?* It was a different chapter, a different day, but it was a tent pole in my thinking. I was aware that I was learning something, but I didn't know what it was.

Spring had not quite sprung; brown leaves still clung to the lower bushes. I stayed there for several moments, and then finally walked away. I felt sad and utterly useless. I knew that being there had helped me with what I was doing. I was glad I hadn't brought my cameras. I didn't want to put this into the film, as it didn't seem relevant. It was relevant to me, that's all. It was teaching me to see in different ways.

CHAPTER 15

Rome and Vatican City

*"Sometimes it's easier to live your life for
others than it is for yourself."*

— NAPKIN #15

I gazed out the scratched window as the rocky coast of the
French Riviera sped by me. Exquisite villas hanging over an inviting Mediterranean Sea would suddenly appear, and then all would
go black as we plunged into a tunnel and the sounds of the train
would be thrown back at us from rocky walls. Bright sunlight and
pitch-black darkness, contrasting flashes of imagery like a scratchy
early film, supported the anxiety I felt within me as we snaked
along the coast toward Italy.

Mr. Chou was doing somersaults in my stomach; we were on
the road again. The quest of *OMG* had been rekindled, and we
were off to visit Vatican City. Yet all I wanted right then was to
be down there on the beach, sniffing the salty air and feeling the
water caress my toes.

Vishnu wasn't with me. He was back in Mexico, stuck on some
commercial gig, so our composer, Colonel Boobs, had stepped in
again to fill the breach and hopefully, record any interesting or
bizarre local sounds that he could then weave into the score. He
had jumped on a plane and joined me in France, where I'd been
attending the Cannes Film Festival and having script meetings
with Andrea Jarach. I had titled the script he'd commissioned *The
Bystander*. It had been a harrowing story to write. I'd woven two
poignant genocides into it and compared Darfur to the Holocaust
as seen through the eyes of a father and daughter. It was a tragic
yet beautiful piece, and I hoped one day we would get it made.

ROME WAS MUGGY AND SCORCHING HOT, with those typical thundery, southern European early-summer skies that fill the air with boiling moisture and periodically erupt into torrential downpours.

We stayed near the Vatican in some ghastly, cheap hotel—which, like many establishments in Rome, had been built years before the elevator was invented. Consequently, getting into and out of the place was a nightmare, as we had to cram ourselves into a box with proportions more suitable to a dumbwaiter than an elevator.

Our rooms were on the sixth floor, and we had mounds of camera equipment. Consequently, loading the elevator to the max was vitally important. Every time we returned from a day's shooting, I would pile cases up and around Colonel Boobs as he stood inside the elevator, holding the ugly blue metallic door open. The problem was, every time I added a new case, the elevator would sink down an inch. By the time it was full and Colonel Boobs was neatly positioned in the midst of our stacked equipments, he would be below sea level, which meant that getting the doors closed could be rather tricky. Once this was executed, I would hold my breath as, with much twanging and straining of steel ropes, Colonel Boobs would shake and shudder his way up toward the sixth floor.

Every time, as if on cue, an old lady with gray hair would appear beside me and wait for the elevator. She didn't speak English and I didn't speak Italian, so we would stand together in silence, and I would nod and smile and generally feel awkward until the heaving, scraping sound of the ancient elevator on the move resumed again, signifying that Colonel Boobs would eventually reappear. The lady was so polite and patient, refusing my offers for her to go first. Instead, she would merely stand back and watch in horror as, once again, I would stack another load of the gear around Boobs, after which he would sink another few inches, and then repeat the whole process again. At that point, the lady would shake her head, point upward, and turn away to take the stairs instead. These encounters happened at least five times during our weeklong stay in Rome.

I'D TRIED TO ORGANIZE AN INTERVIEW WITH THE POPE. We had progressed as far as getting him to see the teaser I had cut, after which we were politely turned down with the following statement: "As a splinter of a thought, the concept is intriguing."

I wasn't upset. The whole point of the film was to keep "professional God people" out of the movie, to avoid having lots of religious talking heads touting their party lines. If I included the Pope, I would have to include the leaders of all the other major religions, and then what kind of a film would I have? Doubtless one that would completely miss the essence of what I was trying to achieve.

Shooting in Rome was easier than I'd expected. Vishnu, who was helping us remotely from Mexico, had managed to get a permit to shoot in St. Peter's Square. I wanted to experience the amazing pull of the Catholic Church.

Having scheduled our permitted day to coincide with the Pope's weekly address from his window, we arrived early so I could pick the best angle to film His Holiness. I chose a spot by one of the magnificent fountains so that I could shoot through the cascading water droplets. Since we were linked by radio, Colonel Boobs went over to one of the great speakers that stood in the square to record the voice of the Pope clean, without the sound of the fountains. I stood in the hot, muggy air and waited as crowds of people arrived. Soon it was elbow room only, and I was very glad to be beside the fountain; otherwise it would have been very difficult to get a shot at all.

While I was there, a very excited woman came up to me with her husband. Seeing me standing next to a professional-looking camera, she wanted to share an "amazing miracle" with me that involved photography. Her eyes were wide with anticipation. She was French and had been vacationing in the south of France with her husband when they had experienced the "miracle." Immediately they had changed their itinerary and taken the train to Rome so that they could share the "miracle" with His Holiness. I was intrigued.

"I have experienced the Virgin Mary!" she declared, almost hyperventilating in her elevated state of excitement. "The Virgin showed me a sign. I have the proof right here." She pulled out two digital cameras from her bag, each carefully wrapped in expensive silk.

They had been at a lake, she started to explain. "There was the most holy of sunsets . . . simply beautiful. It was the most peaceful moment my husband and I had ever encountered together. We both took out our cameras and photographed it . . . but . . ." She started breathing deeply again. ". . . but when I looked at the shot on my camera, there was the cross and a halo of the Virgin Mary in the sky." The woman looked as if she was going to cry, she was so moved. Her husband put his arm around her, to support her in this very emotional moment. "Yet on my husband's camera, it wasn't there. . . . Look."

They switched on the cameras and showed me two images of the same view. In the husband's shot, both the sun and the water could be clearly seen. The shot taken on the woman's camera, however, revealed the shape of a cross and what looked like a weird halo above the water. "There's the proof, sir. Right there. Look! It's the most beautiful thing I have ever seen. Do you think you could get this to our Holy Father? It is a miracle that has to be shared!"

"It's lens flare, madam."

She stiffened. "I'm sorry, sir? I don't understand."

"It's called lens flare. It's—"

"No!" she interrupted. "This is the proof. We took that photo at the same time—and the Virgin Mary made herself known to . . . me." She paused. Tears were now filling her eyes. "I have been blessed. Don't you see?"

"Look," I said. I spun my camera around to the sun and asked her to look at the pop-out screen. There was no flare. "This is the angle that your husband had on the setting sun, shot from right beside you. And . . ." I gently turned the camera a few degrees, and right on cue, a flare, almost identical to the one on her camera, appeared. "Here," I said. "That is the angle you had on the sun. It shows the same shape of distorted light. You see? It's called *lens flare*—it's caused by a refraction of light in the glass of the lens."

I felt really uncomfortable. One could have heard a pin drop, despite the throng of thousands of people. As the news filtered into the woman's mind and shattered her belief, her face slowly whitened. Her husband, who didn't speak English, hadn't understood our exchange.

After several long moments, the woman muttered, *"Merci, monsieur, merci,"* and, deflated, walked off. Her startled husband looked at me as if I had stolen something, before following her. All trace of her former effervescence had gone, and I could have sworn I heard a sob. She didn't even bother to wrap up the cameras in the silk before she shuffled away in the crowd; she just tossed them back in her bag, shook off her husband's arm as he attempted to comfort her, and disappeared from view.

A great sense of guilt enveloped me. All I had done was point out the truth. I was just a messenger, wasn't I?

At that moment, the Pope's arrival at the window was announced over the humongous speakers and echoed off the ancient stone that enclosed St. Peter's Square. I filmed him, raising his arms to the heavens, blessing the crowds in multiple languages.

"WHAT IS GOD?" I ASKED THE YOUNG MAN in front of me with the basilica framed directly behind him. He was about 23, and was dressed immaculately in black robes with a dog collar.

He didn't hesitate. "Even the question 'What is God?' is an example of our search for God in this life," he proclaimed confidently in a Texan drawl. "Because as a Catholic Christian"—he touched his heart—"the real question is *'Who* is God?' For us, God is someone very personal and very concerned about our life here on Earth—not a distant kind of entity out somewhere in space, but someone very near to us, although He's not exactly perceptible in everyday life."

The young man's name was Nolan Lowry, and he was from Tyler, Texas. He had been in seminary for five years and was currently studying at the Pontifical North American College in Rome. We had approached him blind in St. Peter's Square.

"How do you know that God exists?" I asked him.

"Through faith, and ultimately, with philosophy, there are things that show there has to be such a thing as a divine creator

. . . like where did everything come from? How did this beautiful world come to be?"

"Do you believe in the theory of evolution, or do you believe in divine creation?" I asked.

"I believe that God is the ultimate creator, that He could have used evolution if He had wanted to create the world. But, of course, the Book of Genesis is metaphorical in a lot of ways, and we have to see it not as a scientific treatise but as showing that God was the creator of everything."

He had the answers to many tricky questions worked out.

"Is the God you worship the same God other religions worship?"

"Christianity is very distinct as opposed to other religions. We believe that God became man, that He entered into time here on Earth. And He did this through the fully man–fully God, Jesus Christ, who came to dwell among us to tell us about the kingdom of God and the kingdom of peace in the world. And he offered himself for sacrifice for us, and he rose again on the third day.

"Islam rejects that God could become man, that God could enter His own creation as one of us; and that causes a big division. But as far as 'Are we praying to the same God?' there's not an absolute answer. We are and we aren't, because of our disagreements and our theology, so it's not exactly the same belief in God, but we do try to agree that there is one God."

"But the theology that you refer to is really born in the mouths and minds of men. I mean, man wrote the Bible, and man also wrote the Koran."

"Catholics believe that everything we know about God came from God Himself. Yes, God used men as instruments to write the Holy Scriptures, but it was ultimately God's revelation that was writing the Bible. And the Gospels and the New Testament tell us about the life of Jesus Christ—that not only was he a person of faith, but that he actually historically existed, and we try and reconcile what history can show us and what the Bible shows us."

"But Jesus Christ also appears in the Koran. He was a prophet."

"Exactly. The Koran describes Jesus Christ as a prophet of God, but not the incarnation of God."

"So you could say that there are lots of similarities between Christianity, Judaism, and Islam?" I challenged.

"There are many things in common, especially in trying to establish a personal relationship with God. As human beings, God created us to naturally desire Him. There is something innate in man that seeks God, and we believe that God created us with this desire for Him."

I changed my tack. "Let's get back to God Himself. Could He be a woman?"

"God by His nature is . . ." The until-then-very-articulate Nolan stuttered as he continued: ". . . is . . . not of . . . uh, does not have genitalia like human beings have. Because of our incarnation of Jesus Christ, we, we see . . . we use this, uh . . . reference to God, uh . . . we, we find Father, uh, God the Father in the Bible in the Old Testament, but, uh, you can't think of Jesus as—excuse me—uh, or God the godhead, the Holy Trinity, as one, a gender, uh, male or, uh, female, because God transcends our gender differences." He nodded.

"When you pray to God, does He answer you?"

Nolan smiled. "Yes, God dwells in eternity; however, He does listen to us. He's here with us right now, and He desires this loving relationship to be mutual."

"Why do you think so many religions fight with each other?"

"It's very sad. Most religions are founded on charity and peace, but when we take our eyes off God and focus on ourselves, politics come into the picture. We can disagree, and we can agree to disagree—that our faiths are different—but that doesn't mean we have to kill each other or hurt each other as a result of that.

"Sadly, in all the religions you have different groups and sects, and they want to force their faith on other people. There have been times that the Catholics have not always been tolerant of other religions, as other religions have not always been tolerant of Catholics.

"Forcing a belief in God through coercion is the problem. If someone is saying that God is wanting them to do harm to other people, that can't be from God, because God is completely good, and it is contrary to His nature to demand the infliction of evil on another individual."

"The Catholic Church is one of the richest institutions in the world. It seems there are double standards. Shouldn't it be using its wealth to abolish starvation?"

Nolan didn't hesitate—he was off and running. "This has always been a difficulty in the Church because Jesus commands us to help the poor, and as we know so well today, there is so much poverty. However, to the Church's credit, we do a lot of charitable work, much more than secular governments.

"You could ask, 'Why doesn't the Catholic Church sell St. Peter's and all that's in it and give to the poor?' It's because, as Catholics, we see everything that's beautiful, even the things we make with our own hands, as a reflection of God, because God is ultimately the most beautiful being that so far transcends us—that these things on Earth that are created elevate our souls. Everything here can be seen for free. There is no entrance fee for the basilica. Anyone who conducts themselves in an appropriate manner, believer or nonbeliever, is welcome."

Time to challenge: "When AIDS is rife in Africa, do you think it's right that the Catholic Church should dissuade people from using condoms?"

"It's a very difficult issue, because it's a hard teaching. The Church has held its view on sex for 2,000 years, and many other Christian faiths held the same view up until the 1930s. We believe, as Catholics, that life is a gift. Africa is a very difficult situation. As a seminarian, I am not in any authority to discuss this too much, so I am not going to try and explain it, because people have their own opinions. I'm not denying it's a hard issue, even for moral theologians."

I wouldn't be surprised if Nolan Lowry makes it to Pope one day—provided nobody asks him if God could be female.

THE OLD LADY TURNED UP AGAIN THAT EVENING as I was packing Colonel Boobs and the gear into the elevator. This time she didn't wait, but immediately shook her head, pointed up, and carried on toward the stairs.

Every night we would eat at the same restaurant, La Griglietta, which was within walking distance from our hotel. It became our second home, and we became great friends with the owner, Angelini Erminio. I *love* Italian food. The Colonel and I would chew the cud and work out strategies for achieving everything we needed. We even interviewed Angelini, who said that, for him, God was *pasta.* Of course.

One night the old woman from the hotel walked past. She waved and I waved back, but Angelini's dog, Spago, flew out of the restaurant and barked at her. Unperturbed, she hissed at him. Spago retreated, and glanced up at me with what I thought might be a scowl as he sauntered past.

"Very unlike Spago," I commented to Colonel Boobs.

"MY NAME IS MICHAEL COLLINS. I'm Irish. I'm a priest in the Dublin diocese. I lived in Rome for several years, teaching history of religions and cultures." Father Collins was sitting on the edge of a fountain in a square near the hotel.

"What is God, Father?"

"That reminds me of the Latin adage that was coined in this city during the Roman Empire: 'There are as many opinions as there are people.' So I suppose my opinion is only one of hundreds of thousands of millions. God for me is a creator and a sustainer."

"What evidence do you have that He actually exists?"

"Without trying to be smart, you could also ask the question 'What evidence is there that God doesn't exist?' So that kind of leaves you with a 50-50. When you look at all the wonderful things in the world, to me it makes sense that their origin was God."

"Do you believe there's one God for all religions?"

"It is in our tradition that there is one God and that people on the earth worship God in different ways."

"So the God you pray to in your church is the same as Allah?"

"Oh yes," he replied.

"And the same God as all the other religions?"

"Yes. We're the ones that probably make all the complications, the different traditions and forms."

"Then why do so many religions fight with each other?"

"It's not only religions that fight with each other; people fight with each other. It is part of our human instinct. When you look at all the wars and disagreements that have been caused by civilizations, religion is only one part."

"So it's what man does that causes conflict between religions?"

"It's a human condition that we seem to be programmed to violence. Religion is a thing that most people take quite seriously. Those who believe in a particular form of worship or religion hold it very closely and want to guard it, and that's why they want to defend it when they see it threatened in any way."

"Do think religion has become politicized?"

"Yes."

"When you pray, do you feel God answers you?"

"I can't really tell whether I know that or not. It's like talking to a friend. You just hope that the person has listened and that they can in some way respond to your needs, but sometimes friends can't give you the answer you would want. So I presume in your question you are asking: 'Do you feel that I pray to God and expect Him to give me a punctual answer?' Well, that doesn't even happen with my best friends, so I can't expect God to do better."

I liked Father Collins. He was very smart.

"Is God a spirit?" I asked him next.

"That's one definition of God, but that would only be a human definition—a category—so that definition is only partial, and I am sure God is greater than that."

"Do you think God is an all-encompassing power?"

"Yes."

"Do you think human beings make that power into our image?"

"That question is complicated. We tend to try and button down God or compress Him into our own human characteristics and categories, and that's probably because our minds are finite, and they can't deal with something that is infinite."

"Now I'm going to ask you some questions about the Catholic Church . . . about the politicization of the institution." I noticed the tape was running out. "Oh, but first I have to change the tape."

"God occasionally intervenes and makes the camera shut off at the most appropriate time, you see." He chuckled.

We all laughed. "But I'm not going to allow that to happen, because I have a fresh tape! . . . Here we go," I continued. "The Catholic institution seems to be very wealthy, with all their land, art, and history. Why don't they give more money away to the poor?"

"It's a very good question. One of the problems is that most of the art you are referring to dates back to the medieval period of the Renaissance, when the church was a great patron of the arts. One of the Popes—Nicholas V, who lived in the middle of the 15th century—said that if the Church were to build fine buildings and monuments and provide a beautiful liturgy, people would be attracted to the Church; and therefore art was to be subservient to the Church. But in today's terms, I am sure the Vatican would be very happy to have some of the onus of maintaining this art taken away from them, because despite the amount of people that travel to the Vatican museums, they're not able to raise sufficient funds to keep up this patrimony of civilization."

"It still seems to be the doctrine of the Catholic Church to dissuade people—particularly in Africa, where AIDS is spreading so fast—from using condoms, yet it is known unquestionably that the use of condoms can vastly reduce a deadly disease. What's your take on that?"

"I think the most important aspect is in regard to the education of people, to try and help them understand that chastity or abstinence and fidelity are probably—in fact, most certainly—the wisest course. But obviously not everybody can follow that, and not everybody feels that they can go along with that way of thinking; therefore you have to fall back on plan B, which is where condoms and other forms of contraception would be, in some cases, advisable—almost regarded as the lesser of the two evils."

"So you're saying that you would condone the use of condoms, even though this doesn't seem to be the true line of the Catholic Church?"

"Well, if I could put it in a slightly more nuanced way, I wouldn't be in a situation or a condition to condemn."

Even though I liked Father Collins, I wasn't sure that any of the answers I'd heard were bringing me, or the film, any closer to understanding this entity that goes by the name of God. I felt more confused now than when I had started. One thing was becoming clearer by the second: God's own silence was deafening.

WE'D HAD OUR LAST ELEVATOR ORDEAL. Colonel Boobs was outside guarding the gear in the taxi, and I was paying the bill. The woman behind the reception desk was trying out her English.

"Dida you alika the stay?"

"Very pleasant, thank you," I lied. "It would have been better if the elevator was a little larger and more efficient, though."

The woman gesticulated with her hands. "Oh thata thinga . . . is a acurse-ed. It will never work like it should. We try. Old owners, theya try . . . the city, she atry. . . . No good, never, no good." Then she leaned forward and whispered, "Whena they abuilt it, an olda woman fell down dee hole . . . dee big hole from dee topa floor . . ." She clapped her hands. "*Morta! Morta!* When Francisco wenta down there to getta some keys a guest hada droppeda . . . he said there were stilla blooda stains ona de stonea down thera." I couldn't believe what I was hearing. "An olda woman witha da graya hair." She nodded. "True. It's acurse-ed."

"I think I may have seen a ghost," I said as I slumped down next to Colonel Boobs in the taxi. "That old woman who would always appear by the elevator . . ."

"What old woman? I never saw any old woman," he replied. "Where? When?"

"The one Spago barked at."

Colonel Boobs looked at me blankly.

"Um, never mind," I said.

CHAPTER 16

A Brief Trip Home

"Occasionally you have to leave to appreciate where you were."

— NAPKIN #16

I had left the U.K. in 1996 when I moved to California. I hadn't been back much since then, just breezing in from time to time to stay with my mother, Jinx, in our little village in Kent and then breezing out again.

Living so far apart isn't easy for families, but whenever I do manage to get home, it is as if time has stood still. My mother still lives in the same house in which I grew up, the same one my father restored with his own hands. After he passed away, my mother divided the house in two and rented out the other side. But it still retains all its memories, smells of familiar polished wood, and has the same art on the walls. Apart from the trees in the garden, however, the whole place has shrunk. What seemed like a massive space to me all those years ago now feels like a doll's house, and I have to be careful not to bash my head on the Tudor beams.

Every Wednesday night during my childhood was bell night, when the ringers of the church bells would practice. It was the most melancholic of sounds and always reminded me of *The Thing*—that ever-present snake that lived within my father's soul. As soon as the bell-ringing started, I would instantly and inexplicably plunge into depression and guilt. It was one of the reasons I had left home at an early age.

The atmosphere the bells conjured up was as real to me as seeing the old woman in Rome. Only here it would thunder doom, gloom, and dread into my soul; and I could never figure out why. I would discuss it at length with Rana, my sister, who also shuddered at the sound. It was just one of those things we could never put a finger on. I had even tried to exorcise the feeling by taking up bell-ringing myself when I was 14, on the premise that if you can't run away from them, you might as well join 'em. It had helped somewhat, inasmuch as being the creator of one of the sounds somehow made it controllable and I could "own" it, but as soon as I ceased being a ringer, the feeling of despair would return every time I heard the bells toll.

COLONEL BOOBS AND I HAD TAKEN A FLIGHT from Rome to London with EasyJet. The tickets had cost only 40 euros each—about $55 U.S.—but we were held to ransom on our excess baggage. I'd pleaded with the orange-dressed robots at the airport, but they had been unrelenting; they wouldn't allow us to board until we had paid a further 800 euros. The staff was impolite—thoroughly unpleasant—and the true cost of that tiny little flight left a nasty taste in my mouth, rather like the lingering scent of their cheap cologne in my nostrils. Colonel Boobs and I renamed the airline *DifficultJet*.

At Heathrow Airport, we had rented a car with a very polite, male-voiced navigation system that we christened Harold. Harold was suave, sophisticated, and enunciated every direction in proper BBC English. It seemed a long time ago that we had been listening to Harold's American counterpart, Agnes, on our trip across the United States. The more I thought about time, the more Mr. Chou would churn. Would this journey ever come to an end?

It was great seeing my mother. A tower of strength in a tiny frame, she had a strong sense of humor, and a get-on-with-life stoicism that kept her constantly busy like a windup toy. Despite being in her 80s, she still flipped around the world, from Munich to Paris to New York and Tokyo, hosting exhibitions of my father's work. A lot of fun, and occasionally somewhat challenging, my mother is the most lovable human being you could find, and I am a very lucky son. I once read that souls choose their parents (usually for a specific reason) when they come down to Earth from wherever. If that's the case, I chose very well.

My mother's father had been an American Presbyterian minister—actually, a missionary—in the Middle East. She was born in Beirut, Lebanon, and grew up in Syria. When she was about six, her father's church had sent them a brand-new Chevrolet. Grandfather had proudly collected it from the docks, but it seemed every time my mother (whose real name is Lois) was in the car, it wouldn't start. My grandfather would say that there must be a *Jinx* in the car. The name had stuck throughout her life.

It was an uncanny, bizarre feeling being back in my childhood home with all the memories etched into the wattle and daub. I was joined by my childhood friend Jo Todd, whom I hadn't seen for years. I was shocked to find that Jo had gray hair. Was I going gray, too? Our fathers were both named George and were buried side by side. We joked about how they were probably somewhere up there, enjoying a gin and tonic, and laughing down at their little boys. I didn't feel so little, though. I had just learned that the current rector of Smarden Church, Alex Bienfait, was two years younger than I was—the vicar was younger than *moi?*

I wanted a mini-me to represent myself as a child, staring up at the rafters of Smarden Church, dreaming of turning the ship upright and sailing it away—my daydreams of times past. So Jinx had found 12-year-old Will Stevens, who was a dead ringer for me at that age. I filmed Will in the church, gazing up at the rafters—a lonely figure in a sea of wood that still smelled of Mrs. Drury's elbow grease. All those memories of yesteryear, sitting in the church and looking at the patterns of grain in the wooden pews, came flooding back to me. I even found the same knot in the shape of an eye that I had spent so many hours staring at every Sunday as a child.

Then the bell ringers arrived. I filmed them yanking out those melancholic sounds, never in rhythm, constantly out of time . . . the haunting resonance bouncing through my head and into my memories, disturbing Mr. Chou, stirring up *The Thing,* and reviving the snake that had lived in all our souls. I climbed back up to the belfry while the ringers pulled on those ropes, and filmed the great bells crashing back and forth, their thunderous statement shaking the Norman-era tower, just as they had done every single Wednesday and Sunday for several hundred years.

I planted myself on the bell ringers' platform overlooking the nave so that I could film the Sunday-morning service unobtrusively from the rear. Mrs. Randolf still sang in the choir, and Will's grandfather, Jim Carr, read the sermon. I was transported right back in time. I could almost see the ghost of my own father telling the ghost child of me not to look behind him because the crocodile would bite off his head. I'd believed him, remember? And I never had looked back. Not understanding where it had lived at night, I'd assumed that it had feasted on all those little children who couldn't resist peeking behind them. Then it dawned on me, and finally I understood: the crocodile was none other than myself—my daydream had become real.

What had seemed like a lifetime for a child now seemed like a billionth of a second for me, as I gazed back into the past. What my father had been trying to teach me, above the etiquette of church behavior, was to make the most of every day, because if ever you looked back and had regrets, you would be sure to lose your head.

HAROLD THE NAVIGATION SYSTEM GUIDED US politely through wet, green countryside. Colonel Boobs and I were heading down to the West Country of England. We had an appointment with a real, live Druid.

His name was Adrian Rooke, and we found him in a converted garage at the back of a suburban house in Bristol. The house had once belonged to him, but then he got divorced. He looked to be somewhere in his late 40s. He had a strong, kind face and long white hair and was wearing jeans and a sleeveless AC/DC T-shirt. He was a member of the Order of Bards Ovates & Druids.

Modern Druidry is closely associated with ancient pagan religions and certainly borrows certain rituals from times of old, but it's not associated with witchcraft, nor indeed is it a re-creation of the practices of ancient Druids, as so little is really known about that time in history. Druidry today is regarded as both a philosophy and a way of life. It is a way to become more grounded and develop a keen awareness of nature and your surroundings, to focus on your responsibilities, and to serve and revere the land, as well as live as much as possible in balance with the earth.

"Would you like a cup of PG tips?" Adrian asked in a thick West Country accent.

We sat out the rain in his "house," enjoying Britain's most popular brand of tea and talking about many things. Adrian had once been addicted to everything before becoming a social worker who counseled kids on how to keep off drugs, tobacco, and alcohol. His belief—his Druidry—had given him enormous strength. He owed everything, including his survival, to that practice, he told us.

When the rain stopped, we jumped in the car and drove off deep into the Somerset countryside, to a pub that was—aptly—called the Druid's Arms.

It felt surreal, and at the same time very appropriate, to be in the pub. We ordered a "ploughman's lunch"—a popular staple in British pubs, which comprises a chunky wedge of local cheese, fresh crusty bread, and relish—and talked about our location, Stanton Drew, which was the site of the second-largest ring of standing stones after Avebury in Wiltshire.

"These stones are over 5,000 years old. Those were pagan times. There's a lot of power in those stones. A lot of power," Adrian stressed. He gave Colonel Boobs and me pieces of hand-carved birch wood that had a rune etched into them, which he said we were to hang around our necks (I am still wearing mine now). The rune was for protection. "You're going to need that," he said. "You're going to need a lot of that, doing what you are doing."

The sun had come out again. The air was fresh, and the sky was deep blue in parts and white in others. Black storm clouds raced each other across the horizon. We drove up a hill and parked in a farmyard. Colonel Boobs and I carried the equipment out toward a field, from which we could see the standing stones in the distance.

Adrian had asked us to wait there for him. When he appeared, he was completely transformed. He was wearing long white robes with brown symbols intricately embroidered on them. In his hand he carried a staff engraved with runes, around his neck was a necklace of many carved birch-wood talismans, and pinned to his black hat was a silver dragonfly brooch . . . and a silver butterfly. Adrian had his very own Mr. Chou.

"It's not very far. They're just over here." He seemed to glide through the long grass. We picked up the gear and followed.

In photographic terms, it was a very visual site. I filmed Adrian performing his ritual, making offerings, opening the doors to the east, west, south, and north. It was powerful. The stormy clouds closed in as he strode about from one side of the standing stones to another. Thunder could be heard far off in the distance. He raised his staff high . . .

> *"Dorian valianter, listen to the words of the old horned one who is ever young. I am he who opens the doors of life and death, the gates of dawn, and the gates of night. I am Kanunos and Sylvanos and Pan, and the music of my pipes is in the air of the green woods and on the summer hills. My voice is in the wind of midnight, and beneath the stars speaks words of magic. In ancient tongues forgotten and unknown, I inspire panic, fear, and passionate desire. Even now I share the face of a skull. There will be no manifestation of life without me, for without death, there can be no rebirth. The gateway to the south is now open."*

During the ritual, we were startled to see a white owl materialize out of a large barren oak tree and fly over us. It was a powerful omen, Adrian later told us.

"I believe there's an arrogance that human beings can comprehend what God is, or the Goddess—I prefer to use the feminine within that terminology—but even then do we know what God is? Is it a sound? Was the universe created from a thought? I believe it's simplistically arrogant to try and actually sexualize God, or to have some interpretation or conscious understanding of what is beyond our comprehension."

I filmed Adrian as he stood beside one of the standing stones. "I like to think of the analogy of one of our blood cells actually understanding the whole composition of what our bodies do. We're just tiny cells in a massive structure," he explained. "I think at this time in the human evolution, it's beyond our ability to understand God. I think we need to *feel* God, not to *understand* God. I feel God through the land, through nature, through the wind in the air, through the seasonal cycles, the turn of the seasons . . . and I work on harmonizing myself with that sense of nature. Rather than being separate from nature, I strive to be a part of nature."

At that moment nature interrupted us, and the heavens opened with a vengeance. Adrian smiled as he stood by the standing stone, getting wetter and wetter, and not minding a bit. I took shelter under a piece of plastic, desperately trying to keep the camera dry. When the rain died down, we continued.

"One of the great sadnesses of the human dilemma as I see it in this day and age is that religion separates us. I think that we're all ultimately walking through the same forest. Maybe we take different paths to get to the other side of the forest, but we are still in the same forest. Religion, I believe, in its purest form is a great thing for mankind, but it's been spoiled by human beings. If you take the human being out of the equation, some of the teachings of all the major traditions are wonderful; they all express the same ultimate love for one another, as you would love yourself. We all have sparks of the divine within us, and we just need that to be encouraged so that we can all reach our full potential.

"Allah or Jesus Christ or Buddha or any of these great lights that have been here throughout the ages, there's some wonderful truths in all of what they have to say. I like the biblical statement 'Do unto others as you would have others do unto you,' and that's how I live my life." He laughed.

"But there's a great sadness in me that in the 21st century, human beings are still destroying others in the name of religion. We're all living a human experience on this planet and need to pull together. It's absurd that there is poverty today—that people are dying in the millions of AIDS in Africa, when we in the Western world, a so-called Christianized society, live in abundance. With all of the bounty that we have today, I think we have to remember there's more depression, more anxiety, more drug addiction, more alcoholism in our society now than there ever has been. And yet we have abundance—of food, of material possessions—so something is missing. Something is missing."

The bleating of the sheep and mooing of the cows seemed louder. I looked up from the camera to see that all the animals that had been in the fields had come to visit us.

"For me, all I hope to do through my Druidic path is to become the best human being I can possibly be in the time that has been given to me on this planet. I feel that I'm part of a wonderful miracle that takes place on a daily basis."

It started to rain again. I used the time to call home and check in with Soumaya. The rain ebbed; Adrian remained as still as a statue, right where he was, and Colonel Boobs recorded the sheep with the boom mike. A little later, there was a tap on my shoulder. "Hold on a minute," I said to Colonel Boobs.

"I don't think you want to hold on."

"I'll just be a sec . . . one sec . . ."

I continued my conversation on the phone. There was another tap on my shoulder.

"What's up?" I looked up. Colonel Boobs just pointed. "Holy smoke!" I exclaimed. "I'll call back," I shouted into the phone and ran to the camera. Immediately behind Adrian and the standing stone—in the frame of the lens that was still set up—was a *full rainbow.* I turned the camera on, cursing the time it took to warm up, asked Adrian to look out into the distance beyond me, and filmed the scene. As I panned along the rainbow to find Adrian, a large dragonfly flew right past the end of the lens into the scene. Within two minutes the rainbow was gone.

Adrian just chuckled when I played it back to him.

IT WAS VERY LATE BY THE TIME WE HAD DROPPED Adrian off at home, had another cup of PG tips tea with him, and traveled into Bristol to look for a hotel. By the time we had checked in and stowed the gear safely, it appeared all the restaurants in the area had closed. There was only one place that served food late. So we walked over a canal and down a dock and entered *the most happening place* in Bristol. It was one of those ghastly, cavernous chain pubs that seem to be so ubiquitous in England these days. It had laminated menus and ersatz food, but they had local ale, and we were very hungry.

Colonel Boobs and I took our pints and sat down at one of the tables. We gazed mournfully at the sticky, plastic menus as extremely loud (and actually very good) Brit pop poured out of thumping speakers. We had to order food at the bar, so I left the

Colonel to nurse his pint and went to put in our requests. It was about 11:30 P.M., and the clientele consisted mostly of oversized men with extremely thick necks, between the ages of 18 and 40.

Finally it was my turn. The place reeked of BO. A 20-something platinum-blonde barmaid with *Tracy* emblazoned across a remarkably large chest was manning the bar.

"Yes, luv?"

"Do you have any simple salads?" I asked politely.

There was a rude snorting sound to my left, followed by a voice repeating my question in a very derogatory manner: "'Do you have any simple salads?'" I pretended I hadn't heard it.

"Luv, no, there hasn't been lettuce for days."

"Okay, then I'll go for the curry and the ahh . . . what's better, the curry or the chicken?"

"'What's better, the curry or the chicken?'" the voice mimicked.

"Billy, shut it," barked Tracy. "Sorry, luv?"

"What's better, do you think, the curry or the chicken?"

"'. . . the curry or the chicken?'" the voice behind me parroted again.

Following the advice my parents had always given me as a child, I ignored the ignorant bully.

The mocking continued: "What's better? Curry? Chicken? Why not a chicken curry, eh? Trace? Ain't the curry chicken?"

"Shut it, Billy," Tracy reiterated.

Billy didn't shut it. . . . Judging by the warmth of his breath on my neck, Billy was not only edging closer, he was also just getting into his stride. "You gonna make up your mind, sweetheart, or do I have to hear a discussion about the whole fuckin' menu before I get to order my fuckin' pint?" If the situation hadn't been so threatening, I might have laughed at how bizarre Billy sounded, speaking like a Cockney gangster with a West Country accent.

It was time to meet this Billy and see for myself just how much danger I was in. I turned around and looked up . . . and up. . . . No wonder Billy had a big mouth—at around 6'4", about 260 pounds, and with a thick, blemished neck that would have looked quite at home on a bull, he was clearly not the kind of man one argued with. Standing beside him was his partner in crime, an equally large and intimidating Billy clone with a bulbous nose, an empty pint glass, and a glare that could turn living creatures to stone.

"Billy, you've been warned," Tracy said in the long-suffering tone of a mother who was tired of reprimanding her five-year-old.

"C'mon, Trace . . . bloke's gotta right to order a pint, right, Bob?"

"Yep," Bob grunted.

Billy turned to me. "So why don't you get the fuckin'-chick'n-fuckin'-curry, then, so I can order my fuckin' pint," he said in a voice that indicated in no uncertain terms that the stakes had just been upped to a level that I definitely wouldn't care to match. *Uh-oh . . . trouble's brewing.* I gulped, casting a frantic eye around to see if Colonel Boobs was watching.

"One more lip outta you, Billy, and I swear you're not coming back in 'ere. Don't think I won't call the pigs." Tracy turned back to me with a sigh. I could see her life before me: the England I had left behind. "What would you like?"

"The curry, and the scampi and chips, please."

"Oh . . . oh . . . oh . . . sweetheart boy 'ere's changed 'is mind, ain't he? Thought you were a chicken type? Or maybe he's just chicken. Eh, Bob? Smart-boy sweetheart's a chick'n, ain't he?"

"Yep," Bob grunted.

"That's it. Fuckin' chicken."

"£22.90, please, luv."

"Fuckin' poofter chicken," Billy repeated.

"Yep," Bob grunted.

I was doing my best to ignore the situation, but the truth was, Billy and his sidekick, Bob, were very drunk and clearly in the mood for a fight. I was a stranger with a *posh* British accent that several years States-side hadn't managed to eradicate. That made me different. The prognosis wasn't good.

Colonel Boobs was a black belt in karate and could knock these boys across the Irish Sea, despite their size, but he was sipping his pint way on the other side of the pub. I had to come up with a plan—and *fast*.

Stalling for time, I pulled out my wallet and passed over my American Express Platinum card, which, of course, only made things worse.

"Oh, oh, bloody 'ell." Billy was in his element now. "Not only is he a fuckin' poofter, not only is he a fuckin' chicken, but he's a fucking *rich* mother-fuckin' poofter chicken. Bob, ain't that the worst fuckin' combo you've ever 'eard of, eh, Bob?"

"Yep," Bob grunted.

"A fuckin' *loaded* fuckin' poofter chicken. Fuck me!"

"Shut it, Billy!" Tracy yelled.

"I'm not the fuckin' problem 'ere! I'm not a fuckin' poofter chicken, Trace, am I?" Billy said, throwing a proud *Aren't I wonderful?* grin at the snickering crowd gathering around us. I sighed. Billy was really loving his moment in the spotlight. And so, it seemed, were most of the pub's customers.

I screwed up my courage, and decided to face Billy down.

"Aren't you?" I slowly turned and asked.

Within seconds Billy had pulled me in by the lapels and was sneering into my face. Where was the Colonel when I needed him? I could smell Billy's brewery breath, and feel a head butt coming on. I'd just given Billy the excuse he'd been looking for.

"Are you fuckin' accusing me of being a fuckin' poofter, eh?" He stared at me menacingly.

I didn't answer.

"Billy! Billy! Billy!" the chant went up.

"Put 'im down, Billy!" I heard Tracy scream at the top of her voice. "I mean it. I'm callin' the fuckin' pigs, Billy, if you don't back down right now." She was trying hard to get his attention.

But Billy only had eyes for me. "I'll take your silence as a fuckin' yes, then!" He scowled down at me . . .

"Can I interview you?" I asked, as unfazed as I could fake it (while secretly trying not to choke). "I would really *love* to interview you."

"Do what?" Billy's face went blank as his brain groped frantically to catch up with the sudden change in direction of our conversation.

"And Bob. Both of you," I quickly added.

"What?" Billy repeated. I breathed an inward sigh of relief as his grip slackened just a smidgen. *It might just work.* Bolstered by the thought, my mind worked overtime to come up with a plausible explanation before I lost ground.

"I'm from Hollywood, hence the poofy accent, and I'm making a film here about what people think God is . . . and"—the wheels of my brain quickly whirred—"and . . . I'm FUCKIN' FED UP with all the FUCKIN' PUSSIES I've found so far in FUCKIN' BRISTOL!" I shouted, in a burst of inspiration. "I need REAL BLOKES! Like you and Bob. You're fuckin' perfect!"

The viselike grip relaxed a little more. "Really?" Billy's eyes widened.

"Yeah, you wanna be in the film?" I pushed my advantage home. "I mean that's why I'm in here. I mean, why else would a poofter chicken like me be in here, right? I'm looking for real men like you and Bob. You in? You in?"

"You should do it, Billy," grunted Bob. "Tell him how God never got this far west." Everyone cracked up . . .

"So, what about it? You gonna do it?" I asked.

"But why me . . . ? Why would you want me?"

"'Cause you're real, Billy. You're the real deal. Not a FUCKIN' PUSSY!"

"Yeah!" said Billy. "The real deal."

"You're being a fuckin' pussy now, pussying around . . ." pointed out Bob, to a gale of laughter.

"All right . . . I'll do it, then. Yeah, I'll do it. I'll do it. Bob, you in?"

"Nah, Bill, you're the spokes-bloke. You'd be good."

Billy had let go of me completely by now. "All right, then. When, then?"

"Tomorrow—9 A.M. We could shoot it right out there on the quay."

"All right, then. But what I gotta say?"

Phew! It had been a close call, and I was grateful to have escaped it without a thorough beating.

I filled Billy in on what would be required of him, and was pleasantly surprised to see Colonel Boobs standing there right beside him.

As we made our way back to our table, the Colonel said, "Ja, that was pretty smart, the way you pulled that one off. One more second and there would have been blood, ja! Vee have *vays!*" Apparently, the Colonel had been there all along, just in case, and was rather disappointed that the situation had ended with a diplomatic treaty.

As we were eating our dinner, Billy and Bob came over with a couple of pints they had bought for us. We invited them to join us. "By the way . . . you made the right choice, Peeta. The scampi's much better than the chicken!" Billy said approvingly.

When I say I'm going to do something, I always try to do it. So after breakfast the next morning, we made our way down to the quay to honor my contract with Billy, but he never showed up. I wasn't surprised, as the last time I had seen him, he, Bob, and an Irishman called Dazed (I kid you not . . . that really was his name) were drinking vast amounts of beer with chasers and singing, "Put your left leg over my shoulder . . ." I made a mental note that if ever I was cornered in a seedy bar, being threatened with a "Glasgow kiss," I would ask the perpetrator if I could interview him about God.

CHAPTER 17
London

―――――――――――――――●―――――――――――――――

*"You shouldn't judge a horse by looking at its droppings;
you should judge a horse by looking at the horse."*

— NAPKIN #17

Colonel Boobs and I went back on the road, to Merthyr Tydfil
in Wales to film a wet Monday afternoon, up north to interview
a white witch, then zigzagging back south, doing an interview
here and there. The film was beginning to take form. There was
a lot still missing, which didn't best please Mr. Chou, but I was
beginning to see that there was a great commonality in what was
emerging from the mouths of different people.

One thing was clear: it was no longer necessary to arbitrarily
interview strangers; it was time to become much more surgical in
our approach.

IN LONDON WE HAD AN APPOINTMENT with Benjamin Crème, an
artist, author, and the owner of a publication called *Share International* magazine. For several decades, he had been proclaiming
that the Second Coming, as prophesied by many religions, would
come in the form of *Maitreya*, a figure that represents every religion's expectations in one form. And not only was he definitely
coming, *he was already here.*

We pulled up outside a terraced house somewhere in north
London and knocked on Mr. Crème's door. We were ushered inside and set up in his living room, and soon he arrived. He was
then 85, but looked younger and had tremendous energy. I sat
him down under one of his paintings, and he began to talk.

"My job has been to prepare the way for *the one* people in the
West generally call *the Christ.* My direct experience is that there

are 14 masters of wisdom—the mahatmas of the East, the masters of wisdom, the lords of compassion—and I was contacted by one of them way back in January of 1959. A man came to me and told me that the masters were trying to contact me. A few weeks later, I had my first experience when a voice came into my head, late at night—about 11:30 P.M.—and it was as clear as day. It was as if energy, or some pressure, had been exerted at my head, and all my own thoughts disappeared. In the place of my usual thinking was a voice that said, 'Go to Blackfriars Bridge, south side,' and it gave me a date.

"When the day came, I walked over the bridge; there was hardly anybody around but a car waiting at the far end. I sidled up to it and sort of looked in, and there were some people I didn't know inside, but one of them was the man who told me that I was being contacted by the *masters*. And that was the beginning of this process.

"That master told me to get a tape recorder, and he began to give me long dissertations by telepathy. As he said something, I would just repeat it as I heard it, onto the tape, and he did this for about three months. And then in March of 1959 he suddenly said, 'Switch off the machine and kneel down,' and he said, 'Now our master, the master of all the masters, Maitreya himself, has something important to tell you.'

"An extraordinary energy completely overwhelmed me, and I began to shake. I began to cry. My heart turned over. I was filled with the love of all the world. While this was going on, I was inside a great sphere of light; and if I looked to the right, I could see all the events of the past, which were still taking place, and if I turned my head to the left, I could see all the events of the future, which had not yet taken place. I saw myself. I saw millions of people. I saw crowds running about the streets, crying with joy, the tears running down their cheeks. I was talking to thousands, and Maitreya had declared himself and was speaking publicly to millions.

"All this was as real as anything I've ever experienced. And while this was taking place, Maitreya said, 'I myself am coming, sooner than anyone thinks possible. It will be in about 20 years. You will have a role to play in my coming if you accept it.'

"That was all he said. He didn't explain what the role was. I said, 'Whatever you want done, I'm your man. I'll do it.' Then the overshadowing, as I would call it, stopped. I came back to normal. The sphere disappeared. The voice of Maitreya disappeared.

"That was my introduction into this work for preparing the way for what Christians would call the Christ. He is the Christ. He embodies what we call the Christ principle. And he is back in the world today, living in a temple, a Hindu temple, not so very far from where I live here in north London, awaiting the time when he can come forward openly and address humanity. And that's what I've been working on for all this time, for the last 30-odd years.

"The interesting thing to me today is that all the major religions expect a teacher. Christians are awaiting the return of the Christ. Some believe he's coming, like, Tuesday week. Others believe he's going to come at the end of the world. The Muslims await a teacher, too—the *Imam Mahdi,* the great Imam—mainly the Shiites, but some of the Sunnis, too. And they don't have any special time for his coming, but some Shiites already believe that he is in the world, and others believe that he will be in their midst within the next two or three years. And the volatile president of Iran has already announced that he is dedicating himself, his office, and his country to serve the Mahdi.

"At the same time, Jews await the coming of the Messiah. To me, the Messiah came to the Jews as Jesus and wasn't recognized, and was eventually put to death. The Hindus await the return of Krishna or a great being they call Kali Avatar. The Buddhists expect the coming of a teacher called Maitreya Buddha; they are the only ones who have his name right."

I was intrigued. It was such a bizarre story. "It must be pretty hard, though, for one entity to be the Second Coming for all these religions with preconceptions. I mean, how would Mahmoud Ahmadinejad take it if Maitreya, who as you infer is the great Imam Mahdi, came from, say, Boise, Idaho, and was white? Or Jesus Christ was now a gay black man? Or even a woman? . . . How would the Christian Right take that?"

"Well, that is the task of Maitreya. He comes as a world teacher. He does not come as the Christ for Christians. He does not come as the Imam Mahdi for Muslims or Maitreya Buddha to Buddhists. He comes as a world teacher to all groups, religious and nonreligious alike, and he does not come as a *religious* teacher."

"Jesus Christ gave birth to Christianity; will Maitreya's presence on Earth give birth to another religion, do you think?" I asked.

"It will give birth to another approach to God, another understanding of God, which you can call religion. Maitreya says religion is like a ladder: It can help you to get onto the roof, but once you're on the roof, you don't need the religion. You can hand the ladder over to somebody else to help them up or leave it there."

"So, what is God?" I asked.

"That's the number one question. I think God is energy, but that energy isn't just some muscle power. It's made up of qualities, the qualities of God—the love of God; the power, the purpose of God; the intelligence of God; and so on. I believe that all things have consciousness. The tiniest atom anywhere in the universe has the potential of God consciousness within it."

"And why do so many religions fight each other, do you think?"

"People do this out of fanaticism. I find fanaticism ugly and repulsive and far, far from the truth of life. If it's Christianity, it's the 'best of all'; if it's Islam, then that's the best . . . and so on.

"Everything that follows the market is about competition, and that creates commercialization, which is driving the life out of our lives. We are like pawns on a huge chessboard, pushed around by materialistic forces—huge, powerful empires; mass corporations; and rich and greedy countries whose only goal is the heightening of their bank accounts. This is true of all the developed countries. The G8 nations of the world are corrupting the world and destroying it. Competition is a canker. It should be eliminated from the world altogether. Competition separates; divides; creates schisms and eventually wars, terrorism, death, and destruction.

"If we want to live together on planet Earth, we have to learn to share. We can no longer be cavalier in our destruction of the environment. Global warming is a reality, and it is more than just the earth heating up; it is the result of the very destruction of the fabric of our planet. The Christ is in the world again, whether you call him the Christ or the Imam Mahdi or the Messiah or Maitreya Buddha or Kali Avatar—it just doesn't matter. Maitreya doesn't even like these religious terms; he wishes only to be called the teacher. And he's the teacher for all men, of every kind and color, religious or not.

"If one child anywhere is dying of hunger in a world filled with food, then you don't have a spiritual world. That is the reality; that is what Maitreya comes to do battle with, and to inspire humanity to see this.

"Sharing is the first step, because when you share, you create trust. When you create trust, all other problems can be solved. But without trust nothing can be changed. Maitreya comes to do battle with this competition in the world. He comes to free the heart of man to be what it is."

Benjamin Crème stopped for several seconds. His eyes glazed, and he started to weep. His voice quivered, and like a man who has something extremely important to impart, he closed his eyes and continued reverently: "The heart of man is really the heart of God; and when he experiences himself as God, as the reality which he is, then the idea of competition will fall away. The idea of wars, of terrorism and all the rest, the idea of starving millions living in the midst of plenty—all that rottenness in our modern, materialistic world—will disappear. The task of Maitreya is to galvanize humanity to see this."

I liked Mr. Crème a lot. Despite having to listen to his ideas with a very open mind and a truckful of salt, he'd said some interesting things. As he saw us out, he told me that when he was younger, aliens had lived in his house and had taught him to drive a spaceship. He could get from London to Los Angeles in under a second. "It was an exhilarating way to travel," he remarked with conviction.

I said, "If it's still parked out the back, perhaps I could borrow the keys?"

"MY NAME IS AHMED SAAD, and I am the Imam of North London Central Mosque, previously known as the notorious Finsbury Park Mosque. But actually North London Central Mosque is the original name of this mosque; and now it's under new administration, and we are doing a lot of things to bring the youth back and to regain trust and change its image."

An image change was precisely what the mosque needed. A previous Imam, notorious militant cleric Abu Hamza al-Masri, who is now sitting in a British jail, had allowed the mosque to become a haven for radicals—hosting such figures as Zacarias Moussaoui (9/11's convicted 20th hijacker), Richard Reid (the notorious shoe bomber), and reportedly, three of the four London bombers. The British police had stormed the establishment, and a new administration had now taken over.

"What is God?" I asked Imam Saad. I was shooting him by a window inside the mosque. We'd just had two cups of PG tips. He was young, smart, and articulate. He had a commanding yet approachable presence.

"As a Muslim leader, when I think of God, I get at least five words describing Him: Number one is *purpose.* I have a purpose in life that I dedicate my actions to. I dedicate my life to Him. God to me means *conscience,* that I should always be doing things for someone who is witnessing me, who is seeing me even if I am away from people. God to me also means *guidance,* because whenever I am in need of someone to help, whenever I'm perplexed or confused about something, I simply turn—or any Muslim will simply turn—and say, *Oh God, help me.* God also means to me *justice,* because if someone does wrong to me and I cannot reclaim my rights in this world, what will I do? And the fifth word is *love.* I believe that God is loving, and He does not create us to fight each other; He created us to be united to each other. And out of His love He will provide even for those who deny His existence.

"So this is what God means to me—it means purpose, it means love, it means justice, it means soulness. When I'm totally isolated from people, when everyone forsakes me, I'm not alone in this world, because God is there."

"Is Allah the same God that the Christians pray to," I asked, "the same God the Hindus pray to, the same God that the Jewish people pray to?"

"The word *Allah* is the Arabic name, proper name, for God.

As Muslims, we believe the word *God* is not an accurate name of Allah, because the word *God* has got derivatives. You can have female goddesses and male gods. You can have false gods and true gods. You can have Greek gods, Persian gods, Roman gods. But Allah is the proper name of the one unique God. In Hebrew it is *Elohim*. It can be *Allah* in any other language, but it's actually the Arabic word for God. And Arab Jews and Christians worship Allah with Muslims."

"Why do so many religions fight each other?"

"Well, I have been searching for an answer to this question for a long time; and since as a Muslim, I believe there is an answer for every question in the Koran, I came across this verse—it says: 'All mankind, we created you from a male and a female and made you into nations and tribes so that you may know each other.'

"I have been thinking that's why God has created us so different—different religions, different backgrounds, different colors, different geographical locations, and different ethnic minorities as well—so that we come and explore and cooperate to find the commonalities and excuse each other for different opinions. But we shouldn't fight; we should go find commonalities, explore the world, and enjoy the diversity for which God has created us. Diversity and difference are a blessing that people are misusing by killing each other, exploiting the weaknesses of each other, and taking the houses of each other."

"So let's just talk about that for a second," I interjected. "Because we are, as you mentioned, in what is formerly known as Finsbury Park Mosque, which was a place where a radical side of Islam was being preached and taught, and even Richard Reid and Zacarias Moussaoui's names have been associated with this mosque. What is happening to Islam today?"

"What's happening to Islam is that it's been hijacked by a bunch of extremists who have no knowledge of the truth of Islam and who are being, I'm sad to say, promoted by the biased media.

"And in this mess, a lot of true scholars of Islam are being neglected and not given the space to speak and communicate the truths of Islam to people. By shutting down these true scholars, space is being given to these fake people who have no knowledge and no proper education about Islam. What I'm questioning here is who has given them the authority to speak in the name of Muslims? Not Muslims. Of course, we haven't given them that authority, but it might be the media who has given them that authority."

"Not every Muslim is a terrorist, but it seems that, today, every terrorist claims they are a Muslim. How do you react to a statement like that?" I challenged.

"I don't believe this is true, because terrorism doesn't have a religion. There could be Christians who are terrorists, but we don't say there are Christian terrorists. Or Jews who are terrorists, and we don't say Jewish terrorists. Or Hindu terrorists. But unfortunately, lately the media says that terrorists are always Muslims, but in fact if we look deeper, we will find lots of terrorist incidents that have been perpetrated by people who belong to other religions. Like the Tamil Tigers—they are not Muslims; they have no link with Islam.

"It is upsetting indeed that the image people have of Muslims is based on a few personalities who lack understanding as to what Islam is. As much as the West is suffering from the actions of these people, the Muslims themselves are suffering from the actions of these people."

"But we cannot deny that these fanatics exist. Why are they fanatic?" I asked.

"Because of a lack of understanding. If you bring someone from the street who has had no prior contact with Islam at all and has just started practicing, often what happens is that he reads two books and misinterprets them. They are fanatic because of the lack of justice in the world. A lot of people see wars happening, and that the victims are mostly Muslims—look at the war in Iraq; look at the war in Afghanistan.

"Of course, I am for fighting terrorism; however, I am not for fighting innocent people. I am for removing tyrannical regimes, but I am not for punishing people for the guilt and for the sins of these regimes. What did the Iraqi people do to suffer so? They suffered under Saddam for many years, and now they are suffering under the American troops and the British troops as well. It's not fair.

"I believe that there are so many voices, here and in the West, that stand for the rights of Iraqis to have their own country devoid of any foreign troops. But the politicians are not allowing these voices to be heard. So as much as there is injustice being done against the Muslim people, because they are not given the space to speak, there is also an injustice done against the Western people, because the just voices are not given a space to speak."

I didn't want to get too deep into politics, but at the same time, I couldn't help thinking about Sally back in Texas and her friend Cody, who woke up having nightmares because his buddy was blown up by a roadside bomb, fighting a war in a foreign land to help a population who simply didn't want them there. It was so deeply convoluted. I decided not to press too much.

"So do you think that organized religions, including Islam, are politicized?" I said.

"Yes, very much, and this is horrible. Religion and politics should be kept separate. In the world today there is ideological corruption, financial corruption, and political corruption, but the worst of them is religious corruption, where religion is used to serve personal desires and hidden agendas."

I COULDN'T HELP THINKING JUST HOW DIFFERENT these last two interviews had been. The diversity was fabulous—completely different cultures in the same town. Strangely enough, if you really broke down what Benjamin Crème and Imam Saad had said, there were more similarities, perhaps, than were immediately apparent, as objective thinking and tradition had divided the same content like a centrifuge in a chemical process.

As Colonel Boobs and I ventured back across the Atlantic, I felt our trip had yielded some fascinating footage, and although there was still a long way to go, Mr. Chou folded his wings on the journey home as I played over the voices of each of the characters we had met, to the drone of yet another set of jet engines.

CHAPTER 18

Seal and Ringo Starr

"If you think you're good, you're probably some of the way,
but you won't arrive until you know for sure."

— NAPKIN #18

There was a lot of work that had to be done when I arrived home. I desperately needed a backer. Along with the line of credit I'd taken out on my house, I'd sunk all my savings and my writing fee for *The Bystander* into the *OMG* project in order to continue financing it. I wasn't even halfway through shooting it, let alone editing and finishing it. I had a family to support and wasn't earning money from lucrative advertising jobs, as I was never available. My trusted manager and friend, Adam Krentzman, went all out to find an investor for the project. In the meantime, I continued to research and find interesting interviewees.

We never really get to know celebrities on an intimate level. They are usually present in our lives because of their profession or charitable works or the fact that they are often the foundations of gossip. What would a celebrity think about God? I felt that having some well-known people in the film would provide an interesting insight into such a personal age-old question, so I put out feelers to all my friends to find some household names who might be interested in being interviewed.

MY FRIEND ROBERT NORTON INTRODUCED ME to the singer-songwriter Seal. I'd been a great admirer of his for many years and was very happy to make his acquaintance. Seal emerged from England's house music scene in the early '90s to become the most popular British soul vocalist of the decade, and is still going strong on both sides of the Atlantic today. Seal's lineage can be traced to Nigerian, Brazilian, and Afro-Caribbean roots; and one of his middle names is Olusegun, which means "God is victorious."

We had lunch at the Beverly Hills Hotel and immediately got along like brothers. I'd been involved in photography since before I could walk, yet I learned more about cameras and photographic technology from Seal in one afternoon than I think I had in my whole life. As well as being a talented musician, he is a serious photo nut, a great photographer, and a great appreciator of photography. I was very proud and touched to learn that one of my father's most famous photographs of the Nuba in Kordofan—his homage to man's humanity to man—was hanging in a very prominent place in the home Seal shared with his wife, supermodel Heidi Klum.

Several months later, I set up the camera outside Seal's home, and we chuckled like silly schoolboys, as the British tend to do.

"What is God?" I asked.

"My perception of God is that it is this infinite energy that is visible all around us, if we care to look. It's right in front of us," Seal replied.

"So basically, people use the word *God* to describe something that is giving us life?"

"I don't know if it's necessarily giving us life, but I think it's constantly confirming life. God is pretty much everywhere; and you can see that through looking at nature, looking at human beings, looking at your reflection."

"Why do you think so many religions around the world fight with each other?" I asked him.

"Because of man's bastardization of religion. I think that throughout history, religion has been interpreted, reinterpreted, and rewritten by man in many ways. A lot of religion has been restructured for purposes of control. I don't think it was ever meant to cause people to fight—it was a means to determine right from wrong, nothing more than that. Whenever you try and control people, whenever you tell people that your way is right and their way is wrong—or you have the only true path to God or to the Holy Land—that, in turn, causes conflict and resentment. That's probably the reason why it causes so much fighting."

"Do you pray to God?"

"I used to pray a lot more, kneeling down at night or first thing in the morning; that's the way we were raised. Do I pray now? That's debatable because I do believe there's such a thing as silent prayer. I think that meditation can be perceived as a form of prayer. I spend time alone clearing my head, focusing on my thoughts, and trying to reconnect with myself."

"Do you see God in your music?"

"Not always. I've had one or two flashes of it throughout my life; you can experience that when you're writing certain songs. The best songs I've written are the ones that happen really quickly and that write themselves. I remember when I wrote 'Crazy,' it was written literally in about ten minutes. That's one of the songs, along with 'Kiss from a Rose,' that to this day, resonates with people more than any other. I wasn't conscious of writing them; they almost wrote themselves. I think that's probably the closest I've been, in terms of my music, to a state that is infinite and beyond words.

"I think there's God in everything we see," Seal continued. "So whenever I need to connect with God, I always look at this thing I hold around my neck." He pulled out a gold locket and opened it up to reveal a series of coins with pictures of his family on them. "Sometimes it's a photograph or a photo album that I carry with me. But if you look right here, that's four examples of God." He showed me a picture of Heidi and his children. "On the reverse side, that's another one. There's another one. There's yet another one. There are two on the back—that's my wife and me. I think that if I'm constantly reminded by those access points, I need look no further. Over the years, I have chosen to see God in people."

I asked, "If there's one statement or sentence that you could say to promote peace, love, tolerance, and understanding around the world, what would it be?"

"You asked me a question earlier: 'Why do I think religion breeds such war, such violence?' I think it's really down to fear, and fear is promoted by lack of communication. Quite often we fear things that we don't understand. But we don't really stand a chance of understanding if we don't communicate."

At the end of the interview, Seal stared directly into the lens and sang *"Oh my God"* in that famous voice of his. I was flattered. He was open, communicative, and intimate with his perceptions.

MY THEN-12-YEAR-OLD DAUGHTER, GEORGIA, had always been a Beatles fan (as had I). Even when she was three, Georgia used to strut around to her favorite album, *Sgt. Pepper's Lonely Hearts Club Band.* I was downstairs in the basement office in my house one day when I heard my cell phone go off upstairs. I called out: "Georgia! Please grab the phone!" She appeared a few moments later, white in the face, arm outstretched.

"Daddy, it's *Ringo Starr!?*" She looked as if she was about to faint.

Ringo Starr—the British musician and singer-songwriter who gained worldwide fame as the drummer for the Beatles—*was on the phone!*

Doris La Frenais was a mutual friend who had loved the concept and teaser to the film. She'd mentioned to Ringo that I wanted to include some famous people in the film and had asked if he would be interested. Ringo was very forthcoming. His whole mantra is "Peace and love," and he was glad to help. But I hadn't known that at the time, so it was a complete surprise when he called me up out of the blue.

I cleared my throat. "Hello, Ringo!"

"Hello, Peter. Doris La Frenais said you were making a film about God. She thought I might say a few words on it."

"I'd love that!" I said.

"Can you come by the house this afternoon at about 4, then?" he asked.

I enthusiastically agreed.

"You don't have, like, zillions of trucks and stuff, do ya?" he asked.

"No. It'll be just two of us. Real small, down, and dirty."

"All right. See you at 4." He gave me his address.

I was shocked and deeply flattered, and for some reason, nervous. *A Beatle!* For the first time, Mr. Chou danced in elation rather than anxiety.

I immediately rang Colonel Boobs, who dropped everything to come and do the sound, but of course, I couldn't go without Georgia. She would never forgive me. Then Soumaya came home, and a couple of hours later, there were four of us driving over to Ringo's home in Beverly Hills.

I rang the bell outside large gates, and soon they started to creak open and we climbed up a private drive adorned with lusciously manicured California foliage. Birds twittered in the sweet-fragranced air.

Ringo came out of the house to greet us with his wife, Barbara Bach (who couldn't have been more delightful and soon made us feel at home). Ringo looked at the car to see four people emerging instead of two, and as he came over to shake my hand, said, "You've brought a whole bloody army, haven't ya!?"

Georgia was by now at my side, and I answered, "Well, you see it goes like this: I couldn't leave Georgia at home, because you are Georgia's biggest fan." Of course, what I'd meant to say was that Georgia was *his* biggest fan, but it all came out wrong.

Ringo didn't miss a beat. "And that is correct!" he announced. "I've been a fan of Georgia's since as long as I can remember—in fact, I've been a fan of Georgia's since before she was born." And he went down on one knee. "I am so honored to meet you!"

Georgia was beside herself. Then Ringo went in the house and returned with four elastic wristbands with the words *Peace and love* and three stars emblazoned on them, and gave one to each of us.

Within minutes, the camera was rolling, and I was interviewing a legend.

"My name is Ringo, and we are in L.A."

"I'm going to ask you a very simple question, Ringo: what is God?"

"God, to me? My God in my life? God is love."

"Simple, clear, undiluted love?"

"Pure love."

"Do you think that you could consider love, therefore, a power?"

"Love is an incredible power. If you give out love, the reaction to it is so great, even with crazy, violent people. If you give out love, they stop for a minute, because everybody notices love when it's coming their way. . . . I feel that so long as you are doing something with love, the world will support you. That's how the world works."

He continued: "There's a Vietnamese monk whose name I can never pronounce, but he says when you get to the traffic light, it's no good getting crazy. Just love the red light, and when it changes, drive on. And when you're angry, it's no good being angry at yourself, because then you're twice as angry."

"There are a lot of religions that believe their God is greater than everyone else's—"

"Yes, but that's people, not God," Ringo broke in. "I think everybody wants their religion to be universally the wisest, and sometimes they're not."

"So why do you think so many religions fight with each other?"

"Power. Many religions have wiped out indigenous populations. The American Indians couldn't understand the concept of buying land: 'Huh, what do you mean, you want the land? It's for all of us.' And the world is for all of us. We are one."

"So what do you think we can do to promote the fact that *God is love?*" I asked him.

"Well, I do it, in a simple way: I have a wristband that says 'Peace and love.' I'm forever going, 'Peace and love.'"

"With your life and the fantastic career you've had, have you felt that your acceptance of love has helped you along as an individual, as a human being?"

"I think so. But there has been a lot of searching. I feel I had spiritual moments as a young kid and as a teenager. And we went to India with the Maharishi."

"So what did you find when you went to India?"

"I found it was pretty hectic, but Maharishi gave me something nobody can take away from me." (Ringo would later tell me that the discipline and structure of Maharishi's teachings and meditation helped him navigate through all that was happening around him.)

"Do you still go back to what he said at that time in your life?"

"Occasionally. I mean, there are lots of other people who have said things, so it's like you're filling up the ocean with good pebbles. I heard one guy say, 'Carl Jung—he was so great; he was asked, "Do you still believe in God?" And he said, "No . . . *I know!*"' He's the only one I ever knew who said, '*I know.*' How great is that?"

Then Ringo asked *me* a question: "Well, what about you? Where's your God?"

"Me? This film's not really about what *I* think; it's about what other people think," I said.

"Oh no, not you—you can't think. You're behind the camera!" he ribbed.

"If you really want me to say what I think, well, I believe God is power. I believe you do with God what you want to do with God. I think people have access to that power, and a lot of people call that access God."

"Yeah," he agreed. "You know, people are frightened of the word *God*. 'Oh God'—whoa, you can't just say 'God.' Well, you can. Someone asked me once, 'What is your concept?' I went off into these 1960s moments of madness and things like that, and then I thought, *Oh my God.*" He realized he'd mentioned the name of the film and kindly repeated it with added emphasis: "*Oh My God.* God is love. Keep it simple."

"And who do you pray to?"

"I pray to my God, my God in heaven, and I do it on my knees. It's like respect. But you have to remember I was brought up in a Protestant, Christian way."

"As was I."

"As were you, but who cares!" Ringo laughed again. "God is love. Love is love, you know. And the more we put love in our life, the more love there is on the planet. I am not religious, but I am trying my best on a daily basis to have a spiritual life."

"What do you think happens when you die?"

"Personally, I believe I go somewhere."

"So you believe that your spirit is separate from your body?"

"I do."

"Do you think people are frightened of what happens when they die, and so they want to have something larger than life to hold on to?"

"Yeah, well, the churches are full of pensioners. You better get in there quick. God bless them."

Ringo was a delight, and I was very pleased to have such a famous person in the film. He was succinct, gracious, and very funny. We chatted, I took his portrait, and soon we were on our merry way again.

CHAPTER 19

Down Under

━━━━━━━━━━━━━━━ ● ━━━━━━━━━━━━━━━

"In order to set the train squarely back on the tracks, it is first necessary for it to be completely derailed."

— NAPKIN #19

With the help of friends such as Doris La Frenais, I was starting to attract attention, which was a good thing. But like all projects of the heart, I also attracted some bad things—like a seductive siren who sang a great song and talked the talk, but never quite managed to walk the walk, and who actually cost me a great deal of money and wasted time. Promises were made that were never kept, and when the final betrayal came, it was so unnerving that it made me question the very grace of humanity I was experiencing across the world. I will call this person Frau Looney.

Frau Looney was an old friend of Soumaya's. Although a little eccentric, she had always been very enthusiastic about culture, film, and Hollywood. Indeed, she had once been an actress, but was now trying to start a new career producing films. Frau Looney decided that *Oh My God* was the greatest thing since sliced bread and latched onto it. She was going to get me this, get me that, get me in here, and get me in there, she vowed. What's more, she didn't want a penny for her efforts; she was going to do it all purely for the betterment of humankind.

Adam, in the meantime, secured a deal with a wonderful gentleman from Mexico named Horacio Altamirano, who was one of the largest distributors of films in Latin America. He was passionate about the project, and we thrashed out a deal.

Since Frau Looney had already proven useful in suggesting people thus far, I embraced her willingness to help. I wanted to formalize our arrangement, as I had done with others, but she refused to discuss money. There was something about her rhetoric that made me uneasy. I should have listened to my instincts.

To her credit, Frau Looney did introduce us to the actor Hugh Jackman—to have someone so famous talk candidly about God would be a great asset to the project. Hugh was currently on location, filming *Australia* with writer-director Baz Luhrmann and, coincidentally, my dear friend Jack Thompson.

I was excited; it felt like the gods had all come together. Frau Looney assured me she had more famous people and interesting religious figures lined up. She gave me dates and places where these "contacts" would be so I could organize a pan-Pacific flight plan that would take us to Australia, Indonesia, China, and Japan. Vishnu was still not available, but Frau Looney would step in as the producer. It was going "to be spectacular," she said. Colonel Boobs signed on for another adventure.

THE ACTOR JACK THOMPSON IS A LEGEND Down Under as one of the major figures of Australian cinema. He is best known as a lead actor in several acclaimed Australian films, including the popular classics *Sunday Too Far Away, The Man From Snowy River,* and *Breaker Morant.* I'd met him years ago in Morocco at Abdesalam's house, where he vacationed after filming *Star Wars: Episode II* with George Lucas in Tunisia. We had become great friends. A larger-than-life character, Jack is supremely intelligent and can rattle off words on any subject at the drop of a hat. He also makes me laugh. We are like two inseparable buddies whenever we get together.

Every August Jack takes a break from work to attend the Garma Festival—which is an event to enlighten Australians and the rest of the Western world about the virtues, traditions, art, and beliefs of the Aboriginal people. It takes place near a town called Gove, in the Northern Territory of Australia. Jack invited us to attend the festival for an Aboriginal point of view, and then to join him on the set of *Australia,* where I also would interview Hugh Jackman.

Prior to our departure date, I tried desperately to get a schedule from Frau Looney, but it never came. Two days before I was due to leave, she called to say that unless I gave her 20 percent of any personal fees I would make out of the film and an astronomic daily rate, she was going to pull the whole shoot.

I was so stunned that I didn't know what to say or do. I felt that I was being ransomed, especially as she had thus far been unable to provide any indication of what she was actually "producing."

I couldn't let Jack down or miss the opportunity to film the Garma Festival and Hugh Jackman, so I decided that the best thing to do would be to carry on with the schedule and try to work out an arrangement later. Judging by the sudden flurry of activity in my stomach, Mr. Chou shared my uneasy feeling. I started to analyze what, apart from Hugh Jackman, Frau Looney was bringing to the table. I still had no schedule, no list of the "famous personalities" she supposedly had lined up . . . and even more worrying, she insisted that she'd procured visas for China, yet she'd never asked for our passport details. Without this information, you can't *get* a visa, so it was obvious that there was some distortion of truth.

I'd sunk thousands of dollars into this trip already, the tickets were nonrefundable, and I'd made a commitment to pay Colonel Boobs. Had I been too trusting? Was it possible that Frau Looney had betrayed me?

ON AUGUST 30, 2007, the day before our departure to Australia, Adam and I met with Horacio Altamirano and his representative, Penny Karlin, in Santa Monica to finalize the arrangements for financing the rest of the film. Adam Krentzman, Horacio, and an investor from Turkey named Metin Anter were to become my partners and executive producers in the film. It was a huge weight off my shoulders, as it meant that, finally, I could actually continue production (not that I'd really ever stopped). We made the deal, but it was still only a verbal agreement until official contracts had been signed. My credit cards were almost melting under the stress that was being placed upon them, and frankly, so was I. But at least I now had some hopes of paying them off.

THE JOURNEY TO THE NORTHERN TERRITORY was very long, but I was excited again. I'd always wanted to go to Australia. I had so many friends there; and I loved visiting new places, smelling the scents, hearing the sounds, and feeling the "pulse."

Jack Thompson met us at Darwin airport with William Barton, who was one of the world's most gifted *yidaki* (didgeridoo) players. It was wonderful to see Jack and his lifelong partner, Liona, with their son, Billy. We flew on together to Gove, where a fleet of trucks was waiting to drive all the festival attendees into the bush.

On arrival, we were escorted to our tents under stars so bright that they felt like low-hanging fruit, ready to be picked and savored. Above us were the constellations of the Pleiades and Orion, which, to some, represent the shape of the rainbow serpent that the Aboriginal peoples regard as both the source of all life as well as the protector of the land and the people. To the Aboriginals, the stars were only an indication of the existence of the serpent; the serpent itself actually lived in the gaps between them. My thoughts immediately flew back to Rabbi Froman saying that God lives in the gap between us. It amazes me how, when you care to listen, people from all different walks of life and cultures say the same thing in different ways.

The Garma Festival was a wonderful experience. It's not easy getting such close access to indigenous cultures, so we really appreciated the opportunity to spend five consecutive days there, filming the *bunggul*—the traditional Aboriginal ceremonial dance. It yielded excellent footage, and I was struck by how similar it was to the Maasai dance. Interestingly, Aboriginal philosophy is similar to that of the Maasai and Adrian's Druidry. The rainbow serpent is regarded as the controller of water, of life source, which replenishes rivers and slithers across the arid land, defying the strong sun, carving gullies and deep channels; and when the sun shines through water, you can even see the serpent in myriad colors.

I also learned about the *dreamtime*. In Aboriginal culture, there are two parallel streams of time: that of daily life on Earth; and the "dreaming," which refers to spirituality, where everyone exists eternally. The dreaming existed before a person's life and exists after he or she dies, and what happens in the "dreamtime" becomes the foundation of the values and laws of Aboriginal society. Those who are spiritually gifted have contact with the dreamtime.

"GOD IS A SPIRITUAL BEING that gives Aboriginal people the right to live." Jack, Colonel Boobs, and I were on an escarpment near the Gulkula, the festival site, interviewing Galarrwuy Yunupingu— the chairman of the Yothu Yindi Foundation, the charitable organization responsible for the festival. The wind, which was blowing so strongly that it rattled the eucalyptus trees, felt like the breath of Mother Earth herself as Galarrwuy talked.

"As far as Aboriginal people are concerned, gods in our own ways and in our own beliefs—they are the dreamtime heroes. We follow those spiritual heroes to get to things like food and resources for everyday living. The bunggul dances are for everyday enjoyment, and it's a practice to pass on to the little ones so they, too, can come through that process.

"Our form of God is not one god; it is many gods. We tell stories about the gods and the heroes who have created these dreaming tracks, passing them on to the young ones every day in our languages, through learning, dancing, singing, and arts. It's gotta have a backdrop. It's gotta be connected to the soil. It's very important, as all the resources in our dancing, arts, singing, talking, sleeping, and dreaming come out of the soil. The Mother Earth supplies that. The Mother Earth is the book.

"This [dreamtime] place has no boundaries. Spirituality comes from a foundation whereby all human beings of different race understand as one—it's one language. Spirituality is the coming together, uniting, and believing one thing. The very life we breathe is unity.

"We believe gods are our own heroes of the land. When we walk through the bush, we speak to the tree to provide us honey, the sugar bag [the small sac of honey made by the native Australian black bee]. We talk to the tree, say." Galarrwuy vibrated his lips and said, "'*Bbbbbbbb*—give us the sugar bag.' And three minutes later we pray to the hero who lives on this land, he provides us with the sugar bag. I'm of the dreamtime. My land is of the dreamtime."

There was so much beauty and peacefulness in what Galarrwuy had said that I shuddered at the incredible examples of bigoted persecution that the Aboriginal people have endured at the hands of the white man. It wasn't until the 1970s that a white could be prosecuted for killing an Aborigine. In these parts, in those days, the Aborigines were referred to as *Boong,* which was a reference to the sound a body made when hit by a kangaroo bar mounted on the front of a truck—"Run 'em down as they head home"—it used to be a sick sport.

Yet the persecution was still going on, it seemed. If you think the Native Americans had it bad, it's a lot worse in Australia, and 90 percent of Australians are still unaware of the shameful below-the-belt tactics that were being used at that time by former prime minister John Howard's government to reverse land rights and grab vast tracts of territory that had been granted to the Aboriginal people so as to allow lucrative mining projects to tear up the earth. Education was nonexistent in some areas. There were no jobs, yet there were no government incentives to help the local Aboriginal people. Ethnic cleansing was being executed subversively, by splitting up families, enforced relocation, and horrendous—and totally fabricated—stories of sex and alcohol-abuse scandals, used as a wedge to force the Aboriginal people out in order to clear the way for huge uranium mines.

It was a sad state of affairs, and the Garma Festival was designed to educate Australians about some of these hidden realities. The Aboriginal people have always had a philosophy of benevolence. For many, it just wasn't in their psyches to understand the cruelty that was being thrust upon them. They would either take refuge in their belief systems and hold on to the teachings of their culture, or eke out their frustration in confused, erratic behavior. Many would turn to alcohol abuse as an escape—but as with so many other indigenous cultures, this substance didn't suit their systems. Incidents like these were seized upon, in no uncertain terms, by the government to further their persecution. In reality it seemed life's victims were those who were the most benevolent—and the victors seemed to be those who were the most aggressive.

EACH NIGHT JACK THOMPSON; his partner, Liona; their son, Billy; Colonel Boobs; and I—and a few others—would sit around a campfire at the Garma Festival and tell stories. It was like being a kid again. Jack would entertain us with his exceptional wit and an endless supply of humorous tales. Fireflies buzzed about, and the sound of the forest was loud with life, providing a soothing backdrop to stories of Australian yore.

There was one tale about a swagman that still sticks in my memory because of its relevance to the film. *Swag* is an Australian term for a blanket that you roll up, put on your back, and use for camping when out in the bush. During the Great Depression there were tens of thousands of out-of-work swagmen who would wander the land looking for odd jobs.

In his deep, gravelly voice, Jack began: "There was this swagman who knocked on the door of a house which belonged to a clergyman. The swagman went, 'Oh, sorry, Father.'

"The clergyman went, 'No, no, my good man, how can I help you?'

"The swagman said: 'Just thought there might be a job around, you know, for a cup of tea. Slice of bread . . . something?'

"'Yes, some firewood needs cutting out the back. Come on in.' The clergyman leads the swagman out the back.

"The swagman cuts the firewood, then announces, 'Thanks, Father. I'll be on my way, then, now.'

"'No, come on in and sit down,' says the clergyman. Swagman goes in, sits down rather awkwardly in front of the fire. The clergyman's reading.

"Swagman asks, 'Good book?'

"The clergyman says with a chuckle, 'Yes, *the* good book, as a matter of fact.'

"'Ah, yeah? What's it about?'

"'Well, it's the Bible, my good man, the Bible,' the clergyman replies.

"'I've heard of it. What's it about?' asks swagman.

"'Well, it's, ah, it's God's word.'

"'Ah, yeah?'

"'It's about a number of things. The particular part I'm reading now is very exciting. It's about an extraordinary man of God, a powerful man, Samson from Jerusalem. He's capable of tearing down the pillars of the temple; and in this bit he's with his girlfriend, Delilah, out grinding corn, when 5,000 Philistines descend upon them. He picks up the jawbone of an ass, slays 2,000, and he routs the rest.'

"And the swagman says, 'Fair dinkum.'

"Clergyman then says, 'Rest here the night, please. Be my guest.'

"Swagman gets up before the clergyman rises and sets out on the road. Just as the sun is coming up, he sees some smoke, and in the distance is another group of swagmen. One of them looks up and says, 'Come and join us, mate. There's only a bit of bunny stew in the drum there—help yourself. And a cup a' tea.'

"'Thanks, mate,' says our swagman.

"'Whada ya know?' asks the other swagman.

"'Ah, nothin' much.' Our swagman pauses, then goes on: 'Oh, wait a minute. I did hear some news. There's this bloke, um, Simson from Jerilderri. Apparently a big bastard, regular terror, ripping up telephone poles and throwin' them around. And apparently he was out giving his girlfriend, Delicious, a grind in the corn, and 5,000 of them Filipino bastards come along. He's picked up the ass-bone of a Jew and killed 2,000 of 'em, and he's rooted the rest. He's a real bastard, that Simson!'"

Such was a typical evening with Jack Thompson. The yarn made me wonder how much misinterpretation had been interwoven into what would become *God's word* or the *Gospel Truth*.

"IN THE BEGINNING WAS THE WORD, and the Word was God. *God* is a word for the unnamable," Jack said. "*God* is a word associated with our understanding or belief that there is something more than this *self*."

We were out in the bush in the middle of the day under a tree that provided scant protection from the hot Australian sun. It was Jack's turn to answer some questions. "What's your take on paradise, Jack?" I asked.

"I'm pretty much convinced that this is it. I can't imagine better than this. Now that doesn't mean that there isn't better than this, but I can't imagine it. I think this is certainly as good as it ever gets for us.

"There is this classic Judeo-Christian concept that life is a veil of tears through which we struggle toward the light at the end of this miserable tunnel, that light being heaven in the hereafter—our paradise that's due to us for a life of hard-won virtue or whatever. But I propose that those who believe that concept have just got it wrong by one incarnation: that in fact they were in the veil of tears last time, and they have now woken up in paradise, but they are so used to bitching, they can't stop complaining about paradise!"

I loved what Jack was saying, but I had to challenge him. "If it can't get better than this, what about a paraplegic, poverty-stricken person living in the slums?"

"In that case, you would have to imagine that, given the probably nonsensical proposition that they came from a previous incarnation, if *this* is their paradise, they must have had a terrible one before.

"On the other hand, I have been with people in slum areas and in the developing world who have had tragic lives and terrible wounds, who are living on that edge of despair, and yet they are not filled with desperation. Day by day they find little moments of joy and compensation. We are extraordinarily adaptable creatures in this way."

"What is your definition of hell, Jack?"

"I think hell is right here, too. Right here in paradise. If you don't believe it, go take a look. Hell is classically portrayed as the rack, the nightmarish image; it is fear and physical agony magnified. I think the reason why organized religion is so successful is that it's not very difficult for any of us to imagine heaven or hell. It's impossible to imagine God or eternity, but it's very easy to imagine heaven and hell—it's all around us."

THE GARMA FESTIVAL WAS A WONDERFUL INTERLUDE. But when I arrived in Darwin, things started to unravel. I'd been hoping that all would settle down, but as soon as we were back in cell range, Frau Looney called to announce that she would not now be on the set in any capacity, even when we were in Sydney. The reason, she explained, was that *Oh My God* had "created a poltergeist" that was inhabiting her "son's space," and she believed that any physical proximity to the actual filming would only increase the power of the poltergeist. Although she wouldn't be able to travel to Indonesia or China, she still wanted her daily rate to produce by remote, along with 20 percent of any remuneration I would receive from the *entire* film.

If I had written this in a screenplay, nobody would believe it. Apart from an introduction to Hugh Jackman, there was still no word on any of the meetings with (or even the identities of) the other "incredible celebrities and personalities" she supposedly had lined up.

I was beginning to suspect that Frau Looney was dangerously delusional, and if that were true, then any thought of continuing our association could be disastrous for the film. I knew right then and there I was in very deep trouble. Even though our tickets included a trip to China, it was now certain all that was a sham. Anytime I brought up the word *visa*, I received a fogged reply. My whole shoot was in ruins, and the massive investment I'd made in it was lost. I was meant to be in Australia for three more weeks, then in Indonesia and China. My long-haul tickets were nonrefundable. The entire project was unraveling because of a crazy woman and a poltergeist. I had been duped. What was I going to do?

I decided the only thing was to continue with what had already been arranged and come up with an alternative plan—quick. I felt sick to the core—it seemed Mr. Chou had started hula-hooping lessons in my stomach.

CHAPTER 20

Hugh Jackman and Baz Luhrmann

"When I hear the wind in the trees, I know it's not my breath that causes the breeze."

— NAPKIN #20

Beautiful forests stretched for miles on either side of the road. Wallabies could be seen hopping through the trees. We stopped the car so that I could walk down the road a few paces. With the engine off, all I could hear was the sound of the wind rustling the leaves. There were no planes or cars, just the sounds of nature itself. Viewed from the Aboriginal perspective, you could say I was listening to the sound of God Him- or Herself. I inhaled the warm, sweet fragrance of space like a breath of life.

For a few seconds the world actually stood still. It was a profound moment, and it occurred to me that if we could understand the words of the wind's song, we would understand that it helps balance the scales of nature. Perhaps, then, *wind* and *nature* are equally appropriate words to describe God. Did that mean I was actually acknowledging the existence of God? Had I come that far? I didn't think so, but then, one could argue that the very fact that I was asking, "What is God?" by definition was an admission of His, Her, or Its existence.

A wallaby glanced questioningly in my direction, and I stared into its eyes. I could have sworn it nodded a wise thought. The wind tickled my hair as I watched it bound off into the bush. Then I climbed back into the car, and we continued on our way.

We followed signs and soon came out of the forest to arrive at a clearing dotted with baobab trees and hundreds of trucks. It was the set of Baz Luhrmann's film *Australia*—in the middle of absolutely nowhere.

On a knoll overlooking a river inhabited by crocodiles was a lone trailer with a tent beside it that was filled with racks of weights. We knocked on the door, and Hugh Jackman's assistant, Ryan, greeted us. "Come on in," he said warmly. "Make yourself at home. He'll be back in a minute."

Before long a truck pulled up, the door opened, and Hugh bounded into the trailer, full of energy. He couldn't have been more delightful. I've met many movie stars in my time; and Hugh was by far the kindest, most polite, and down-to-earth of them all. I was so used to hearing him playing American and British characters that I was taken aback by his natural Australian accent. Half an hour later we were set up under the shade of the tent with the river in the background.

"My name is Hugh Jackman, and we're about an hour's drive from Kununurra, which is on the border of West Australia and Northern Territory."

"So, Hugh, I'm going to ask you some very simple questions, and I'm going to start with the simplest of the lot: what is God?"

He laughed. "Simple question—'what is God?' Take about a lifetime to work it out." He paused to think. "I suppose what God is, for me, is my idea of consciousness. God is not a thing, something that you can necessarily see. It is somehow separate from the laws of time, matter, and space. And that is about as close as I've come to any realization as to what God is."

"So you don't see God as a bearded chap up in the sky, telling us to be good or we'll go to hell?" I asked.

"I don't see God as a bearded chap, although I used to. I was brought up with a very strict Protestant view of what God is and our place next to God; and that consisted of some deity, a guy with a beard, telling us what to do, marking us on our behavior, and hopefully granting us entrance into heaven. I fully bought it. But around the age of 14 or 15, I thought my father's idea and this church's idea of what God is just didn't make sense. How can only 5 percent of the world be admitted into heaven under these laws?

Why is it that largely wealthy white people are the only people heading there? Why aren't the Buddhists going?

"I do believe there is an element of faith to life. There's an element of, God is . . ." He paused. ". . . unexplainable. It is a concept that you can't put into words. I think it's a really interesting idea to make a documentary and ask people what they think God is, because I don't believe you can actually explain it. It's an experience. God is an experience.

"I was introduced to meditation about 15 years ago. And if I ever feel close to knowing what God is, it's somewhere in the boundary of that half-hour period, twice a day, when I meditate. In a little time, ideas of Hugh Jackman as a father, as an actor—all those roles we play—just seem to melt away. And somewhere in there is where I have some glimmer, some glimpse, of what God is. It's a feeling, and it's blissful. And the minute you try to grab on to it, it's gone. I've spoken to some incredibly wise people, and sometimes the wisest of them said to me, 'No matter what we talk about, don't hold on to it; just listen to the sound of my voice, and somewhere in the sound is the truth.'

"As a child, God was very much wrapped up in good and evil, God and the devil. And for many years I thought everything that was good was God, and everything that was bad was the devil. Now my understanding of it is that it's neither and both at the same time. There is something beyond that—there is something linking all of us. That to me is God."

I thought I'd reference Rabbi Froman and what I learned about the rainbow serpent. "So maybe God exists in the gap between the yin and the yang, the black and the white?"

"It's amazing you say that," Hugh replied, "because often, if you're really listening, it's the space between words. If you listen to great music—the greatest composers understood the space between the notes; and when you feel that, it's so uplifting, it's amazing.

"The experience of God is restful. It is, I feel, rejuvenating. In modern life, we often feel quite tired and run-down, and that may be because we don't always observe the laws of nature and the laws of this body and how we should live our life. But I wrestle with this all the time. Is there a way that you can experience God when everything is crap in your life?

"I try to do little things every day, and I know you probably think I'm weird, but at the end of a shower I will always turn on the cold as a little reminder that it's not going to affect who I am. The experience of being warm, pleasurable, in a hot shower—it's just an idea that it's better than cold. It's not comfortable to have a really cold shower, but why can't God exist in that uncomfortability? Why can't you be able to find rest in that? Why am I wasting my life only wanting the pleasurable, only wanting the comfortable? A lot of life is uncomfortable. A lot of this experience is not easy. I don't care who you are—it's not easy waking up first thing in the morning; you don't always want to get up out of bed. But can you find God in that? I think that's where I am right now.

"I think that fear is the greatest disease of modern times. People call it stress, but it's just fear. Lately, I've been practicing this whole idea of just resting in the idea that I'm scared."

"What happens when you die, Hugh?"

He laughed heartily. "I've just been reading about it this morning."

"Oh, somebody knows? Somebody wrote a book about it?" I jokingly retorted.

"Yeah. It's called the Bhagavad Gita. I was reading that it tells you what to do at the moment of death. And I remember thinking, *Ah, man, this is like a fairy tale to me because I've never actually faced a moment of prolonged knowing that I was going to die or thinking I was going to die. I haven't had that moment yet.* But I have had a glimpse into what it would be like for me.

"I was researching this movie *The Fountain* in which I played a brain surgeon. I was invited in to see some surgery on a woman who was going to die; she had a tumor the size of a tennis ball in her brain. It was the most extraordinary thing: they kept her awake so that they knew as they were cutting into the tumor whether they were cutting into speech parts of the brain, or movement. She was lying down with the top half of her skull off. And they were cutting in and asking her questions. She had to play this video game.

"She had blonde hair. My wife has blonde hair, and for a second I was almost sick from the fear of thinking, *What if that was her?* And then, I won't lie to you, almost straight after that came the idea *What if it was me?* And I was just absolutely terrified. Because the bottom line is, for all the work you might do in your life preparing for that moment, I realized I was miles off being ready.

"You said at the beginning of this interview, 'I'm going to ask you a very simple question: what is God?' I think death is as simple as that. It's another moment. Whatever happens beyond death will be due to what's been going on in your mind at that moment of dying."

My mind flashed back to Marrakech and Abdesalam talking about the billionth of a second as the bullet hits the brain.

"What about the concept of paradise being your life on Earth now? What about hell being your life on Earth now?" I immediately asked him.

"I truly believe there is a way to find the Garden of Eden here in this life, wherever you are. You don't have to go to a top of a mountain to do it. I think you can find it in a suburb of Sydney. I've had a few moments of experiencing it sometimes in meditation. I've had a few moments onstage, some moments in relationships."

"So paradise could be here on Earth?"

"Yeah."

"What about hell? What's your definition of hell?"

"The definition of hell that I was taught, when I was younger, is absence of God. I don't think you can be absent from God, because God is in everything. But I do think that you can get so far away from the laws of nature that the experience of life is hell. It must be. I haven't been close to doing it, but people take their life. I think that *they* must be in hell—for there to be no other option than to end it."

"Why do you think religions fight so much between themselves and each other?"

"There are no questions more important in life than 'Who are we?' 'Why are we here?' and 'What do I have to offer to the world?' And some people, I believe out of fear that they might be wrong, can't accept someone else's opinion. That's why there is so much fighting over religion.

"If you put Buddha, Jesus Christ, Socrates, Shakespeare, Arjuna, and Krishna at a dinner table together, I can't see them having any argument. All the things they have to say seem to have a commonality. I was brought up by a father who became a missionary in China. I'm sure missionaries always feel that they are right. I mean, we can look back in history now at what some missionaries and churches did throughout Africa, and out here in the outback of Australia, that just seems so incredibly imperialistic and aggressive, but I'm sure they thought they were doing the right thing; they were doing their duty."

I couldn't help thinking about Reverend Peter Ole Kasingi back in Shompole.

"Do you feel that God is us?" I asked.

"Yeah, I do. God is us and is not us. It's inside you and me, and it's outside you and me. It is everything. I understand the concept that everything around us is an illusion, and I struggle with that because it feels real to me, and the pain and the thoughts feel incredibly real. I think the truth is that God, consciousness, is what binds all of this together. And really, through all our ideas, quite simply, what a gift this creation is—everything about it. Whether it be times when you are hurting, this human experience is amazing. It is here to be enjoyed. Not just the happy times, but the sad times are here to be fully experienced. I think that if we do that, it is probably about as close to God as we can get.

"You know the Aboriginal people, I have read a lot, and in speaking to them, they see what they call *The Magic*. They see it in everything. And I suppose that's what I mean by saying God is us—you, me, the land, the creek, the interplay of so many different things that have to make this creation work . . . it's kind of magical. It's wondrous."

Hugh Jackman was a deep thinker and very generous toward us. We spent three days on the set of *Australia*, and he extended a warm welcome to use his trailer for checking our e-mails and introduced me to director Baz Luhrmann—a Golden Globe– and Academy Award–nominated director, writer, and producer. I had admired his work (*Strictly Ballroom, Romeo + Juliet,* and *Moulin Rouge,* just to name a few examples) for many years.

"IN SIMPLE LANGUAGE, FOR ME, it's that which is bigger than all of us, but that which we all participate in." We were shooting Baz at his camp in the bush. He had been living out there so long during the shooting of his film that he'd started growing vegetables outside his trailer.

"I think that human concepts always fail you when you try to have a conversation like this. The simple idea of creation is a human concept. You know, one very small portion of our brain is being utilized now. What are the other portions there for? What will happen when they become fully evolved? These feeble things that we have in our hands, these tools of communication and understanding, are so human, that's probably why they're beautiful to us, because they're so tragic, really.

"I have no direct criticism of religion, because it comes from a very good place. It is man's attempt at communicating with God. It comes from a search for signs and meanings and a language. I notice religions tend to start out as an individual quest, but end up very much the collective. And anywhere human beings gather, there's a dollar to be made, so bureaucracy, economics, and those things that go with clubs and organizations grow very quickly. That doesn't mean it's all bad. I think there are enormously positive things in religion. Some of the scriptures and texts, be they of any religion, are some of the greatest stories in the world. But it's just the way they're edited; human hands have been involved. If you look at them as story, they have great power and great use."

BACK AT OUR BASIC MOTEL IN KUNUNURRA, I had to come up with a plan very quickly. Frau Looney had continued to live up to her nickname. She was never available by phone and had reneged on all her promises.

An old producer friend of mine from years back, Peter Ker, had moved to Bali, which was just a 90-minute flight from Darwin. Since I loved the color and philosophy that came out of that island, I decided to move the production there. I could employ Peter and get as far away from Frau Looney and her craziness as possible.

I finally tracked the Frau down by phone and told her that our relationship was over and that I was leaving the country.

As soon as I hung up, a mutual friend called to say how wonderful it was that I was in Australia and that she had heard that Frau Looney had *employed me to direct the Frau's film, which she was calling Oh My God.* I was shocked that even Frau Looney could have told such an outright lie. I explained that I'd been working on the project for well over a year before she'd become involved. Our mutual friend laughed—not because she thought it was funny, but because, she said, she wasn't surprised.

CHAPTER 21

The Island of the Gods

"If you are true to your heart, then you give heart to the truth."

— NAPKIN #21

I left Australia with mixed feelings. I'd had a wonderful time and got some great footage, but the situation with Frau Looney had also thrown me for a loop. I'd spent a lot of money on tickets I couldn't use, I still had no contract from Los Angeles, and my credit cards were on the verge of maxing out.

But that wasn't the only thing bothering me. The movie really needed a fanatic's point of view. It was the same old problem: all the people I'd captured on camera so far were so tolerant of each other that it was as if the film was becoming one huge group hug. *Let's all get along!* Vishnu, and everyone I knew, had been trying to find a group or just *someone* who would talk to us and spell out why people do really evil things in God's name. We all know they exist! What was I to do? Call 411 and ask them to put me through to al Qaeda?

WE LANDED IN BALI, OTHERWISE KNOWN AS the Island of the Gods. My old friend Peter Ker picked us up at the airport and took us to an incredibly sumptuous house that cost just $75 per night.

I had known Peter for more than 20 years, having worked for him in London as a keen young whippersnapper of 19. We'd made quite a team. I moved on to become a photographer, then a director, and eventually had relocated to the United States. Peter had become very successful and had then semiretired to live in paradise.

Bali was a whirlwind. It was fabulous to have a real *producer.* Peter enlisted his son Jack, along with Jack's friend Ricky Ricardo, and together with Colonel Boobs we now felt like a proper film crew. The Balinese people are the friendliest, kindest, and most wonderful human beings you could meet. The weather was perfect, the beaches seductive, and the food enticing. We stayed in an area called Seminyak, which was full of Brits and Australians.

Peter Ker found us a great character who soon became our adopted host of the island: Ida Pedanda, Gede Putra Telabah, Dr. Ida Bagus Ngurah Narendra—his name was so long that we nicknamed him *Grandmaster P.* He was like a blissfully happy, tall Yoda. A holy man who occupied a high position in the echelons of Balinese Hinduism, he had apparently died for a whole week and come back to life. Wherever we went, people stopped, put their palms together in prayer, and muttered, *"Om Swatiastu, Om Şanti Şanti Şanti, Om."* May God bless you. May peace be everywhere.

We traveled all over the island with Grandmaster P, from Hindu temples to paddy fields that stretched for miles, with villagers tending to the rice. It was phenomenally peaceful to be among those hills and to listen to the rushing streams of all the intricate irrigation canals and channels that fed water to the millions of terraces carved out of the mountains, like a lush green multilayered wedding cake.

It would rain; it would thunder; and then the sunlight would pop out through tremendous clouds of billowing blues, blacks, and fluffy white. The people smiled regardless. There was such grace and kindness in the air. We filmed kite fliers, a local wedding, a Buddhist village, a diplomat, ceremonies, and traditional Balinese dancers. We shot footage of puppet shows with intricate figurines projected onto a screen by fire, mile-long processions with drums, and women walking in step, with massive baskets perched on their heads filled with petals and fruit.

If you believe in magic, Bali is where it probably lives. There are certain places on this earth that inspire, and this island inspires your sense of spirit. In Bali, you don't have to have a large imagination to believe in ritual, ghosts, and the lost ancestors of the dead. It was so refreshing to be with human beings who threw their heads back in laughter all the time, instead of scowling with anger, heads down, spitting and kicking stones. Just the attitude of the place could lift one's soul and free one's breath.

GRANDMASTER P WANTED TO TAKE US TO KINTAMANI, one of the most beautiful and sacred parts of Bali. It poured with rain as we snaked our way up winding roads that climbed high into the mountains.

I had finally received the contract for the financing deal for the rest of the film, and I took it with me to read on that journey. My heart sank; it bore no relation to our verbal agreement. I felt so sick to my stomach again; Mr. Chou started performing aerial gymnastics. Expenses were mounting daily, and I was now tapping into an emergency line of credit. It was unnerving.

Grandmaster P sensed what I was going through (he was Yoda, remember?). When we stopped for a cup of tea in a little shop on one of the mountain roads, he looked me in the eye and said, so quietly that no one else could hear: "It's only temporary. Things come. Things go. Things come back, and they go again. When you understand that, you will be able to breathe again." I hadn't mentioned a thing to anyone, but his words gave me enormous strength.

The volcano at Kintamani rises upward from the earth and the waters of Lake Batur—hence its name, Mount Batur. It is the largest volcano in Bali, and the area is guarded from evil spirits by temples, which isn't surprising, as the volcano has erupted 24 times in the last 200 years, destroying all the villages around it; and when earth-shattering activities like that occur in Bali, they are usually attributed to upset spirits. A karmic protective shield of temples with pagodas dotted the landscape and the shores of the lake. They looked as if they had been put there by Peter Jackson's production designer—except these were hundreds of years old. Most tourists are disappointed when they arrive at Lake Batur because it is very rare to see the volcano, as it is usually completely shrouded in clouds. Since visibility that day had been reduced to just several yards, I was beginning to believe that, despite Grandmaster P's words, it was my own overcast vibe that was causing the downpours. But Grandmaster P said that if the mountain wanted to show itself to us, it would.

And it did.

One minute we were in a quagmire of mud, with the rain hammering down from boiling clouds above, as if to echo my own despair . . . and the very next we topped a ridge to see a completely cloudless sky. And there, glistening across the waters of Lake Batur, was the volcano.

Grandmaster P chuckled in a gentle *I told you so* kind of way, and directing us to a spot with a great view of the mountain, climbed up on a rock and began to chant. I panned the camera from long grass blowing gently in the breeze to reveal the mountain behind, and then on again to find Grandmaster P on the rock. He raised his hand and flicked a fuchsia petal into the air in blessing to the spirits that surrounded the mountain. It was a powerful shot and probably one of the most beautiful in the film. I felt the same sense of connection I'd felt several months prior when I'd been out in the open air with the rainbow and the standing stones of Stanton Drew and Adrian the Druid.

ON OCTOBER 12, 2002, a suicide bomber had walked into a nightclub on Kuta beach in Bali and blown himself up. The crowd had run out into the street and there, perfectly timed, was a ton of explosives in a truck. The ensuing explosion had killed 202 innocent people. It was a heinous crime, instigated by a particularly radical group of militant Islamists. All the bombers (bar one) had been arrested and were currently being held in Cilacap island prison off the coast of Java. Having shown no remorse, the militants had attracted considerable attention from the Western media. I wanted to interview them.

Peter Ker and I tried to reach the right people so that I could finally get the dark side that I felt was so necessary to the film. We attended meetings, made phone calls, and sent out e-mails and faxes. We enlisted help from production friends in Jakarta. We contacted politicians and government ministers—you name it, we tried it.

Going to the memorial site in Kuta was particularly disturbing. The goal had been to kill as many *infidels* as possible. The bombers had also killed dozens of local Balinese—many of whom were also Muslim. The ripple effects of the crime had all but destroyed Bali's tourist trade. Many families suffered. The local economy crashed. Indonesia has the largest Muslim population in the world; and the citizens felt hijacked by these unrepentant, unremorseful individuals who celebrated the announcement of their upcoming executions with glee.

But trying to get into the prison to interview them became an impossible task. When I vented my frustration one evening, Grandmaster P said to me, "Hindu, peace, Islam, peace, Christianity, et cetera, they are all peace. But now, *the followers,* it depends on the level of consciousness of the followers. Religion is politicized. So I ask you the question: When you are making a film about God, why do you want to interview these people? What on earth do they have to do with God? You are barking up the wrong tree." Although it was frustrating at the time, in retrospect, he was probably right.

ONE NIGHT WE THREW A DINNER PARTY at our rented house. Peter's wife, Fiona, had cooked spaghetti Bolognese and had invited a fascinating author, explorer, filmmaker, and doctor of comparative religion named Lawrence Blair to join us. A larger-than-life character, Dr. Blair, who had lived in Indonesia for 35 years, was not only tall and charismatic, but with his pirate-esque eye patch, also looked incredibly exotic. His lifelong work was *psycho-anthropology,* the study of the human mind. The following Sunday he sat before my camera.

"Lawrence, what is God?"

"Even though I'm prepared for this question, of course, I'm completely speechless. I think it's a very personal and private thing. And I don't think we really have any clue as to what it is, if it is, in fact, anything we can give a name to. I'm rather in favor of what the Buddhists say when they say, 'If you feel that you can name it, you haven't understood it at all.' I suppose if I had to define it, I would say it is the sum of all and everything in its highest sense."

"Do you pray to a god?"

"I don't pray to a god. The more I study other religions, orthodox religions, the less convinced I am that they are making any sense as far as my God is concerned. I suppose it's hard to divorce God from religion. That's the trouble. But quite frankly, as my old professor used to say, to update it, we are only in 2007. It's early in history; we are still a bunch of little primitive bacteria that barely have a clue as to which direction the sun is coming from."

"Were you more religious when you were studying for your doctorate?"

"I think I've got things more in balance now than I did then. I'm still religious, but it's just that I'm much slower to put any sort of a name to it."

"But after studying so many different religions, there must be a way of describing God other than the sum of all and everything?" I challenged.

"I'd like to say it is a glimmer. If we are fish living at the bottom of a very dark sea and we're vaguely aware of light, mainly bioluminescence from other fish, we will see these glimmers going past us. Some very bioluminescent fish will go past us, and lots of us will follow it as the brightest light. But still, we've little idea of what the luminosity is like on the surface of the sea. So as I say, God, for me, is more a direction, an indication of a course, rather than a continent or a destination."

"Why do you think so many religions fight each other in the name of God?"

"Because we're primitive little animals; we haven't a clue about ourselves or about the effulgence of existence in which we find ourselves. It's all a form of tribalism. It has nothing to do with God itself. A lot of the sages and mystics, whichever religious background they come from, report the same phenomena, seeing the same thing. Many Buddhists, as I indicated before, would agree it's a sacrilege to put a name on Him, because He doesn't belong to the area of thought, of language, of mind. It's probably belonging to a deeper faculty in us, which is not particularly evolved yet—may have been something that we had more clearly as young children or have as very old people, or in those moments of transparency when we're terrified that we're about to die. Then there is a sort of a clarity about the broader significance of things, the meaning beyond the two-dimensional world that we are destined to live our lives in."

"Did man create God, or did God create man, do you think?"

"I think God is more distant than either of us. I think it's much bigger, much vaster. I mean, I think there is an analogy when we look in the garden here. We see little communities of ants, and on the ants' legs there are little communities of bacteria. We belong in that sort of area, without a clue as to the broader picture."

"So what do you think happens to us when we die?"

"My personal experience, from when I was 6 and again when I was 11, when I had to have a series of operations in hospital, is that I did get this tunnel experience that people describe—coming back through a white tunnel. And I remembered as soon as I could wake up in my body that I had seen an enormous amount, much more than I could pick up with the spoon of my mind.

"I think some of what happens after we die is the sort of thing one experiences in these out-of-body experiences, which are very genuine for me. Whether or not those last particularly long and whether or not the individual, the personality, the self, exists after death for particularly long, I rather doubt. I think what does last is probably consciousness itself, and *that* you can find in anything."

Near-death experiences fascinate me deeply, and I had studied the subject quite a bit. "Let's get back to this near-death experience you had, because there are a number of philosophies on this," I said. "One, it could be endorphins kicking in, causing hallucinogenic experiences to the individual. Two, it could be exactly what the Christians, Muslims, and all organized religions would like to believe—you're passing on to a higher state, meeting God and your ancestors. Three, it could be that entrapped in your body are DNA memory sticks of everything that's happened from different experiences that you had in an altered state and that you are actually tapping into again during the process of death. Would you opt for one, two, or three?"

"Probably three, because that would be where consciousness exists. Occasionally, we have access to consciousness beyond our own limited selves. I think reincarnation, which is part of some of the religions, is a fairy story for something much more extraordinary that is actually happening. Because if, as you suggest, we do have memories locked in our cells of everything we have ever been through all the way down to single-celled creatures in the sea, then we do have a feeling of what has happened in our whole history. And sometimes, in certain out-of-body states, we can connect with it.

"And there are a lot of people who say they are reincarnations of Cleopatra or something, which obviously sounds a bit silly. But maybe enormous events in our history resonate through time. We still carry their imprint, their shadow, in us. And in certain states we can receive those, we can feel those. And this isn't as different from modern physics' current thinking as we might imagine. Everything that ever was, or ever will be, is arguably in contemporary physics right here, right now.

"And what that has to do with God really doesn't matter, because this discussion of God is a very old-fashioned atavism that really belongs in the past, before we could think as three-dimensionally as we can think now. But it is no less extraordinary, because if God doesn't exist, something out there exists that is every bit as extraordinary as God." Dr. Blair paused. It was a complicated but fascinating road down which we were traveling.

"God is famously irrational, famously beyond reason," he continued. "In a way, we are living in the irrational all the time. The odds of us all being here alive, born at the same moment in time, are completely against the odds of chance."

"Do you think paradise exists on Earth today, and also hell, for that matter?"

"Yes, I do. I'm sure one can have nothing more horrific than what takes place on this earth today. And indeed, the ecstasy is a little harder to believe. I do have a feeling that there are out-of-body experiences that are more ecstatic than incarnate ones. But yes, I do buy into heaven and hell existing here on Earth, except it does rather describe the end of everything at death, doesn't it?"

"It could also mean that you could create your paradise here, or you could create your hell here."

"Yes, except I don't think that we create our own heavens and hells. I don't think we create much. I think we're only instruments, and the degree to which we surrender can be shaken like a candle flame."

"So you don't think we are in charge of our own destiny?"

"I don't. Modern neurophysiology suggests we're not even fully in charge of our decisions to pick up a cup of coffee. Something has taken place at the subconscious level where the decision is made before we decide, *Okay, I'm going to reach out my hand and grab it*. I think we're living under an amazing illusion.

"I think we're laboring under the illusion that we are the captains of our fates, the masters of our ships. I think that something is unfolding through us, and the greatest degree to which we can be aligned, in tune with the *godliness*, is by letting it happen consciously. Consciously, being very specific, being simply aware. And consciousness, surely, is seeing the broader picture. We're like cells in the body. The leg cell doesn't know that the ear cell exists, but if it sees the broader picture, it realizes it is part of the whole."

"If there is one thing you could say that would help break down the tribal battles between religions, what would it be?"

"Only that those who have any intimation of God don't talk about it so much. As soon as somebody tells you who God is, mistrust them!"

AFTER THE INTERVIEW, WE GRABBED Lawrence's boogie boards and went down to Legian beach. It was another perfectly balanced day. The waves crashed on the wide shore in just the right motion to enable me to catch one and be pulled along for hundreds of yards. It gave me an odd sense of equilibrium, and I repeated the process again and again. I was never too hot, never too cold. The muscles in my body worked when I wanted them to work. I caught every wave I concentrated on, and after Lawrence's out-of-body descriptions and analysis of the odds of that kind of circumstance taking place, the whole beauty of the experience came home to roost. Perhaps, in wider terms, that is what God really is: *balance*. Paradise, definitely that day, for me, was catching those waves.

I thought about those souls who had been blown up in Kuta— 202 people in 2002. How many of them had visited this same beach on the day they'd died? And what kind of mood had they been in? If they had known that come that evening they'd be dead, would they have had more appreciation for the paradise surrounding them?

That made me think of a report I'd read in the media about how several of the deceased's loved ones had developed the habit of returning year after year to Bali to reconnect. I wondered if any of them ever found their way to this beach; and if they did, would those people perceive it as paradise or hell—or neither?

And finally, I wondered about the human beings who had caused so much destruction, devastation, and pain. *What could possibly have possessed them to carry out such acts in the name of God?*

CHAPTER 22

Japan

"Like salt in a wound, pain can be an indication of healing."

— NAPKIN #22

Several months prior to our Australian and Balinese trip, I had been contacted by John Halpern, M.D., assistant professor of psychiatry at Harvard Medical School. He'd seen the trailer I'd put together and had encouraged me to go to Japan. He used his considerable influence to set up a shoot for me there and brought in a friend of his, John Munroe, to produce the segment for us. I was amazed by how the passion of someone I'd never met had been responsible for us being on a plane to Tokyo.

John Munroe picked us up at the airport. While we hadn't been able to communicate fully with him from Bali, he had the brief, and my instincts had told me that even though he'd never worked in film before, he would do a great job for us—which is precisely what he did.

It was a shock when John took us to our hotel, however, having become used to the opulence and space of Bali. The hotel rooms in Tokyo cost three times as much as our Balinese house and were the smallest I'd ever been in. My legs stuck out over the end of the bed, and there was only about 18 inches between the bed and the opposite wall, which meant that some of the equipment bags had to share the bed with me.

The bathroom was hilarious; it was like a plastic porta-cabin within the room. I had to almost double over to get inside. The toilet seat had all sorts of electric buttons that did weird things when pressed and scared the hell out of me. My room looked out onto a busy street with a massive concrete overhead pass running right by my window. Knowing we were in a severe earthquake zone, I used my school mathematics to ascertain whether I was in any danger should the big one hit here. My calculations showed that if the overhead pass collapsed, it would miss my window by about ten feet, which would be fine, providing a big truck didn't happen to choose that particular moment to pass by.

Everything is very precise in Japan. The taxi drivers do everything perfectly. They wear white gloves and they'd jump around like frogs when they were packing our equipment bags in the trunk. Tipping is not part of the culture. They do a good job because they're proud of what they do. Everyone we met was kind and scrupulously honest. Every meal was exquisite and healthy, and it made me salivate just thinking about eating. The people were punctual, ultra-polite, and if I left my camera on the street in Tokyo, I guarantee you it would be there the next day, untouched.

I couldn't understand the disconnect between the horrific stories of World War II, the kamikaze pilots, and the prisoner-of-war camps (as depicted in the movie *The Bridge on the River Kwai*) and the people I was meeting.

The more locals I interviewed, the more sense the Shinto and Buddhist philosophies made to me, which made the mysteries even more baffling. The cruelty of yesteryear seemed so far removed from the country I was discovering. It reminded me of my experience in Bergen-Belsen, which had brought home to me just how much time can change the pulse of nations and create an alternative reality.

John Munroe took us everywhere. We shot the city of Tokyo, with its throngs of people milling about like ants; and Kabukicho, the red-light district. In Machida near Yokohama, we visited John Halpern's mother-in-law, Ruriko Nitta, who was a very well-respected tea-ceremony hostess—and was famous in Japan for perfecting this tradition. We had the great privilege of filming the kimono-clad ladies performing the ritual in Mrs. Nitta's tatami-floored tearoom. She then demonstrated the ancient art of calligraphy to us, drawing the symbols for God and Buddha and explaining the origins of the way the shapes of the characters were used. What was effortless for her was almost impossible for Colonel Boobs and me when we tried our hands at the ancient art.

We filmed Taiko drummers, and horseback riders firing arrows at a gallop. We visited a sake factory in Mumazo. We were invited to a sumptuous lunch and a performance of song and traditional dance in Kanagawa Prefecture.

John's mother-in-law arranged for us to visit the Shinto Fujinomori Shrine in Kyoto to interview the head priest there, her father, Fujimori-san.

I seated him, dressed in his immaculate white robes, outside in an elegant Japanese garden at the back of the temple.

"To the Japanese, there is not one God that has absolute power—the Christian God and the Japanese God are equal," he said. "There is no way to confirm the existence of God, as He cannot be seen. It's something you need to feel in your heart." It was the exact same song as Adrian the Druid's, just a slightly different tune.

In Osaka, I interviewed the Dalai Lama of Japan, Sonkyo Takito—the 105th superintendent priest of Shitennoji Temple—one of the most revered Buddhists in the country.

I filmed him in the very center of the temple, in a beautiful garden that was dominated by a pond of lotus plants, one of which was in bloom. Birdsong echoed across the inner sanctum, and in the distance you could hear the gentle roll of thunder.

"God is something that is always present and fulfills our wishes with His almighty forces. God is our best ally. He guides us onto a proper path. As long as you have faith in God and meditate on Him with all your heart, eventually all your fears will go away. You will feel the intense presence of the mighty power that protects you."

After the interview was over, Sonkyo Takito presented me with a wonderful gift of calligraphy, by his own hand—a deep, beautiful blessing for the film and the message it was to portray.

But it was our meeting with Kanju Tanaka, a Zen master from Kouunnji, Nanzenji Zen center in Kyoto, that really made the Japanese trip shine for me.

IT WAS A BITTERSWEET DAY. John Munroe, Colonel Boobs, and I arrived at the 700-year-old temple half an hour early. It was supremely peaceful. Every stone of the gravel in the front gardens had been raked to utter perfection. It was part of the meditation practice of the temple to make the monks rake the gravel for three weeks before a single word was spoken.

We were invited in to a beautiful room with a low table. Classic sliding doors opened out onto the inner gardens, which were as meticulously groomed as the gravel, with bonsai trees and a stream that was neatly guided to flow through rocks with myriad glistening patterns on their jagged faces. Oddly enough, just as with the Shitennoji Temple, we could hear the sound of distant thunder. It started to rain.

Then Tanaka entered. Bald and tall, he wore immaculate gray and black robes and a cream silk scarf neatly draped across square, erect shoulders. His eyes blinked behind round-rimmed glasses, as if he had a tic. We bowed to him, and he motioned for us to sit down at the table. Tea was brought in, and we talked.

We talked about all the things I'd been thinking while making this film. He spoke slowly in broken English, but the simple words that he chose described a profound wisdom. We talked about both paradise and about hell, and about love and pain. He described the people who came to him for help and how even the most serious of cases—even the terminally ill—would change their thinking and leave the temple happy. It was so simple, he assured me. *So simple.* He worked with the sick at heart, the sick of mind, the possessed, and the dispossessed; and they all left with a different perspective on life that eased their pain.

In all the traveling I had done on the film thus far—in all the holy places, from churches to mosques to Hindu temples to synagogues—I had only experienced mere slivers of any spiritual feelings . . . mostly stimulated by beautiful art, the singing of a choir, or chanting and clapping in India. I'd felt a little bit of something at the standing stones; I'd felt something strongly years before, up a mountain at night in Thailand. But most of the obvious places, even the Church of the Nativity, were mostly devoid of peace but filled with the remnants of desperate prayers, questions, pain, disappointment, and betrayal. Yet here, with

Tanaka, I experienced an extremely intense peace. Somehow, the place balanced the acidity, soothed the burning, and allowed something deeply relaxing to emerge. It was a profound feeling that made me choke back tears; not only did I feel very safe, but as I was to discover later, my meeting with Tanaka couldn't have come at a more fortuitous moment.

When we checked into a local Kyoto hotel later that day, we found it had no Internet service. I was in the process of renegotiating the contract and needed to be in regular contact with the world, so we changed hotels.

My new room was very high up. The evening sun was gleaming off railway tracks down below. It was oddly surreal. I turned on the computer and read my e-mails. I just sat there and stared, unable to believe what I was seeing.

My bank had reviewed my line of credit, and because I hadn't paid any money into my account for many months, they were now calling in the loan. The next e-mail was from my lawyer, informing me that all the changes to the contract we had submitted had been rejected. I had no deal.

No deal, no money, and I had to find almost 100 grand—like *yesterday.*

Adam was in Italy. My lawyer was at the Toronto Film Festival. Horacio was in Mexico; my wife and family were in Los Angeles; and I was in Japan, thinking that I was finally, without any doubt, staring my own version of hell right in the face.

I felt as if I'd been hanging on to the thin rope of hope for so long, and now I was suddenly plummeting. It was all over. The movie was never going to be finished, and I was devastated.

I curled up on the bed in a fetal position. I felt I'd let everyone down—my family, myself, and all the others who had believed in me. As I lay there, I imagined myself flipping into another dimension for a second, like Abdesalam had said you could do when you're dead. I knew that when I awoke, I would still be in exactly the same space, but I didn't care. Even if only for ten minutes, I had to get away; I was in too much pain.

They say when you're backed into a corner and have nowhere to run, you come face-to-face with fear—and I didn't like fear. I was fearless, wasn't I? I had *faith!* Someone once told me that *fear* stood for "false evidence appearing real." But there was nothing fake about what I was facing in that moment. I was in serious trouble.

As my anxiety oddly induced an incredible wave of fatigue, my mind went back to the interview with Tanaka.

"I'm a Japanese Zen monk. I am 59 years old. I became a monk at the age of 28, and I'm living in the happiness of pleasure."

"Sir, what is God?" I asked.

"What is God? The essence of nature . . ." He paused, stock-still, before concluding his statement: "That's all." I was about to ask him another question when he suddenly started speaking again.

"When I attained enlightenment, I didn't sleep for three months. I discovered a fundamental experience of emptiness—nothingness—and I recognized for the first time that there is no self, ego, subject, or object, so our fundamental being is selflessness. We have no enemy at all.

"So your happiness is my own happiness. Your unhappiness is my own unhappiness, so I can easily cure your mental problem. When people with mental problems visit me, I never try to solve their problems, because when I try to solve their problems, they become sick. I don't want them to become more sick. According to the Buddha's enlightenment, and also to my own experience of enlightenment, we have no problem at all. In other words, we are all perfect beings. No problems. We are already saved, so never mind. We have no problem at all."

"Why do you think so many religions around the world fight?"

"Because most religions have their own egotistic thought and practice. They should abandon their egotistic thought and dogma. We have no dogma in Zen Buddhism."

"When you experienced your own enlightenment and discovered you have no self, and you discovered the bliss of emptiness, for you was that like a communication to God within?" I asked.

"No. No God. There is no God at all, according to Buddhism. We don't have to desire or seek God around us. According to the Buddhists—especially Zen Buddhists—we only seek the true nature of ourselves. It is then that you find the true nature of emptiness. One of the famous Japanese Zen masters, Hakuin, said, 'Your true nature is no nature,' so no God at all, according to our Zen Buddhist teaching and experience."

"What do you think happens to us when we die?"

Tanaka's whole face lit up. His eyes sparkled, and he laughed a hearty laugh. "The master Hakuin said, 'If you don't want to die, you should die before you're dead. If you die once, you never die twice.' We say the greatest death is our thinking; we should kill the thought of death and birth."

"Do you believe that paradise exists here on Earth?"

"Yes!" Tanaka nodded with great conviction. "I am living in the middle of paradise, right now, every day. Zen monks say every day is a good day; even in the midst of unhappiness, I'm living in the happiness."

"Do you think hell exists here on Earth?"

Tanaka laughed even more heartily. "There was a famous episode. One day, master Hakuin asked a young samurai, 'Do you think hell exists or not?' The samurai got angry, took a sword, and was going to kill Hakuin, and Hakuin said, 'There, that's hell!' The samurai stopped and said, 'Sorry!' Hakuin said, 'And that's paradise!' Hell and paradise live in our mind." Tanaka's eyes blinked with utter conviction, and he nodded to emphasize his words.

"What would you say to promote peace, love, tolerance, and understanding?"

Tanaka thought deeply before answering. He was very serious. "I am feeling a lack of confidence from a lot of people who visit me—so, we need self-confidence. In other words, when we *believe we are living in the midst of happiness, I'm sure we'll be happy. If you have no self-confidence to live in happiness, and you are always living in unhappiness, I'm sure you will be unhappy. So please abandon your negative thinking. This is a shortcut to paradise. Thank you."*

Recalling Tanaka's words, I felt very humbled, and very grateful for having met him on that day, of all days.

All I wanted to do was walk out of that hotel and learn how to scrape gravel.

PART III

CATCHING BUTTERFLIES

CHAPTER 23

"My God Is Greater Than Your God"

"When you're not looking is usually when you find."

— NAPKIN #23

We flew home to Los Angeles completely burned-out. Grand-master P had predicted: "It's only temporary. Things come. Things go. Things come back, and they go again." He was right.

The day after I returned, we agreed upon all the terms of the contract, and I finally had a partner on the film. It was a wonderful feeling. Horacio turned out to be the most honorable and supportive partner I could wish for, and he agreed to give a substantial amount of any income the film might generate to world charities. I'd felt adamant that I couldn't make a film about what people think God is without giving back.

Despite the ups and downs and many moments of despair, the footage we had collected from the adventure was worth it. Now that I had financing, I enlisted John Hoyt as the editor. John and I had collaborated on many commercial projects in the past; and I trusted his patience, his expert eye, and his objective opinion. Colonel Boobs started weaving sounds from the trip into a preliminary score, and I started working in earnest on the missing elements of the film: Native Americans, atheists, and fanatics.

In the meantime, news was spreading about the project. Doris La Frenais (my friend who had introduced Ringo Starr to it) was championing it around the world and called to say that Sir Bob Geldof had agreed to be in the film.

I called him, and he said, "What do you want to interview me for? I don't even believe in God."

Perfect, I thought. *A well-known atheist.* I'd reached out to many famous names, from Christopher Hitchens to Richard Dawkins, without any luck. I was very excited about Sir Bob Geldof and worked out a time to see him back in London.

It was the militant fanatics who were causing the problem. Vishnu had been working for weeks to get someone to talk on camera, and it was proving to be very difficult. It seemed that no one wanted to take the risk. There was only one thing for it: fly to Peshawar, in Pakistan, and Afghanistan and go look for them there. I mentioned this one day on the phone to Chandi in India, and within minutes Mr. Gill was on the line. He was very blunt: "If you go to any of those two countries looking for what you are looking for, Peter, you will not get out alive."

I certainly wasn't going to ignore advice from someone who knew my hotel room number before I did, so we abandoned plans for Afghanistan and northern Pakistan.

Then Vishnu got a call. He had a lead—a strong lead. We started making plans.

A MONTH AFTER RETURNING FROM JAPAN, we were off on the next— and potentially most exciting—leg of the journey. Metin Anter, one of the investors and executive producers of the film, invited us to Istanbul. He and his wife, Ela Barlas, would produce a shoot for us there; and my manager and executive producer, Adam Krentzman, would join us. After Turkey we would travel to Kashmir, via London, where we had set up interviews with Sir Bob Geldof and others.

I'd filmed in Turkey 17 times over the years and knew it very well. The people were famous for their kindness and hospitality, but I hadn't been back for at least ten years. I was amazed by the transformation of Istanbul. What used to be a rather dull city full of people with downcast eyes, wearing ill-fitting suits and old-fashioned polyester sweaters, had turned into a modern, progressive metropolis brimming with life and vitality. A decade ago, I'd seldom seen pretty girls on the streets, but now the young elite were out in droves. Ultramodern shopping centers had cropped up everywhere. The restaurants were innovative, and the quality of food was right up there with New York and London. The only downside was the terrible traffic—you could spend hours getting from one side of the city to the other.

When we arrived at the airport, lo and behold, British Airways had lost our baggage—yet again! I couldn't believe it. Fortunately, it wasn't quite as bad as the last time, as we had the camera, lenses, tapes, hard drives, cell phone, and computer with us in the cabin; it was the chargers, spare batteries, tripod, and boom mike that didn't make it this time. We quickly managed to rent what was needed, so we didn't lose any shooting time.

Ela Barlas took us on a whirlwind schedule. We conducted many interviews with politicians, peace activists, and sociologists. We filmed the city from all the best vantage points. We climbed the minaret of Sultan Ahmed Mosque—more famously known as the *Blue Mosque*—and shot a rare angle of the Hagia Sophia church. We filmed in the souk and managed to get some beautiful footage of the whirling dervishes performing at the Sema Cultural Center. I loved the city. It was full of life, the weather was beautiful, and it was a visual feast.

THROUGHOUT THE *OH MY GOD* ADVENTURE, I had filmed in the places of worship of most of the major religions, but we'd had a terrible time getting to film inside a mosque. For me, it was vitally important to illustrate the faithful, bowing and praying in unison. We had tried in Indonesia, Morocco, and Ramallah, to no avail.

In Istanbul, luck was on our side. Ela arranged for us to be invited to Friday prayers in one of Istanbul's largest and most famous mosques, the Conqueror's Mosque, or *Fatih Camii,* so-named because it had been constructed by Sultan Fatih Mehmet, the conqueror of Constantinople, sometime between A.D. 1462 and 1470. (It was Fatih Mehmet who was responsible for changing the city's name to Istanbul.) It was breathtakingly beautiful. The original mosque was built to rival the Hagia Sophia. Legend has it that the sultan had the architect's hands cut off, because, despite being built on a hill, the mosque still didn't reach as high as the church. Destroyed by two massive earthquakes and rebuilt twice, the present building dated back to 1771.

We were invited onto the raised platform where the Imam sings the prayers. The mosque was packed, and I managed to get exactly the shots I needed. I was ecstatic.

As I was walking out of the mosque, clutching the camera, a man with a long beard that had been dyed orange and a white headband, dressed in a beige suit with pants pulled up so high that they almost reached his rib cage, approached me and, bizarrely, asked in broken English with a north London accent, "Are you a Muslim?"

"No," I replied.

"Then what are you doing in the mosque?" he demanded to know.

"I was filming in there."

"You're not allowed in there!" He was outraged.

"Am I not allowed in there because I was filming or because I'm not a Muslim?" I asked him.

"Because you are an infidel. It is forbidden for non-Muslims to enter a mosque."

I stopped for a second and gasped. *Wow!* Someone had actually said it! "Sir," I began politely, "I'm making a film about what people think God is. Would there be any chance for me to interview you? I would love to hear your views."

"Really?" There it was again, exactly the same reaction as I'd had from Billy, the drunken thug I'd met in the pub in Bristol.

"In fact, it's vitally important that the world hears your views, sir," I said.

He didn't hesitate for an instant. "I would be delighted."

I cancelled our afternoon schedule and spent the rest of the day with him. His name was Abdullah Irzek. He wouldn't tell us much about himself, apart from the fact that he was a very devout Muslim—evidenced by his dyed beard. He seemed to fit into the mold of disenfranchised first-generation European minorities, but any attempt to delve deeper into where he came from was immediately deflected. I wasn't concerned with labeling him. It was what he had to say that mattered.

"What is God, Abdullah?"

"God is the creator of all. He created our forefathers and has given directions, guidance, and intelligence to man. He created life after death. I have a copy of the Koran in my hands, in the Arabic language, which He Himself revealed to His servant Mohammed. And I would like to translate it to you in the English language how He explains how to know Him and worship Him."

Abdullah held his copy of the Koran high and started to sing. Then he stopped and translated, as if presenting a sermon: "I take refuge in God from the rejected devil. In the name of God, the most gracious, the most merciful." He started to sing again. Then he stopped and translated. This went on for such a long time that I was glad I was shooting HD and not film. He finished up by saying, "God always speaks the truth."

"But, sir, I still don't quite understand. What is God?" I tried again.

"God is the all-powerful creator that created man, and has given him intelligence and guidance."

"And the God that you pray to is called Allah?"

"That's right."

"So is the God that the Christians, Jewish, and Hindu people pray to the same God as Allah?"

"God says in the Koran that whoever says Jesus is God is a disbeliever. Or whoever says Jesus is son of God is making a false statement against God Himself, because God has taken Himself neither a wife nor a son."

"So Allah is not the same God that the Christians and the Hindus pray to?"

"No."

"How do you know Allah exists?"

"I can see His signs within myself and within the creation around me that He has created the seven heavens and the earth. And He has revealed His signs to His messenger Mohammed. So that is a faith that I carry, and I believe that He created the angels and the devils."

"Does that make God a power source?"

"That's right."

"So, then, the God that the Christians pray to through Jesus Christ, and the God that the Hindus pray to through Brahma and Vishnu and Shiva, must surely be the same power?"

"That's right."

"So their God is the same God as Allah?"

"That's right."

"But you just said it wasn't the same God as Allah."

"No, Allah is the same for everybody, but for everybody not the same, because He has revealed Himself in the Koran to explain to you who He is."

Oh boy! This was getting confusing. I decided to change my tack. "Okay. Well, then, let me put it this way: do you think that Christians will go to heaven?"

"No."

"Do you think the Jews will go to heaven?"

"No."

"Do you think anybody who is non-Muslim will go to heaven?"

"No."

"So you think the only way to get to heaven is through Allah and leading the life of a Muslim?"

"That's right."

"Why do you think that?"

"Because this is what is revealed in the Koran."

"But in the Koran, it does not say, 'If you are a nonbeliever, you are not going to go to heaven.' It doesn't—"

"It does say in the Koran that the Christians and the Jewish people will be in the hellfire forever," Abdullah interrupted.

"Would you mind reading me that passage because I just don't—"

"I have to look up the right *sura*, if you wait."

"Yeah, yeah, absolutely. Love to," I said.

It took him two and a half hours to find it. At one point he disappeared into the mosque to call some friends to pinpoint the precise passage. I waited. Vishnu and I walked about, took shots around the mosque, came back . . . he was still there. We paced, we ate a sandwich, I downloaded the footage, and then, finally, he announced that he'd found what he was looking for. He stood bolt upright and triumphantly sang from the Koran before delivering his translation.

"This is Chapter 98 of the Koran," he preached in an authoritative voice, swaying back and forth. "'There is no doubt, the people of the book, i.e., the Christians and the Jews, and the people who set up rivals and partners to Allah, will go forever to the fire of hell, and stay there forever. And they are the worst of the people.'" He lowered the book and announced victoriously, "Allah always speaks the truth. And that is the statement, Sura 98 of the Koran."

I WANTED TO GET TO THE BOTTOM OF THIS. It didn't make any sense to me, so let's briefly jump forward in time to Los Angeles and my subsequent interview with Imam Jihad Turk, the Director of Religious Affairs at the Islamic Center of Southern California, whom I specifically sought out in order to check the accuracy of Abdullah's statement.

"This is a problem we face as Muslims, with both the non-Muslim community and with Muslims themselves. Misinterpretation, taking out of context, and just lack of education about the Koran overall—the teachings of the Koran as a whole," said Jihad Turk. "Let me read you the Arabic and the translation—the *correct* translation," he emphasized. In front of him on the desk he had a beautiful copy of the Koran open at the right page.

Jihad sang the same passage, Sura 98, which Abdullah had delivered in Istanbul, and then translated: "'Verily, those individuals who are bent on denying the truth from the people of the book, i.e., Jews and Christians, or from amongst the polytheists, they are destined to abide in the fire of Gehenna. They are truly the worst of creatures.'

"The important part of this verse," Jihad continued, "is the first part, which says, 'Those who are bent on denying the truth.' The Koran guarantees anyone who is bent on denying the truth a consequence in the hereafter, including Muslims. So, accepting Islam is not a ticket to heaven, and not accepting Islam is not a ticket to hell, because Chapter 2, Verse 62, in the Koran clearly states that 'whoever believes in God, Jews or Christians, and who does good deeds, has nothing to fear for their soul, nor shall they grieve.'"

BACK IN ISTANBUL, I'D WANTED TO TRY TO UNDERSTAND what made someone develop fanatical views, what made him or her think that it was okay to kill in the name of God, and why such a person felt his or her God was superior to any other.

I asked Abdullah, "In the United States and Europe, the words *Islam* and *Muslim* seem to be dirty words since 9/11. Are you upset with the way that the West views Islam?"

Abdullah continued to shift from foot to foot, like a child who needs to visit the bathroom. His eyes mimicked the move. "No, I am not upset. I can say without fear that God reveals in the Koran that the Christians and the Jewish people are friends of each other but not the friends of Muslims."

"So you really don't have much respect for anybody who's not a Muslim, then?" I challenged.

"Well, I wouldn't put it that way. What I am trying to say is what my faith and what my book allows me to say."

"But in the Koran there are a lot of passages that preach peace and tolerance. In fact, Islam preaches that one has to be tolerant of other people and their belief systems," I remarked.

"The Koran never explains what you have just said. The Koran explains peace and tolerance among the *Muslims*," he countered.

I upped it a notch: "What do you think about the small group of fanatic individuals who are creating terrorism around the world in the name of your religion?"

"Well, I think there is a counteraction for everything, and the poor people are just counterattacking the West within their own ability for what the West is doing, with its technology and mechanical powers."

And there it was, plain and simple. Abdullah thought terrorism was *justified*. I was finally getting somewhere.

"But why would they attack the West? What has the West done to them to make them do this?" I asked.

"The West, after the collapse of the Ottoman Empire, has been taking resources, lives, blood, and property from Muslims; they are being attacked by the Christians and by the Jewish people in Palestine. They have lots of people and lots of material power to bomb, to kill a lot of Muslims."

"It's pretty intolerant not to accept other religions, is it not?"

"Allah is very tolerant, and He is inviting the non-Muslims to His religion, Islam, because what Allah is saying is: 'If you don't accept Islam, and the message I have conveyed through My messengers, then you will have a very painful punishment forever after your death.' So He is just trying to help you and the non-Muslims, to rescue them from the fire of hell, because evil is enemy to man."

This was getting interesting. *Join us and you'll be fine.* I remembered those horrible videos of journalists who'd been captured by militants, being made to say they had converted to Islam, in front of hooded men with guns.

"And you think that gives Muslims the right to use violence?" I confronted Abdullah.

"There are different ways how the message can be put across to the non-Muslims, but the best way is by the Koran."

"But the Koran preaches peace."

". . . if a non-Muslim accepts Islam and then comes and lives in the same community as a believer and to learn the ways of Islam."

Abdullah was now sounding like a more militant version of Peter the Pentecostal Maasai back in Kenya.

"So do you think it is part of your mission to make non-Muslims Muslim?" I asked.

"That's right, because at the end of the day, there will be a punishment if they don't believe in the message of Allah, and then they will forever have punishment in the fire of hell."

"But why do you think your God is the only God that's right? Don't you think that's intolerant of other beliefs?"

"No. He *is* the only one."

There was no doubt at all in my mind that Abdullah's motivation was driven purely by fear, just like so many other glazed faces with shifty eyes that I had come across. "Abdullah, what does *jihad* mean?"

"Jihad means struggle in the path of Allah, or to fight in the cause of Allah."

"When we in the West hear the word *jihad,* we think of terrorists who blow people up in the name of Allah. Can you try and explain that from your point of view?"

"Well, the Muslim and the Koran's point of view is that to fight is obligatory for every Muslim, and it is written down in the Koran, whether you may not like it."

"Really? I have never read that in the Koran. In the Koran it says that you should not kill anybody unless it's in self-defense."

"No, unless it is an *unjust cause.*"

"And so Christianity and Judaism are unjust causes?"

"Unjust causes."

"They are?" I asked incredulously.

"Yes."

"But the Koran teaches tolerance and peace."

"No. I just read you the Sura that . . ."

". . . that was a misinterpretation."

"No, I have said the meaning of it from the Arabic. Have faith in Him, believe in Him, trust in Him, and take Him as the only protector, but do not associate partners to Him. He is the only one."

There was no doubting Abdullah's tenacity. I'd met many others over the course of filming who had spoken like him, used the same justifications, the same language, displayed the same *My way or the highway* attitude—but none of them had had the courage to say it in front of the camera. Abdullah was dying to speak up. What's more, what he was saying reflected the same ideals I'd heard time and again from those who wanted to stay anonymous.

"When I was in the Palestinian Territories recently, I spoke to a few people, and they said that they would love to kill Americans, and if they did so, they were promised a place in paradise. Can you try and explain that from a—?"

"Well, I can explain from the Koranic view that whoever fights for the cause of Allah and has been martyred will go to paradise."

"But they were saying they were promised virgins in paradise."

"That's right. In the paradise, Allah has created maiden women, beautiful women, but not from the providence of Adam, but from the creation of Him. So these women will be given to those martyrs, and they will have her in the morning and in the evening, their foods to eat, and their enjoyment. And they will wear silken clothes, and there is no getting tired in heaven, and the fruit of the heaven will be near at hand, and they will be given wine to drink."

"Isn't there a conflict here? People believe that by killing others they will be rewarded in heaven with virgins and alcohol that they are forbidden on Earth, yet they are inflicting evil—"

"Well, the oppression is worse than killing. Allah orders Muslims to fight until there is no more oppression. Because Allah has revealed in the book, the clear pages, to purify people from evil, from sin, and from illegal sexual intercourse, from homosexuality, from other evils. But if these evils are not stopped in society, and if evil grows more, Muslims are obliged to fight the evil and the cause of the evil in the name of Allah to make society, children, and people more safe."

"Thus creating more evil," I protested.

"They will be leading a better way of life instead of living the way of evil."

"So if somebody kills someone for being a homosexual, is that not an act of evil?"

"No, it is an act of good action. To kill a homosexual is a good action in the sight of God, because a homosexual is not a man of man."

"So you support people killing?

Abdullah held the Koran high. "This book is the law. And this is not man-made. This is God-made. The law of God, if that is broken, that would be a crime."

"What about suicide bombers? Are they justified?"

"Well, that is something done in the name of God to protect the Muslim community. It is ordered in the Koran to fight, because the Christian people and the Jewish people are fighting the Muslim people to get their lands, to get their resources, and to get their attention."

"No," I argued, "the Christian community and the Jewish community are very accepting of the Muslim community—"

"Well, it doesn't look that way, because I don't believe in any Muslim living under the protection of a non-Muslim. That is not allowed in the tradition of the prophet Mohammed. I believe that Muslims should be more free from the non-Muslim governments."

As usual with those who have fanatical points of view, there was no arguing with him. "Some say that the word *Islam* means 'peace.' What do you think *Islam* means?"

"Well, what I understand from the Koran, Islam means to submit, to give in to the will of God. And to accept His greatness and to bow down to His will."

"And that could involve killing people?"

"That's right. For those who oppress Muslims and the Muslim community, we have got no other choice but fight."

And there you have it.

And no wonder the world has such a problem. Polite as Abdullah was, it was extremely disturbing to hear such ignorant, misinformed bigotry. There's no point in just saying, "Oh, the man's brainwashed. He's mad. He's uneducated." The truth is that Abdullah's kind of thinking is growing exponentially across the world, and not just among the uneducated. There have been rings of doctors in the U.K. who have militant fundamentalist ties and have been arrested for being connected to recent airport bombings. I'd heard the same rhetoric time and again, and it wasn't going to just *go away.*

A HOLLYWOOD WRITER/DIRECTOR FRIEND OF MINE, Dale Launer, mentioned while I was interviewing him, "There's nowhere in the Koran that says that a person who gives up their life for the cause of Islam will get 72 virgins. It doesn't exist. But it could be, maybe, a translation thing, and that it's not 72 virgins, but one 72-year-old virgin."

Joking aside, I asked Imam Jihad Turk to try to throw some light on this problem of misinterpretation.

"One of the challenges, one of the beautiful things, and one of its greatest shortcomings at the same time is that Islam recognizes no clergy. There's a scripture; there's a source for interpretation, for guidance, but there is not an individual that can say this is the authoritative interpretation, and so it's a great responsibility we have individually as human beings to approach the scripture without our own biases being imposed upon the text.

"I think Islam currently has a negative image around the world, particularly in the United States, because it's being conflated with terrorism. While terrorism is an abomination, and the criminals who commit it are, unfortunately, claiming Islam, I feel they have hijacked our religion and taken it off course. Our religion condemns terrorism. The Koran specifically says that to take one innocent life is as if you take the life of all humanity, and to save one innocent human is as if you save all of humanity. So the onus is on the rest of the community to stand up and speak out loudly against those who would commit such acts in our name. It's a big challenge, but we're trying our best to meet that challenge."

"Why don't we hear those voices that you just referred to? We don't get it in the press. We just get the negative. Where is the majority's voice?"

"We are screaming at the top of our lungs, fighting in the front lines against the war on terror. We are screaming against those who are committing such acts. The problem is, we don't have outlets for our message in terms of mass media, and so we thought we'd devise something quite clever by issuing a *fatwa* against terrorism. We got the media to show up, but unfortunately, the story didn't make the headlines. We are doing our best, but we don't have the influence in the media to have our voice heard."

BUT THE "MY GOD IS GREATER THAN YOUR GOD" syndrome is pretty commonplace and wasn't only, as the media pushes us to believe, coming from the Muslim faith.

Adam Krentzman managed to organize an interview with Dr. Tim LaHaye, the best-selling author of the *Left Behind* series of books. An evangelical minister, well-known religious right-wing activist, and member of the ultraconservative Council for National Policy, he is also openly antihomosexual. He co-authored a scary book that encapsulated his own interpretations of biblical prophecy, entitled *Global Warning*.

Adam and I traveled out to his home in Palm Springs to inter-view him. Dr. LaHaye was gracious. Slight in build, he had beady eyes and a good sense of humor. He started in prayer:

"Dear heavenly Father, we thank You for the privilege of living
in a technological day where we can sit here and communicate
about You, and it can be carried to many parts of the world.
I pray that You will give us wisdom and guidance, clarity
of speech, and make it a blessing to those who see and hear.
Thank You for those men who are willing to do something like
this and get truth out. In Jesus's name we pray. Amen."

"Let's start off, sir, with the most profound question of all: what is God?"

"God is a spirit, as the Bible makes very clear, and He reveals Himself as a personal God. And I'm convinced after many years of teaching the Bible that the Bible has the answers to the problems of life and many of the unseen things about the world. God is the uncaused cause of all things. And as such, He is the creator, the savior. That's the thing that the world doesn't understand: God is a merciful God Who loves mankind. And the best proof of that is that He has given His only begotten son to save mankind."

"Is the God you pray to through Jesus Christ the same God that all other religions pray to?"

"The God that I pray to is the same God that the Jews pray to because He is the God of the Old Testament, as well as the New, but He is not the God of Allah. Allah is a polytheistic God that Mohammed made up and hijacked some of the teachings from the Bible. And the Hindus, I don't believe they believe in the God of the Bible, the God of creation. They have a different formula for creation. You have to be very careful when you get outside the God of the Bible."

"Some Muslims have told me if you don't believe in Allah, then you're not going to go to heaven, yet you're dismissing Allah as being a good representative of what you would call God. As there are 1.7 billion Muslims in the world, who is not to say that they are right and you're wrong?"

"They don't have the Bible like we have. See, there are signs of the supernatural within the Bible. It's called fulfilled prophecy. The Koran does not have that. In fact, if you've ever read the Koran, it's a mumbo jumbo of things that are confusing. I'm convinced that calling God *Allah* is blasphemy, because there is no likeness between the God of the Mohammedan faith and the God of the Bible. In fact, the Bible makes it very clear that God Himself identified Himself as a merciful God, gracious, long-suffering, slow to anger, plenteous in mercy; and I believe *that* kind of a God, mankind can trust. But the God of the Muslim world is 'You believe in Me and you accept Me or off with your head.' That's a cannibalistic, barbaric way to live. And it's not a merciful religion. And I don't see how they can be equated.

"In fact, I've had Muslim women say they don't like the God of Allah because He is so cruel to women. I don't understand how any woman would want to voluntarily become a Muslim woman. They're the object of some sexual individual here on this earth and then up in heaven. Everything's against them. I find that Jesus Christ, by expressing his love for womanhood, did more to raise the stature of women's life; he's given them an honorable position.

"Remember, when Jesus was born, women were traded for cattle. And a man wept when he had a girl child, because he had to raise animals to peddle her when she got of age. And yet Jesus came into that kind of environment and made women real human beings, and everywhere Christianity has gone and had an influence in society, it has raised the status of womanhood. You can't say that about Islam."

"Do you believe in the Second Coming?"

"I believe in the Second Coming for a number of reasons. One is the Bible teaches it, but most of all, because it's prophesied by the Old Testament prophets."

"How would you react if Jesus came back to Earth again as a Muslim?"

Dr. LaHaye's jaw dropped. He looked at me incredulously. "As a *Muslim?!*"

"As a Muslim," I confirmed.

"There's no chance that he would do that."

"Why not?"

"Because there is no prophecy in the Bible that supports his coming back to such a cruel-taskmaster slavery as the Muslim faith."

"But Muslims are human beings."

"Well, they are human beings, but they sure don't love all mankind. I don't understand the question. The comparison is so bizarre!"

I decided to explain my thoughts. "Well, Jesus Christ is about humanity, and if there is a conflict in the world among different human beings—and obviously, you believe there might be one between Muslims and Christians—therefore, as a humanitarian representative of God, there might be incentive for him to come to Earth again as a Muslim so that he can teach love to all human beings, whatever group they may belong to."

"That's conforming God to the ambitions and desires of man, instead of man conforming to the issues of God. Let's understand: there is only one God, and He has revealed Himself in His word. And if we are not willing to conform to what He teaches in the Bible, then it's tough luck for us."

"What if Jesus came down and he was a she?"

"For that to happen, you'd have to throw the Bible away and say it doesn't have the signs of the supernatural; it isn't a message from God. When He speaks, it's true, and I'm convinced that the Bible is true. No other book has that kind of thing. I mean, Mohammed going into a cave and getting this from the devil spirit, or some spirit; and he comes out with something that's contrary to the Bible, which makes it that he's the prophet and not Jesus? And he didn't rise from the dead? He wasn't crucified? I mean it's bizarre."

"In your book *Global Warning*, which I think is a frightening book for me—"

"Good!"

". . . it's a very frightening book. There are a few statements that I find to be contradictory for somebody who I would term a Christian. It's like you've taken the word *Islam* or *Muslim* and made them dirty words. And the Western press is doing this as well. I want to know why that would be, with a religion that says it is based upon peace."

"Well," answered Dr. LaHaye, "I think it's a false premise to assume what they say is peace really *is* peace. Like the Communists said, 'We want peace, a piece of this country and a piece of that country, and put it all together.' Well, the Muslims have done this for years. They're not interested in peace. They're interested in dominating the world, and then kill Jew or Gentile or anyone who refuses to accept their philosophy.

"I don't find that Christians are violent and want to force people by losing their head, and yet the Muslims do this. And they do it in the name of religion and have the ludicrous idea that killing thousands of people in a suicide attack is going to get you to heaven. What a bizarre idea that is! That's nothing like the God of the Bible."

"But those are fanatic evildoers," I suggested.

"But they scare the bejabbers out of everybody else, even the Muslims! You will find that Muslims, even in our country, the safest place for them in the world, are afraid to oppose their own Muslim people—these fanatics, as you say—because they know that they will do them harm. It is not a peaceful religion."

"You are talking about a very small group of people, but in your book you make it out as if *every* Muslim is like that," I pointed out.

"I don't see how anyone can close their eyes to the fact that the Mohammedan religion is not a peace-loving religion. If you go back and study about Mohammed and how he was a murderer, a child molester, he was a very evil man; and he murdered everybody that didn't agree with him, and would lie and cheat and steal—just as many of the terrorists do today. I think that we are closing our eyes to the reality of how dangerous they are. And in our book, we try to be fair, but we try to point out that it is a dangerous religion."

"But where does it say ever that Mohammed was a child molester?"

"In history."

"In the Koran?"

"The encyclopedia will tell you that. I've read enough about his background to know that he married a girl when she was 12 years old, and he took her as his wife. That's kind of bizarre. And then she was his fourth wife, I think."

"Does that make him a child molester, then?"

"Yes."

"In those countries at that time people did take wives at that age. In fact, wives were married off in families at age 12 even in Europe and places. In Texas today, with parental consent, you can be legally married at 14. Would you say those people were child molesters as well?"

"Well, I'd have to know more details about them, but I know enough details about Mohammed, who, when you've already got three wives, then you marry a girl who is 12 years old, there is something wrong. I mean that's never been acceptable in a Christian world. And that's why I say that Jesus Christ has done more to help womanhood than anyone who has ever lived. And you will not find Christians teaching that that's the way women should be respected. That's why we campaign for one man, one woman in marriage as long as you both shall live."

"But don't you find it's a little bit much to be critical of 1.7 billion people? Wouldn't you say that it's a little unchristian to say that the holy prophet of Islam, Mohammed, is a child molester? That's pretty strong, isn't it?"

"There's not very much at all holy about Muslims, about Mohammed. He was a very evil man. As a matter of fact, I think much of the Koran was inspired by the devil himself. He gave him this message in a cave somewhere, and he wrote it down.

"See, I look down the road and I'm convinced that the Mohammedan religion has a multifaceted attack on humanity. One is by the terrorist routine. That's the quick routine. But the other is Khomeini gave his instructions to his people before he ever took over Iran that they should have big families and infiltrate the other countries. And when I go to Washington, D.C., and I can't find a taxicab driver that can understand English, that came from

Iraq or Iran, and realize how these people are reproducing and they have these mosques all over the country built by oil money, I realize that they have a plan to take over America and Europe and the other countries of the world. The world should wake up to the fact that they are being infiltrated for the purpose of world domination. It's an invasion."

"But shouldn't we love the Muslims like our neighbors?" I asked.

"Oh, I love the Muslims! I'd love to lead them to Christ, but I don't want them coming to my home and cutting off the heads of my children."

Dr. LaHaye invited Adam and me out for lunch and insisted on paying for it. He asked me not to sandbag him. I hope he doesn't feel I did. I merely printed what he said, and I will again use this opportunity to thank him for his time and the lunch, throughout which I couldn't help thinking how interesting it would have been if Abdullah Irzek could have joined us, to see what they would have said to each other.

IN LONDON, A FEW DAYS AFTER FILMING Abdullah Irzek in Istanbul, a young Muslim actor by the name of Sami Hall Bassam said this to me: "I'd like to say to all the ignorant people out there, and you know who you are, just take five minutes of your time to find out about our religion and what our religion stands for. And then when you fully understand what our religion is about and what our people are about and where we come from, and you understand what the fanatics are doing, then I think you'll be able to differentiate between the two—that they are fanatics who use violence and murder to get whatever they want. That's not what our religion preaches."

CHAPTER 24

HRH Princess Michael of Kent

"Happiness belongs in the space between reality and fantasy."

— NAPKIN #24

Vishnu and I continued on to London. Once again, we traveled via British Airways, but much to my relief, this time (unlike the previous occasion) they managed to deliver our luggage to us safely at Heathrow Airport.

A dear friend of mine, Simon Astaire, was a longtime associate of Her Royal Highness Princess Michael of Kent and had set up an interview with her.

It was a remarkable coup and would turn out to be the first time a member of the British royal family had talked about God on camera. What made it even more interesting was that Princess Michael is a Catholic married to a member of the most prominent Protestant family in the world: Prince Michael—first cousin to Her Majesty Queen Elizabeth the Second, Supreme Governor of the Church of England. A historian and author, Her Royal Highness has published several books on the royal families of Europe.

WHEN WE ARRIVED IN LONDON, as usual we hit the ground running. First off was shopping. Vishnu and I had nothing suitable to wear in order to meet a real princess, so we rushed around looking for suits. The one I ended up acquiring didn't really fit, but at least it wasn't soaked through and wrinkled, like the getup I'd worn when Abdesalam, Vishnu, and I had visited the Royal Palace in Rabat.

Adjacent to Hyde Park, Kensington Palace sits completely self-contained in its own grounds. The contrast between what lay on either side of the security gates couldn't have been more startling. I felt as if Scotty had just beamed me up from the dirty, dusty urban sprawl of London and dumped me into a sleepy picture-postcard hamlet in the country. My first impression was of huge lawns, birdsong, and a veritable village of buildings. There was a low hum of traffic, but it was so muted by distance and foliage that it was barely noticeable. The noisy, bustling streets of London were separated from this bucolic paradise by an avenue of gorgeous mature oaks—their dry, rusty brown leaves still intact.

Anna, Princess Michael's assistant, ushered us past the myriad buildings along a path to Princess Michael's private garden, which had once been a place of sanctuary for Princess Diana.

We were to film in the Indian Pavilion, which was situated in the secluded walled garden. Furnished with many comfortable chairs and cushions, it was a very special place.

"Would you like a cup of tea?" Anna asked.

Vishnu and I accepted, and she was just about to leave when it suddenly occurred to me that I had absolutely no idea as to the appropriate etiquette when meeting a member of the royal family. I asked Anna to explain to us how we should greet the princess.

"Oh yes. Please refer to Her Royal Highness when you first meet her as 'Your Royal Highness' and again when you leave. Do not extend your hand to shake Her Royal Highness's hand unless she puts out her hand first. Please bow when you first see her. Thereafter, please address her as 'Ma'am.' That's 'Ma'am' as in 'spam,' not 'Ma'am' as in 'marmalade.' The police say 'Ma'am' as in 'marmalade'; you don't," she fired off in rapid succession. Anna was an utter delight.

A few minutes later the princess entered, accompanied by Simon Astaire. Vishnu and I bowed. Tall and extremely elegant, Her Royal Highness held a couple of jackets in her hands. With her delightful personality and grace, she immediately put us both at ease.

"I brought a couple of changes of wardrobe, just in case I was wearing the wrong color!" She smiled. In fact, the navy blue jacket she had on was perfect. Once she was settled and the camera was rolling, Her Royal Highness started to talk.

"I believe the title of this film is *Oh My God*. And I think it's very apt, because we say that in times of crisis. We say that in times of humor. Something terrible, the reaction is: *Oh my God!* I know when 9/11 happened, in interviews with people, they all said, 'Oh my God!' So it's a phrase which goes very deep, I think, and a good title for this film."

"Thank you, Ma'am." I paused. "So, may I start by asking, *what is god?*"

Her Royal Highness replied, "I think probably my earliest connection with God was that He was going to punish me if I was bad, so He was an all-important authority in my life. But when I went to convent school, I learned that God was good, and all goodness came from God, and we had to be good to please God. And I was caught very early. They say when the Jesuits get you before you're six, they have you for life, and they got me for life."

"Do you think God is a spirit? A power? Or what do you think?" I asked.

"I always think of it, of God, as a great umbrella of powerful goodness that we on Earth sometimes misinterpret. So we, in different parts of the world, do things in the name of God, but we all have different ideas of what God is."

She continued: "I see God as Christians do, as a forgiving God. That's the point of Christianity for me. God is goodness, and I'm not quite sure why we fight for this forgiveness and goodness. Fighting seems to be evil. I don't understand that very well. As a historian, I'm always conscious that there seems to be financial reasons for most wars, but they were often fought throughout history in God's name—in a particular God's name. They're fighting for their God."

"Why do you think so many religions fight?"

"Why do children fight in [the] school yard?" she countered. "I think that confrontation is in the nature of man—less in the nature of woman. I don't really know the answer. If I knew, I'd fix it."

"Ma'am," I began, "forgive me for asking this, if this is too personal a question. You're a practicing Catholic . . ."

"Yes."

"Is it important for you to go to Mass every Sunday?" I asked.

"I was brought up with the Latin liturgy," Her Royal Highness explained, "and a great joy for me, as someone who travels a great deal, was to be able to go into a Catholic church in any country in the world and understand what was going on. But my husband made a very fair decision when we married that we would take it in turns—one Sunday, Anglican; next Sunday, Catholic—so that the children, who by law, and by family decision, have to be brought up as Anglicans, have a pretty good idea of both religions. When I married my husband, there were people who wouldn't speak to me because I was Catholic, in the family even . . . you know, relations. It wasn't personal. This is historical; this is ingrained history."

"Do you think the God that you worship as a Catholic is the same God that the Muslims worship—Allah?"

"Absolutely. I think God is all-encompassing—a huge, great mushroom in the universe who embraces all who believe in a superior being. It's just that the Christian God is a forgiving God. But He's up there for everybody."

"What do you think about all these people who fight in the name of God—for instance, fanatic terrorists?"

"I think any fanatic is very dangerous. And there are fanatics about everything—exercise, golf. Any extreme, I think, is foolish, because it leads to conflict. Conflict leads to confrontation. Confrontation leads to war. War leads to killing people, and we must at all costs try to avoid war."

"It must have been very hard for you, Ma'am, marrying into a family that didn't accept your faith in a way. How did you deal with that on a personal level?" I probed.

"I ignore it," she answered. "They've got their faith; I've got mine. I go to their church; my husband comes to mine. It's a very personal thing. When I came to England, I was 21, and my mother had a lot of English friends who took me about and introduced me to young people. And a friend of my mother's would say to me, 'That's so-and-so, and his father is so-and-so, and he's going to inherit so many acres and a lovely house.'

"And I'd say, 'What about that young man?'

"She replied, 'That young man is absolutely charming—lovely house, yes, very nice young man—but, oh dear, he's a Catholic.'

"And I would say, 'But so am I.'

"'Oh, dear, yes, of course you are, my dear, of course you are.' And this struck me, it was: 'Oh dear, he's Catholic.' I'm just a very quiet Catholic. I don't bang the drum at all."

"Do you have one statement that promotes peace, tolerance, love, and understanding?"

"I just wish I knew how to do it. I wish somebody who is important in our lives, our governments, knew how to do this. It's the most important thing there is. And if all these different religions would accept that we all believe in something that is spiritual, superior, that binds us together, so that we could say, 'Love one another, be tolerant of one another, and accept one another.' It's just terribly hard to know how to do it. Reconciliation is the most important thing, but I don't know how, except by gentle persuasion. But it's not the people who are listening who are causing the conflict. It's the people who are *not* listening who cause the conflict."

When the interview was over, Her Royal Highness took us out to show us the garden. She spent a lot of time with us. We chatted at length about all sorts of things, and she noted, "I'm a passionate gardener, so I believe my God is in the garden. I'm a farmer's daughter. I think it's a miracle every time I put my finger in the soil, I put a seed in, and something grows and it becomes a flower. That to me is paradise—that's a miracle."

CHAPTER 25

Sir Bob Geldof

"Logic can be complicated."

— NAPKIN #25

Right at the appointed time, the doorbell rang. Vishnu and I had commandeered his sister's house in Fulham to conduct our next interview. At the door stood a very tall man with long gray hair, wearing a pinstriped purple suit, cream scarf, and beret. He looked very grumpy. He was also a legend—Sir Bob Geldof. Irish singer, songwriter, author, and political activist, Sir Bob rose to prominence as the lead singer of the band the Boomtown Rats. As I mentioned earlier, he raised millions of dollars for famine relief in Africa as one of the organizers of Live Aid in the 1980s.

"Hi, Bob."

"Hi."

I led him in. Vishnu and I had set up our filming area at the back of the house, where there was just enough natural light, despite the ubiquitous London drizzle.

We exchanged small talk about our mutual friend Doris La Frenais (who had connected us) and also discovered we had a few other friends in common. But apart from that, Sir Bob was very quiet.

"I don't know why you want to interview me. I don't believe in God." He repeated what he'd said to me earlier over the phone.

I murmured that that was precisely the reason I wanted to interview him.

It wasn't until he was sitting in front of the camera that what had started off as awkward ended up being one of the most enjoyable and colorful interviews of the project.

Gazing right down the barrel of the lens, Sir Bob Geldof said, "Apparently this film is called *Oh My God* . . . except I don't have one."

"What is God, Bob?" I pressed.

He still looked very bored. "God is a cultural construct, to explain ourselves and the universe, which is probably beyond our comprehension, certainly at the moment. And God differs from culture to culture. It's a sort of cultural conceit, in fact."

I dived straight in: "Why do you think so many religions fight each other? Do you think it's a politicized situation?"

"I think it's beyond politics. Politics, too, is a form of cultural construct. Culture is a function of survival. We need a purpose. We keep saying, 'Who are we? Why are we here?' The answer is: *it doesn't matter.*"

"You said something earlier about being fed up with God. Why?"

"I'm fed up with the idea of it. I don't believe in God. It doesn't make any sense to me."

"But do you believe in a sort of power?" I asked.

"I don't believe in a bigger power, no."

"What do you think happens when you die?"

"Nothing."

"Rot?" I suggested.

"Yeah," he agreed, "the same as humans are not immune to the third law of thermonuclear dynamics: entropy. Everything decays, you know, and I think it's the end, like the end of that cat outside the window or that chair, whatever. That's it. Over. You stop being a chair. You stop being a cat. We have this attribute to ourselves, a sort of uniqueness in the natural world, which frankly is untenable. And I personally welcome the prospect of oblivion. *Blessed* oblivion, if you want to put it in religious terms. You know, the end, finally. Thank God, you are nothing. Great. You do what you do, and that's it."

"Do you think paradise is here on Earth, now?"

Bob's eyes bore piercingly into me, and he shook his head in exasperation. "It's rubbish. Why are you looking for a reason? That cat isn't looking for a reason for going 'meow.' That's it. You know, we say 'meow' all the bloody time, but we pretend it makes sense.

"It's not that I'm a nihilist. I'm not on a crusade. You asked me to do this film. I have a very pedestrian point of view. I don't believe in God. I think believing in God is an impediment to living this life. People who believe in God—good luck to them. Well done. Don't impose your views on me; I won't on you. You know, great. I'm not trying to prove a point. I don't care if there's an afterlife. I don't want an afterlife. I can't think of anything more boring than any proposition that has been put to me as an afterlife. I don't want to wear a white shroud. I don't want to have wings. I don't want to be in the constant presence of a superior being. Fuck off."

I was about to ask another question, but Bob continued: "You know, boring. And all the language that we attribute to it is so *Star Wars*–y, you know. *Superior beings, our Lord, the Master of the . . .* you know, shut up! So what if He can make universes if He existed? That's what He does. He's a God! He can do it. I can make a table; the table doesn't go, 'Oh, Master.'

"It's such a ludicrous proposition that we wear funny clothes and we do these things to this thing that can make universes— so, he can make universes . . . and? So adoring a superior being, I mean it's so farcical. I'm not being superior; it's just that all the theologies are just silly. That is not to say, the sense of the spirit of something beautiful doesn't move within you. Of course it does. When I'm in the desert, I am as moved as anyone else. And though our greatest brains who work in this area constantly try and come up with, *Well, it must be this, it must be that, it must be the other,* they are wholly and entirely and almost universally wrong. Because when a proposition fails to be proven, or throws up another conundrum, we then go off on another theory. We don't get it. We probably never will. It's fascinating. But it ain't somebody up there who's going, 'That's not how it works.' And even if it does, so what? It's so intellectually implausible, I just can't get my head around it, but I'm not a missionary about it. If I'm asked about it, like you asked me to do this, I'm doing it because we've got mutual mates who insisted I do it."

Bob was getting wonderfully into the conversation. I was enjoying the interview, and in a way I think now he was as well. "What do you think of terrorists who kill in the name of God?" I asked him.

"Terrorists, period, are scum."

"And why do you think they do this in God's name?"

Bob replied, "Amongst young men there is this constant search for status—that's one of the things that males do. I suppose females do it, too, but in a different field. There are many statistics where, if you have a bell curve of young male populations, then you see an increase in violence; and at the moment, the bell curve is with the Islamic societies, but that will change to, say, the Chinese within 20 years, because of their one-child policy. And you see a bell curve of young males who find it difficult to find female partners.

"Often in those cases you see conflict. Especially if those people have no other outlet, no way of obtaining status to obtain a female. They don't have jobs, they don't have money, and they don't have societal positions. If you've got entire cultures disenfranchised from all of that, wishing to be heard, feeling that they're being put-upon by more powerful cultures, they will react. Unfortunately in our world, the way to get noticed is to kill, and almost in a postmodern *spectacular show* way. And if you are offered something better than this current life, and you lack viability in this life, then it becomes an interesting proposition. If you are offered heroism, then you do achieve status.

"It's like the romanticism of suicide," Bob went on, "and I don't get it, because *you're dead.* And this life is staggeringly amazing. This life, this thing that you're living now, that's it. Before and after—nothing. That's it. Hard for people to take on board—I find it, as I said, comforting—but it is *it.* And then, *basta!* Hopefully, by the end, the last conscious thought I'll have is: *Fuck me, that was interesting.*"

There was something about the way Bob was talking about the "now" that made me think of Tanaka back in Japan. "That sounds very *Zen*," I commented.

"I don't know what Zen is," Bob admitted.

"It's like we are empty, emptiness . . ."

". . . I'm not empty. I'm a bag of neuroses, trying to fill my time, because if I don't keep frantically busy, I become chronically bored."

I asked, "If you could say one sentence that would promote peace, tolerance, love, and understanding around the world, what would it be?"

"I don't think peace is possible, but it's wonderfully human to reach for things that are beyond your grasp. And we should never, ever stop reaching for those understandings beyond our grasp— the notion of infinity, the notion of universes, the notion of all those things, and the notion of peace, which is aspirational. But since the beginning of the species, and pre the species, we have been defined by conflict, by the Darwinian notion of survival. If that's so, then it just simply isn't in our nature that we will last satisfactorily in a peaceful environment.

"If that is true, it's equally plausible, therefore, that we actively enjoy conflict. And if you look, if you read decent literature—let's take Michael Herr's book *Dispatches,* probably the best book on the Vietnam War, there is a great passage where he is under fire, and he's a journalist, and the Vietcong are 10, 15 meters away; and he picks up a pistol and he starts firing. And his description of that point is totally understandable; he suddenly realized he's exhilarated. It's the reduction of everything, the confusion of being human.

"A lot of the time we abrogate our responsibility to God. We blame God, or we say, 'God willing.' *If God wants it to happen, it'll happen. Otherwise it won't, and it's not my fault; God didn't want it to happen.* It's very immature. We put upon God so many things that we don't want to acknowledge for ourselves. And it's not just *inshallah;* we all say it, you know, 'God willing,' and it sort of hides our own failures. 'I hope you get the job, *God willing,*' you know. And you know you didn't get it because you're a fucking loser. Or you weren't as good as the other guy. Face it! Or you did a crap interview. It's nothing to do with God.

"And with regard to conflict," Bob pressed on, "because it reduces the complexity of being human to its essences—live or die—we become like the creatures around us who live on a daily basis with that *live or die*. It's almost relaxing to be human at that point, and afterwards there's that buzz. It's why we go for the extreme experience, which we've modified, of course, into funfairs, where we have an ersatz experience of *live or die*. It's why we like going to horror movies. It's the same thing. What is that prurience? And it's why we like looking at the pornography of poverty on our TV screens, and wars and hunger, because it is the human experience *in extremis*. We're living it vicariously, and that's prurient. And it's awful.

"At the same time, being human, we don't want it happening to other people. And we do a political thing: we say, 'not in our name.' And the most that individuals can do is put a dollar, a euro, a pound, whatever, into a charity box or something—'We hope that they'll be okay.'

"So I think it's that part of humanity that is exalted, it's not Godlike. It's human. And that's what's so great about it. And that's why we're so profoundly interesting. We like both of it. Some say that's our better nature. I don't know. But I strongly suspect we enjoy conflict, because it's reductionist. At the same time, we laud what we see as good human endeavors, which is why you keep going on to me: 'You have to admit you've done this!' It's not a big deal." (Bob was referring to my praising him for having raised so much money for Live Aid.)

"It's a sense of admiration, actually," I clarified.

"I'm in pop music, you know. I can get in front of a camera and crap on about things."

"How do you think fear coerces all, manipulates all . . . ?"

"Well, I never had fear of the Catholic Church," he replied. "I mean, I did—I was afraid of my sins, pathetic as they were, as a little boy. I don't know if 'the fear of God' is an Irish expression—'Geez, he put the fear of God in ya'—I did have the fear of God about wanking and things like that, which is fairly universal, I understand.

"I once chatted with the Dalai Lama in a monastery in Budapest, and I asked him, did he wank and stuff like that, and like, 'How come you don't? You're a man.' Did he when he was a kid? And he said, 'No you are not allowed to,' and I said, 'Why not?'

"It's basically the same thing; you are not allowed to spill your seed on fallow ground. What does that mean? What happens if your wife can't have a baby? What happens if you're on the Pill, you know? It's complete and utter rubbish; it's so ridiculous. And, uh, his notion of you get to different levels to get to ultimate peace and that, I said, 'It's nonsense. I don't want to come back as a parrot or the leg of a table or something,' and he said, 'Well, too bad—you're gonna have to!'" Bob laughed.

"So, none of them interest me enough," he continued. "I read, and I get exasperated with the low level of intellectualism—that's really it. That's what exasperates me about these ideas. You can only accept them on a very primitive belief basis. And that's what they all say. The mystery of faith—well, it's mysterious because, you know, it makes no fucking sense! If God did make us, he gave us the ability to intellectually analyze propositions. It's called sense. Talk sense to me.

"This not-very-successful Arab carpenter annoyed the authorities, pissed them off; they executed him; three days later he jumps on a cloud and hops off to heaven." Bob shook his head to indicate incredulity. "That's the basis for entirely successful cultures? Apparently so. And it works. Being human, of course it works. Because we are this sort of, as I say, bizarre psychedelic experiment. We are bonkers, you know, but wonderfully so.

"And all these cultures that are unfortunately rapidly disappearing—it's a shame, because they are wondrous. They are wondrous examples of being human. And each separate language contains its own code, and those languages are disappearing, and with them jokes, philosophies, theologies, economies, policies. We should really get all those things before they go.

"I'm not a humanist," he hastened to explain. "I'm not talking about, in a hubristic sense, about mankind *in excelsis* . . . far from it. We are entirely flawed, but nonetheless—let me use a religious term here—*miraculous*. Compare us with every other species. It doesn't mean we go around chopping down trees and killing everything that moves. In fact—again, entirely, stupidly human—we are destroying the very things we need to exist.

"All this stuff"—Bob pointed to his arms, hands, and legs—"is just a support system for this." He tapped his head. "That's all it is. I have hands so I can pick up food and eat. I have legs so I can walk to the point of food to get it with my hands and pick it up. But what have I got all this for, you know, for burning entrails, and going, '*Ooooh wonga, wonga*'? Oh, shut up!"

OUR INTERVIEWS IN LONDON WERE OVER, and it was finally time to get out to Kashmir and meet the militants with whom Vishnu had managed to make contact.

There was a problem, however. We hadn't been notified by his "contact" until the very last minute before we'd left the U.S., and Vishnu had been unable to secure an Indian visa before our hurried departure. He thought he'd pick one up at the embassy in London while we were shooting Her Royal Highness and Sir Bob Geldof, except the rules had changed. Unlike a few years ago when a visa could be processed on the same day, the Indian embassy said it would take a week, and there was no way in the whole world that it could be done any sooner.

There was only one option. I dialed one of the six phone numbers Mr. Gill had made me memorize in case we ever needed any help. I got through immediately and explained the situation. "Okay," was all he said in his familiar dulcet tone after I gave him the address of where we were staying.

Early the next morning, the day before we were to fly to Delhi, a man from the Indian embassy appeared at the house. He picked up Vishnu's passport, smiled politely, and said he would return later. Two hours passed, and the same gentleman dropped it back off complete with a valid Indian visa. Such is how the world works.

CHAPTER 26

Kashmir

"Loneliness should only be a problem if everyone else is dead."

— NAPKIN #26

Vishnu and I were sitting on the terrace of a hotel somewhere in Kashmir, northern India (although, of course, the Pakistanis would like to say we were in Pakistan). We had all but disappeared off the beaten track. Even though we'd only received "the call" just before we'd left for Turkey, Vishnu had actually been working on this expedition for months. We had instructions to turn up at the hotel and . . . wait. A contact would arrive to take us into the hills and introduce us to some radical militants who were working against both the Indian and Pakistani governments. Part of the deal of the introduction was that we couldn't divulge to anyone how we came to be there.

It was all very exciting, and a little daunting at the same time. So, to kill time, we'd started to write all sorts of silly poems.

I started this film on a whim,
I was bored with going to the gym,
So I got on a plane,
Was I really insane?
But with courage in hand
You must understand,
I was trying to get under God's skin.

With neurosis brewing inside,
But really with nothing to hide,
I traveled abroad,
In search of our Lord,

With questions to ask,
I took people to task,
With many a dent to my pride.

The results of my journey, who knows?
Have I found something that shows,
That religion's to blame
That we're not all the same.
It builds walls and division,
'Tween man and his vision,
And we all end up where the wind blows?

Three days after we arrived, a gentleman who shall remain nameless came to visit us. We were to move out the following morning.

After checking, double-checking, and even triple-checking the equipment, Vishnu and I were waiting outside the hotel at the appointed time when a convoy of jeeps tore into the drive. Our point man got out of the head jeep, took one look at all the camera equipment sitting in a ring around us, and shook his head. "We must travel light," he insisted.

That was all right. Vishnu and I were used to shooting from the hip. We knew what to do. Quickly, we pared the gear down to what we call *guerilla mode,* which meant just the bare essentials; stowed the rest back in our rooms; and were back outside in five minutes.

We drove off in a cloud of dust and headed into the hills. A couple of hours later, we were in the middle of nowhere, bouncing along dirt roads, when we abruptly turned off into a forest, descended down onto a dry riverbed, and climbed up a track into the bush on the other side. We came to a very scruffy-looking village hut, where we were advised that the interview would take place. I didn't complain. It was visually excellent.

For some reason, whether it was "photojournalism syndrome" or utter naïveté, I felt absolutely no fear whatsoever. In fact, Vishnu and I remarked on just how laid-back the whole operation was. Despite the presence of many guns, and the fact that we were going off into the unknown and weren't even allowed to talk about where exactly we were or would be going, it didn't seem to make us fearful at all.

I have been much more scared in domestic situations, in South Central L.A. or parts of New York or London. Here it just seemed surreal. I remember in Zimbabwe once, we were stopped at a roadblock by a unit of boy soldiers while I was making a commercial for Save the Children. The heavily armed youths were absolutely drunk or drugged out of their minds, and made us get out of the car. They looked moronic with their wide, crazed eyes. I felt fear then—real fear, the kind you can smell—as none of us knew if the mad, armed children would just decide to shoot us on a whim or not.

Anyway, soon our Kashmiri subjects arrived. Bearded, with deep furrows between their piercing black eyes, they were dressed in muted greens and dark browns. They were all wearing black headbands and shoulder straps full of ammunition, and were carrying Kalashnikov rifles. The militants were here. There were three of them, and they had agreed to talk to us—*on camera.*

"I don't feel remotely fazed about this. Shouldn't we be scared?" I asked Vishnu.

"Why?" he retorted.

"Well, they're all armed militants, aren't they?"

"They wouldn't invite us to film them if they didn't have something to say. They wouldn't harm us. Unless we looked utterly unprofessional and were taking the piss out of them—which we're not."

They sat outside the hut while Vishnu and I quickly prepared for the shoot. They looked menacing with their guns and deadpan stares, devoid of jokes, of fun, of humor. I announced to "our man" that we were ready, and turned on the camera. *Nothing happened.* I turned it off and turned it on again. And . . . *nothing happened.*

We had filmed in 20 countries by then—in freezing conditions, in heat, in rain, in snow, up mountains, down dales, on water, and in deserts. The camera had been tossed off planes and stripped down by security staff. It had been manipulated, manhandled, maneuvered, pulled apart, put together, disassembled, and reassembled hundreds of times. And on the one day that had taken many months and all our contacts and influence to organize, the camera decided not to work. The one interview in which I was surrounded by countless armed men, somewhere in the middle of *Kashmir*—asking dangerous, self-confessed terrorists intimate questions about God—*the camera refused to work!* I could hardly believe it.

I looked around me, and all I could see were gun barrels. . . . *Unless we looked utterly unprofessional!* reverberated in my head.

"Ah, Vishnu," I said out of the corner of my mouth, "the camera won't work."

"What?"

"The camera won't work."

"What, here, today, *now?*" he whispered.

"Yep."

There was a pause, followed by the immortal words: "Icy calm."

"What do I do?" I asked.

"Shoot it on the B cam," Vishnu said.

"I can't."

Vishnu nodded. "Oh, bugger. It's back at the hotel, isn't it?"

"Yep."

Vishnu let out one of his *Oh, now we're completely screwed* high-pitched giggles.

"Yep," was all I could say.

"Try turning it on and off a couple of times," he advised.

"I have."

"Our man" looked at me and splayed his hands in a *We don't have much time* gesture, then, just to make sure I got the message, said, "Mr. Peter. We don't have much time."

"We're screwed," I hissed to Vishnu under my breath. "Should I be concerned now?"

"Not if you fix the camera." He smiled through gritted teeth.

I tried all the things one can do to a camera in this situation, which isn't much. I realized that it must be a power thing. I changed the fuse—no-go. I checked all the connections from the big battery—no-go. Then I realized I could bypass the battery and use the mains plug to power the camera. I had the transformer; all I needed was a cigarette-lighter socket from one of the jeeps.

There was nothing for it. We had to level with "our man." I explained the problem to him. To his credit, the look he gave me wasn't as incredulous as I had anticipated. His reaction wasn't a problem, but there *was* a big problem—none of the jeeps had any cigarette lighters.

Now all the armed men were talking in Urdu around us. The militants were speaking *very* fast. *This is it. They think we're unprofessional morons . . . that we're a joke. They'll probably shoot us for wasting their time.* I began to imagine the series of unfolding events.

But that was not the case. "Our man" told us to leave the setup with some of his guards and pile into the jeeps. We did, and along with the three militants, we were soon tearing through the bush at breakneck speed. Soon we came to another village, if you could call it such. It, too, was not only far off the beaten track, but also consisted of many more small huts similar to the village we had just left. The convoy pulled up in front of one of them. Despite the noise and the dust, it wasn't enough to wake a large rotund man who lay snoring beneath a muddy plastic tarpaulin. When he awoke and saw the crowd of menacing-looking armed men with two startled white guys, he leapt to his feet remarkably nimbly for a man of his size. There were more rapid, machine-gun-fire-like exchanges, and soon the bewildered rotund man led us into the hut.

It was dark inside, and it took a while for my eyes to adjust, but when they did, I was amazed to see every conceivable piece of domestic electronic equipment one could think of. There were reels of wires, digital clocks, innards of TVs and radios, soldering irons, tools, and a bench with a magnifying glass and work light. I pondered where I was and what I was seeing and what all this electrical stuff could possibly be used for. Suddenly, the rotund man made a triumphant sound, which I took to be the Urdu version of "Aha!" and he held up a cigarette-lighter socket in one hand and a 12-volt battery in the other. Within minutes he had expertly soldered the two together and we were on our way.

We slammed the battery down beside the camera. I fished out the adapter from the grip case. One of the men intelligently pulled the jeep up close and connected the battery via jumper cables to the vehicle to ensure there was enough power. I plugged everything in, closed my eyes, took a deep breath . . . and turned on the camera. *It worked!*

THE MEN'S STORIES WERE PITIFUL AND SAD. Two of them had come from very poor villages. With little money for food, they ate only what they could grow. But owing to the droughts, they had been barely scraping a living. One day, a group of militants had come to the village and offered to feed their families, educate their sons, and pay them a wage if they signed up to join them. The militants were an offshoot of the Taliban led by a warlord bent on fighting for Kashmir to be made into a strict Islamic state and to enforce *sharia* (Islamic law). The faction was vehemently anti-West, but the men we were interviewing had successfully divorced themselves from the main group, and explained to us that they were more victimized casualties than active terrorists and that was why they'd agreed to speak.

The third militant had been kidnapped by a similar militia group at the age of 20 and had been trained to maim and kill anyone who opposed their agenda. They made it clear that if the young man tried to escape, his family would be murdered. That had been 12 years ago. He hadn't been home since, and didn't even know where his village was anymore. But the militia fed him regularly, so he did what he was told.

Militant number one was the youngest. He sat on a rock clutching his Kalashnikov. "Definitely they teach us that we must fight in the name of Allah. We were told that when we are buried, we will go to heaven if we fulfill our responsibility of killing the people who are torturing us," he told us via a translator.

Etched into militant number three's Kalashnikov was the word *love*. His eyes seemed resigned to something I couldn't put my finger on as he told his story: "I was about 20 years old when I was kidnapped. I was picked up from my home by the militants and was asked to show them a route. Thereafter, they did not leave me, and they made me a militant. I was uneducated. I was taught that Allah wants me to do jihad, and Allah will be with you. And on Judgment Day, I will be rewarded accordingly by Allah. In training, we were taught about weapons, how the weapon was to be handled and used. The training is all about weapons."

Militant number two spoke sparingly. "We were told that people are in great difficulty. We have to fight against forces. They tell us to fight in the name of Allah. I can't read, and we have been taught that God will help us, especially after death. We will have the fruits of fighting in the militancy."

All three of them seemed very conflicted, downcast, and forlorn. It was as if they'd lost their souls. The very fact that they were talking to us said a lot about how they felt. Out in those parts—from the region we weren't allowed to disclose, and farther west into Swat and Afghanistan—terrorism wasn't really being fought out of religious fervor. Rather, it was the economics of controlling land and resources, the basic need for food and shelter, and the fear of what would happen if they didn't join up that filled the new recruits' boots and souls.

I wanted to interview the recruiters—the leaders—but "our man" made it very clear that any attempt to do so was likely to result in *us* becoming the news that day. Since politics and terrorism were not the focus of this movie, it was a point well taken. I had my militants. It was time to move on.

That night Vishnu and I went into the local town to find someone who could help us fix the A camera. With amazing Indian ingenuity, three inches of wire, and a couple of micro plugs, we got it fixed. The price? About $1.50.

WE FLEW DOWN TO DELHI AND WERE PICKED UP at the airport by familiar faces in uniforms. We couldn't come to this part of the world without popping in to visit an old friend! A police convoy whisked us away to Mr. Gill's for dinner. It was wonderful to see him again—like coming home. We had a hilarious evening with his family, then piled into his bulletproof Tata and, accompanied by a full motorcade, drove down to Vrindaban to join Chandi.

We spent two days in Vrindaban. The weather was beautiful and not too hot. I managed to pick up some shots that I'd missed the year before. We told stories late into the night and visited

the hospital and the villages during the day. Some of the sick patients we'd met the year before came to see us, including the little
boy who had fallen off the train. He looked so much better and
beamed from ear to ear. It was heartwarming to see children who
had been so near death now fully recovered. I interviewed Mr. Gill
again so that he could fill in some narrative gaps, and then all too
soon it was time to fly back to reality and carry on with the film.

CHAPTER 27

Dr. John F. Demartini

*"My pocket is full of thoughts. My mind is full of ideas.
But my heart is full of nothing more than what I need."*

— NAPKIN #27

"What is God, John?" I asked.

We were in Hollywood, California, and I had the great privilege to interview Dr. John F. Demartini. One of the teachers featured in the inspirational hit film *The Secret,* John is a human behavioral specialist, an educator, a best-selling author, and the architect of numerous personal and professional development courses, including The Breakthrough Experience and The Demartini Method® training program.

"I like to think of God as the Grand, Organized Design of the universe," John answered, "or the Grand, Organized Designer, if you want to animate or personify God. It's basically, as some scientists have described, the intelligence and order that permeates the vast universe, which gives rise to or governs all natural laws. It is also that boundless presence of being that we inwardly sense when we experience an open and grateful heart for our lives and for the magnificent world and universe we are part of."

"So you consider God to be like a power or a reservoir of divine force, or the *anima mundi?*" I continued.

"Yes, the *anima mundi* is still an appropriate phrase. The more I've probed into the mysteries of universal cosmology, the nature of existence and of human behavior, the more appreciation I have for, and humble myself to, an intelligence that somehow governs the order behind them. Even the events that we think are chaotic ultimately have a hidden order behind them. Great scientists, theologians, inspired writers, and dedicated researchers would have never continued to probe and endure their long-term focus on the solutions or answers to the mysteries of the universe if they had not somehow felt that there was an underlying rationale or intelligence behind its laws. So I believe there is a hidden order in what is often thought of as apparent chaos—not only in the universe, but also within human and social behavior."

"Do we as human beings create God in our own image, or are we a result of the creation and evolution of that great cosmic force?"

"There are different levels of awareness of God. We have an anthropomorphic awareness where we tend to project our physical image onto our idea of divinity and imagine God to have a sensory function (omniscient) and a motor function (omnipotent) like we do so we can communicate and have a personal relationship with our projection. And we tend to project onto God those actions that support our values, instead of those things that challenge our values. And whenever things support our values, we feel connected; and whenever things challenge our values, we ask for guidance or we pray for protection so that we may again feel this connection. And that's an anthropomorphic form—so we make God in our own image.

"And then there are the natural laws of the universe," John continued, explaining, "the 'intelligence' that's inherent in nature, which provides both support and challenge to human beings, and which is transcendent to the limits any human beings project onto God. This is what I consider truer religiosity. It's something that we can humble ourselves to, and not be limited by our own projections. And it is something that governs life, not only within the world around us, but within the world inside us.

"So we have one form of God that we try to please and to communicate with so we can feel safe when we're challenged. And then there's one that permeates the universe that actually continually bathes us with the balance of nature, which some call love. We, as individuals, grow most at the border of chaos and order, and the truer divinity simultaneously provides us both."

"Why do you think so many religions fight?"

"Many religions are based on the anthropomorphic idea—creating God in *their* own image, according to their individual or institutional values, and based on whoever has the most power. They limit God to a force serving some human need. This creates pairs of opposites, and so for every person that has a need or value system, there is someone else that has an equal and opposite one. And so they come into clash, when really both of them are there to teach each other how to appreciate and love each other, since divine love is the balance of opposites."

"John, what is prayer?"

He replied, "I often say that there are different levels of prayer. The lowest form of prayer is asking God to fix things according to your needs, when people or events aren't supporting you. The very things that challenge you actually make you grow, and you're unknowingly staying juvenile by praying for the anthropomorphic God to take care of them. The highest level of prayer would be one of 'Thank you—I love you,' to the universe, because you see the hidden order, and there's nothing to fix. There's only something to gracefully embrace."

"Do you think it's faith in God that makes people think they're being helped with their challenges?" I asked.

"True faith occurs when you have faith in the hidden order and balance of the universe—which is demonstrated by the synchronicity of both supportive and challenging events—which helps you develop, adapt, and grow. And false faith occurs when you have faith that some anthropomorphic God is going to guide and protect you from the events or people that you're most frightened of, or challenged by, and will someday reward your supposed suffering.

"Ultimately, if we look through our fears carefully enough, the challenging crisis that we are frightened of has a supportive blessing that is something to be grateful for. The yang has the yin inside it. The terrible has the terrific inside it. When we look for both of them simultaneously, we come to a state of poise, gratitude, and love, which I call the truer religious experience."

"What do you think happens when we die?"

"I am now convinced that we don't actually die," John affirmed, "or to rephrase, our energetic essence doesn't die. Our physical body may undergo a degeneration and decomposition, from dust to dust, but it appears that the expression of our consciousness, or energetic essence, continues. I have clinically worked with hundreds of individuals who have had deaths in their families. Nobody comes to me and says, 'I miss their screaming. I miss their dirty clothes.' They only miss the things that they admired. They often say that they miss their hugs, their eyes, their smiles, or their friendly conversations.

"So as long as we are infatuated with people, we will fear their death. The traits we resent in people—we fear their gain. What's amazing is that if we itemize exactly what they think is in their lives the moment their loved one dies, and ask what are the new forms that emerge immediately around them, they discover that the things they're now missing actually emerge around them in family members, friends, and sometimes even in animals. So I have been able to develop a methodology to help a grieving person make that transition—to see the new form that the deceased person's energy is in. Once they make that transformational balance, the person no longer grieves."

"Could mysticism and science have the same polarity as the yin and yang, the yes and the no, the black and white?"

"Well," John began, "I commonly say that true science and true religion are presenting the same message. Pseudoscience and pseudo-religion are at odds with each other. And truly meaningful and somewhat mystical experiences occur when we bring these assumed pairs of opposites into unity. The same thing occurs in particle physics. When we take positrons and their complementary opposite—electrons—within particle accelerators and slam or merge them together, we create vast powers, energies, and/or light. So the very higher states or frequencies of energy that we have access to in particle physics may be what religious people have described as the origin of existence and life, sometimes called God. Maybe true religion is the re-ligation (joining together) of complementary charged particles or ions of mind within the universe."

He continued: "So when somebody says that science and religion can't be intertwined, I think that true science and true religion are already entangled. The underlying inherent order of the universe is there—what we do with it is our own interpretation."

I was intrigued to hear what John had to say about paradise and hell.

"In religion there are gradations of awareness," he explained. "Fundamental religious followers often seek only one-sided existences—like pleasure without pain, kind without cruel, positive without negative—and in looking for things to support their tribal values without challenge, they stay juvenile and frightened. They are looking for a god that will protect them from the very moments and events that actually make them grow. This stage of religion leads to the concept that life is not fulfilling unless it's pleasure all the time, and the idea of an eternal paradise in the afterlife. Since physical life has both sides, they believe that in the afterlife they will get permanent pleasure. This makes them subordinate to those who sell the idea that in the afterlife they will finally have peace and happiness, instead of embracing the true balance of life, which requires a beautiful equilibrium of both support and challenge, positive and negative, in order to grow.

"This magnificent balance of the universe is something we can call the perfection—the synchronicity of all complementary opposites. This is what true love is about, what true fulfillment is. Half fulfillment is seeking one side, the other half fulfillment, which you may unsuccessfully try to deny keeps you from having true fulfillment. When you embrace the pains, the pleasures, and all the polarities at the same moment, the kind and the cruel, you awaken yourself to the true hidden order, and you don't become addicted to a fantasy in the afterlife that's going to rescue you from the truth and balance that makes you grow in this life."

John continued: "If I told you that I would give you a billion dollars if you could give me a one-sided magnet, a positive without a negative, you would search, if you were ignorant. But if you understood the universal laws of nature, you would realize it's futile, and instead embrace the two sides of the magnet wholeheartedly. How can you have magnetism with only one side? How can you have life with only one side? So those who are only seeking one side are missing out on the magnificence and the magnetism of opportunity. Those religions that radically and fundamentally sell one-sidedness are in an initial stage of awareness.

"So let me define heaven and hell. There are two types of heaven: The pseudo-heaven that we fantasize about when we are looking for that which only supports our values and keeps us juvenile. And the truer heaven, when we embrace that everything actually is in order. And there is a balance of polarities, when that heaven is embracing both sides together. The first heaven is seeking one side, while the latter is embracing both sides.

"Now pseudo-hell, on the other hand, is the idea that life is not matching our one-sided fantasy; we are frustrated because we are not getting our delusion and our addictive outcomes—it's the idea that we are only supposed to get one side, happy without sad. So when we are striving for a one-sided life, life is hell because the desire for that which is unobtainable is the source of human suffering. When we finally embrace both sides of life, we have the truer heaven, because now we're grateful."

"So what do you think of these fanatical terrorists?" I asked.

"Let me answer that by saying there are hundreds of millions of children who go to elementary school, tens of millions who go to high school, millions that go to college, hundreds of thousands who become professors, thousands who become professors emeriti, but only hundreds who become Nobel Prize winners. There is a natural gradation of awareness in every field. Even in fields of sport the same principle occurs. So, too, in the field of religious understanding. Fundamentalists seek and live by one-sidedness. And at the very top are the Universalists who see things with more relativity and are more adaptable and gray.

"I'll use an analogy: If you could take a top and spin it at infinite speed, where half the top is black and the other half of the top is white, it would stand steady. It would radiate heat. It would be neither black nor white; it would be gray. But if you were to lower its vibration or rate of spin, it would start to wobble and you would eventually start to see black, white, black, white." John slowed his words as an illustration of the top losing its spin: "Black . . . white . . . black . . . white . . . black . . . white . . . and eventually it would topple over and become either black or white as gravity ruled it.

"Well, the more *grave*"—John changed the cadence of his voice to illustrate the similarity between the words *grave* and *gravity*— "the situation, the more black-and-white it is perceived. The more awareness you have, the more awakened you are, the more you see the gray. So terrorists are those who see things as black or white; and the more rigid they are in their one-sided perceptions, the more conflictive they potentially become, because whoever their opposition is represents a part of them that they haven't loved within themselves.

"Whatever we condemn in others, we breed, attract, and become. Whatever we run away from, we run into. Whatever we resist, persists. And so terrorists are individuals who are running away from half of their own nature. The very people they are condemning and wanting to eliminate are actually part of their own selves, and their opposition is brought into their lives in the form of conflict, to teach them how to love that part of themselves. So both of the polarities come together in war in order to teach them to embrace their disowned selves.

"These are all stages of awareness. So the person who is more awakened and aware will embrace both sides of their nature. You don't need to get rid of half of yourself in order to love yourself. True love is embracing both sides of you: the things that you both like and dislike."

"So, how do we stamp out this terrible problem?" I asked him.

"It's unrealistic to think we are here to stamp it out, because what we try to stamp out, we are obviously at war against. And it's wiser to see the old Christian statement: 'Pluck the mote out of your own eye before you try to pluck it out of others'.' I think it's wiser to just focus on sharing inspiration and education with people, and honoring our similarities and differences. Otherwise it's like saying, 'I want to get rid of all kindergarteners and first-graders because I want them all to be professors who are awakened.' You need each stage and level of awareness in society.

"When you love people for who they are, they turn into who you love. The truth is, the opponent is yourself, and when you finally embrace yourself, you love people."

I LOVED WHAT DR. JOHN F. DEMARTINI HAD TO SAY; and although sometimes difficult to grasp off the bat, his way of explaining life and emotions by applying simple physics and the laws of nature was refreshing. I wished those who caused harm to others around the world could be exposed to some of the points he'd discussed so that maybe they could understand that they were fighting the very things the universe had sent to them so that they could learn to grow as human beings.

CHAPTER 28

Eagles

───────────────●───────────────

"A feather alone may be light,
but many are needed to maintain flight."

— NAPKIN #28

I climbed onto the rock and looked down. Adam Krentzman handed the heavy camera up to me, and I framed the scene. Below me stood Mark Standing Eagle Baez and his son, Calvin Little Eagle. They were in full Native American traditional attire, complete with myriad eagle feathers. They stood together on a ledge, inches from a precarious 1,000-foot drop into the Canyon de Chelly in Arizona.

Mark Standing Eagle began hitting a small drum, and in a high-pitched wail, intoned a melancholic spiritual song. Crouched down in front of his father, Calvin Little Eagle flapped wings of golden eagle feathers. The song ripped at my emotions and bounced off the stark, deep red rocks with their pockets of bright white snow. The air was crisp and thin. There were five of us there, and it seemed we were the only inhabitants on the earth.

Dr. John Halpern from Harvard, who had been so helpful in organizing our Japanese trip, had studied Native American culture for years. I'd tried, without success, to get an authentic Native American point of view about God. So John had arranged for Mark Standing Eagle and his son to perform the sacred Eagle dance for us. With their mixed heritage of Mohawk and Pawnee tribes, Mark and Calvin were a wonderful representation of American indigenous culture, and the dance was truly beautiful.

"When I think of God, the great creator," Mark said, "I think of who He created, a man; my responsibilities to myself, to my family, to my people; and also a responsibility as a keeper of this great land we call Turtle Island. I believe that God is a holy man that brings blessing to all that are open to healing. The medicine that He gives us, the medicine that He has, is to teach humankind to help each other and to pray for one another. When I think of God, I think He has created only one race, and that race is the human race. I see God in my children. I see God in these rocks. I see God in the eagles. I see God in all that is created.

"One of the reasons I believe there is so much anger between cultures is there's too much religiosity. We should be open to each other, as God intended, to help and pray for one another and accept that there is only one God on this land, and in this universe."

I wanted to highlight some of the same references we had talked about in Kenya with the Maasai, especially considering how the white man had treated the Native Americans. "What are your feelings about restrictions and boundaries?"

"The only boundaries that exist are the boundaries that man creates," Mark replied. "There is only the law of God, the natural law that we should focus on. We believe there are many paths to reach God; and there are certain songs that we sing to invoke the creator and our relatives, the eagle people, to be with us, to walk with us, and to dance with us. We hold that dear and try to ensure that we share these songs with our children, so they can share these songs with *their* children, to be open to the human race and to be there for each other.

"The eagle represents an opportunity, a blessing for each of us from the creator, because the golden eagle flies the highest of all eagles and of all birds, and as they fly so high, they are with God, the creator. They are very sacred to our people. We take care of these feathers. They take care of us, because of what they represent, and that is God."

THERE WAS SO MUCH SIMILARITY between the Aboriginal people, the Maasai, and what Mark Standing Eagle had talked about. After our interview, I took the camera and went exploring. Topping a ridge and looking out over the canyon, I came across an amazing sight: there was a rock, standing alone, which must have been at least 300 to 400 feet high. Snow speckled its surface, and because of the play of white in the contours, it looked exactly like an eagle. Without the snow, it would have just looked like an everyday rock.

After hearing those words, and after looking out across the canyon and experiencing the immensity of the silence, the space, the giant rocks, and an eagle painted by snow, I felt surrounded by an immense power. It put to shame all those angry words that I'd heard from Christians, Muslims, and those of other religions— those who thought their God was greater than someone else's. The immensity of scale made me realize how insignificant and tiny these bitter religious zealots were.

I imagined John Demartini's metaphoric spinning top as it slowed so we could perceive the black and the white. We had heard the vitriol. We had heard the bigotry from all sides. It seemed so very clear to me that, however certain they were in their hearts that *they* knew who or what God was, they were missing the point.

As I was walking back to the others, I thought about an interview I'd recorded in Australia with David Ngoombujarra, a wonderfully charismatic Aboriginal actor I'd met on the *Australia* set.

"Me, I call it the higher power, spirit, and controller," David had said. "I got my own personal relationship with Him, yeah. It's about religion and land. That's what all the wars in this world start from. Religion and land. When the Christians came to Australia and put that religion on Aboriginal people, they broke every one of their Ten Commandments."

I thought about all the indigenous populations who have been persecuted throughout history. *When are we going to stop destroying people and start learning from them?*

CHAPTER 29
David Copperfield

"Magic exists when you believe it does."
— NAPKIN #29

As we were speeding across the Arizona desert on our way back toward New Mexico, the familiar *"Duh-duh-duh-duh-duh-duh-duh-duuuuh-duh"* sounded out.

"Don't you ever get sick of that Pink Floyd ring tone?" Adam asked.

"Nope," I said as I answered the phone.

"Hi, is this Peter? This is David Copperfield."

David Copperfield, the Emmy Award–winning illusionist described by *Forbes* magazine in 2006 as the most commercially successful magician in history . . . it was another Ringo moment. Graham Bradstreet, an old friend, had mentioned that he was reaching out to the entertainer, but still, I was again taken by surprise.

A FEW WEEKS LATER, ADAM AND I FOUND OURSELVES in Las Vegas. David invited us to his show. We sat front row, center, and I have absolutely no idea how he pulled all those tricks off. We were so close that I thought we'd spot at least something to give the game away, but there wasn't a hint. It was extremely impressive.

We spent the next day at his private museum, the International Museum and Library of the Conjuring Arts, which was housed in a warehouse on the edge of town.

Over the years David had collected an enormous amount of paraphernalia associated with illusion and magic, from Houdini's famous tank to priceless clockwork figurines from the 17th century, to card tricks and fairground attractions from the 1800s. It was a phenomenal collection, and I spent a lot of time filming it while David and I chatted and got to know each other.

In the afternoon, I sat him down and interviewed him.

"God is something that I believe in, and I'm not sure why," David explained. "Probably 'cause I need to. Certainly, the older I get, the more questions I have, but God is someone I reach out to when I need hope. God has been a part of my life ever since I was a little Jewish boy in New Jersey.

"The fact that people fight each other over something that's supposed to bring out the goodness just doesn't make sense, does it? Why can't we just get along? I don't get it. I think that God, and being spiritual, is perhaps the most passionate thing you can believe in. It brings out the best in us and the worst in us."

I said, "When we first spoke, you mentioned that illusionists and magic performers were the first religious leaders in a way, because they could 'prove the existence of God.'"

"It's amazing that I still believe in a higher power," David replied, "with the knowledge that I have about the biblical things that could have been created by someone who had the ability that I have."

"What about faith?"

"I think that within ourselves we can change many things by believing in them. I believe that our health can be better through a positive attitude, and energy. About ten years ago I was walking around at Caesars Palace, and a guy came up to me and said, 'Can you please fix my son's headaches?' I looked at him, and he said, 'No, I'm serious. My son has headaches, and I want you to cure him for me.'

"I said, 'What do you mean?'

"He said, 'I've been to every doctor in the world, I have lots of money, and I just need your help, because I know you can do it.'

"I said, 'Well, you know I'm an illusionist. What I do is create the illusion of enhanced reality. I don't really claim to have special powers that could accomplish that.'

"He said, 'And I know you can because I saw you last night take a chicken and rip his head off and then take a duck and rip the duck's head off and put the chicken's head on the duck's body and the duck's head on the chicken's body, and they were walking around. I know that's not one of the illusion parts of your show.

That's the real part of your show, and I know you have a special ability. Please help my son. I really need you.'

"I couldn't help him. I was flattered that my magic looked so real to him that it gave him an element of hope. But I realized if I had been alive many centuries ago and was a little disreputable, maybe I would have been encouraged to start my own religion. I could understand how a guy would want to use such an ability to create many followers. I could understand how that line got crossed a lot."

I asked, "Do you think God is power?"

"I think God is an anchor that we can hold on to when we are off balance," David replied.

"What is your definition of paradise?"

"Paradise is moments—moments where everything is aligned properly. Paradise can exist in my show, when the cues are right, the lighting's right, the audience is right—that's paradise in the theater; when things are just magic. Paradise can be a place that's really beautiful and takes your breath away. And paradise for me is just watching people going, 'Oh my God, this is amazing.'"

"What's your definition of hell?"

"Continuous physical pain," he answered. "I think hell is not having control of your destiny or your immediate situation. It's having the dream where you're being chased down the street and not getting anywhere. Someone breaking your heart is hell. Somebody clipping their nails in front of you is hell—I have a problem with that."

"Mine's people putting their socks on drywall." I had no idea why I'd said that. It just came out.

David stared at me with an incredulous look. "Socks on drywall?"

"Aaaagh, yeah . . . !" I cringed. "Even thinking about it makes me go crazy."

"I don't understand what that means." David was clearly confused.

For some people it's fingernails on a chalkboard. But for me it's the feeling and sound of wool being scraped on a dry surface.

"The sound of people's socks . . ." I started to say.

"Socks?" David repeated.

". . . wool socks on drywall . . ." Just the thought of it was enough to make my voice quiver.

"On drywall?" David must have thought I was crazy, but he broke into a smile. "And how often does this particular thing happen?"

Behind camera, everyone cracked up.

"Well, when you have children, quite a lot!" I insisted. I was lisping now . . . my mouth was so dry that my lips were sticking to my teeth. "Ooooh." I shivered. "It makes my teeth go on edge . . ."

"Well, why would they put their socks on drywall?"

"Because they're watching TV, and they're, like . . . kids, you know . . . and they've got their feet on the wall and . . ." The more I tried to explain, the more uncomfortable I was feeling. "And they're, just like . . . moving . . . and suddenly I"—my voice was rising—"hear this hellish noise going on in my head . . ." I couldn't stop myself from squeaking as, body shuddering, I buried my face in my hands.

David looked at me as if he was someone who had never in his entire life had an OCD moment of his own. "Here it is," he advised me, calmly. "Get a bigger house."

I stared at him, dumbfounded.

"The walls are farther away," he explained. "And it would be less likely these problems could exist."

He then told me a great story: "I was picketed by a picketer. There was a guy outside the theater in America's South with a sign that said 'David Copperfield is the devil,' which is only partially true. He strode about in this little outfit, and a friend of mine went outside and took a Polaroid picture of him, which I proudly kept in my dressing room wherever I traveled, because it made me smile that someone could think that my magic was from the bad spirits.

"A few years later, I went back to the same theater in the same town, and there he was again in the same outfit with the same sign. I decided I was going to have some fun. So I took the picture from my dressing room, put it in my pocket, and walked outside with a Polaroid camera and a friend. I walked right up to the guy and said, 'I'd like to introduce myself: I'm the devil.' And then I laughed and said, 'Would you mind if I take a picture with you?'

"He said, 'No, go ahead.'

"So I put my arm around the guy; and my friend took a picture of me, the guy, and the sign. When the Polaroid came out, I put it in my pocket, took two steps away, and said, 'You know, sir, I want you to have this picture.' I reached into my pocket, pulled out the picture from two years before—the one without me on it—and handed it to him and walked away. And he won't be coming back."

DAVID WAS FASCINATING AND VERY GENEROUS with his time and passion for the subject under discussion. It made me think about the theatrics of many religions—especially Catholicism—which rely on a great deal of pageantry, singing, incense, and even the lighting of candles to create an atmosphere of holiness. Although we feel we live in a modern age, our instincts often guide us to places of comfort and worship—sometimes just to feel safe, to give thanks, or to be at peace and have a sense of belonging. Those were certainly the fond memories of my upbringing.

But David's take on how humans can be manipulated by those who created the illusion of something greater than our everyday experience was to resonate very strongly in our next adventure.

CHAPTER 30

Mexico City

"It's difficult to love unless you have been loved."

— NAPKIN #30

I walked through customs into an extremely crowded arrivals hall in Mexico City. Vishnu was there waiting for me, dressed in an off-white suit, having just flown up from his home in Acapulco. He looked like one of Her Majesty's diplomatic envoys in some far-flung banana republic.

He flashed a Vishnu grin and mumbled, "They banned smoking in here—can you believe that? Mexico City and they've banned smoking in the airport. I'm gasping."

"You're mumbling again."

"You're deaf."

"I can hear perfectly well," I retorted. "The lack of nicotine is definitely making you mumble more."

"Well, if you heard me, why did you tell me I was mumbling?"

"Because you were mumbling. You're doing it now."

"But you can hear me."

"I can hear you fine."

Outside in the fresh (or not-so-fresh) air, Vishnu immediately stopped and lit a cigarette. "So what's wrong with mumbling?" he asked as, like a starving man, he sucked the nicotine in.

"Nothing when I can hear you."

"Gawd, that's better," he said, exhaling a massive plume of full-strength, unfiltered Camel.

"And now you're not mumbling," I remarked. "Amazing. If I do go deaf, better make sure you keep up that habit, otherwise we'd make a right pair . . ."

"Ahh!" he breathed.

". . . what with me deaf and you mumbling—what are you *Ahh*-ing about?"

"A perfect excuse."

"For what?"

"To keep smoking."

"So this is Mexico, huh?" I remarked as I took in my surroundings.

I had been to Mexico before a couple of times—but not the real Mexico—just Tulum and Baja, which don't really count. We were in the capital to document the yearly pilgrimage to the Virgin of Guadalupe, during which 10 million to 15 million people, mainly peasants, visit the basilica and line up for days for a glimpse of the miracle cloak that bears the image of the Virgin. It was a huge event that literally brought the entire city to a standstill. Peasants slept on the streets during the day and partied all night in a joyous, festive atmosphere.

"Ah, here's Francisco," said Vishnu, lighting up his second Camel.

A bald man pulled up in a rental car. I did a double take. He was the spitting image of the actor Telly Savalas, albeit somewhat younger. Vishnu had hired Francisco to be our production manager on this leg of the shoot, so of course we immediately nicknamed him Kojak.

Soon, the three of us were speeding through the streets of Mexico City on another adventure. The old Basilica of Guadalupe was a beautiful church known as Templo Expiatorio a Cristo Rey. The building of a shrine on the site had begun in 1531, the same year that the now-famous peasant Juan Diego had allegedly met the Virgin. The basilica wasn't finished until 1709. The cloak used to be housed there, but in 1921 an anticlerical activist had planted a bomb in a vase of flowers, seriously damaging the church, although the famous cloak had survived. Years later, in 1974, a new, circular basilica was built next door to accommodate both the cloak and the pilgrims who came to see it every year on December 12—Our Lady of Guadalupe's feast day.

Based on the number of pilgrims it attracted, the new basilica was the second-most-important sanctuary to Catholics after the

Vatican. My heart sank when I saw it. Creating something visually interesting out of it was going to be a challenge because it was an eyesore. I could not comprehend why anyone would construct a place of worship that resembled a massive public toilet.

We arrived in the square super early on the morning of December 11. It was going to be a long haul. Everything was leading up to the big televised event at midnight, which would welcome in the feast day. Kojak had done a spectacular job. We had all the right paperwork and permits, and I claimed my camera positions along with hundreds of other crews. One position was on the balcony of the new basilica, which overlooked the square and had a great view of the Templo Expiatorio a Cristo Rey.

But first we went to meet the big cheese: Monsignor Diego Monroy Ponce, Episcopal and General Vicar of Guadalupe and Rector of the Basílica de Guadalupe. He kindly received us in a private room on the top floor, where I filmed him sitting in front of a huge replica of the cloak. His voice thundered and his r's rolled as he explained the story of the peasant Juan Diego, who came face-to-face with the *Virgen de Guadalupe.*

The monsignor explained how Juan Diego came across the lone girl in the hills, who looked to be about 15 or 16 years old, surrounded by light, and how she gave the man the task of building a church in her honor. "I want you to go to the bishop's house to show what love is," she instructed him.

The bishop listened, but of course didn't believe the peasant. So Juan Diego returned to the Virgin. When he told her the result of his meeting with the bishop, she replied, "Come tomorrow. I will give you proof." The next day, she apparently asked Juan Diego to gather some flowers from the top of Tepeyac hill. Even though it was winter, when no flowers bloomed, he found Castilian roses, which were native to the bishop's birthplace but not indigenous to Tepeyac.

Juan Diego gathered the flowers, and the Virgin herself rearranged them in his peasant cloak, known as a *tilma.* When he presented the roses to the bishop, the image of the Virgin miraculously appeared, imprinted on the cloth of Diego's tilma.

And that was why millions of pilgrims came each year—to get a glimpse of the miracle cloak. I couldn't help thinking about the French couple in St. Peter's Square who had abandoned their vacation to travel to Vatican City to show a lens flare to the Pope.

Outside things were heating up. There was a sea of people stretching in all directions. From my vantage point on the balcony, I filmed nuns, pilgrims, teenagers, and children walking on their knees toward the basilica, lining up in an orderly but festive fashion to be ushered in to see the famous cloak.

There were also many performances—theater groups acting out ancient Mexican folk law; mariachi bands; and colorful groups of Aztecs dancing in circles with massive headdresses made of multicolored feathers, and bells attached to their feet. There was a welter of sounds from every type of musical instrument you could think of. This went on all day.

Vishnu and I would make forays down into the square to get shots of vigorous dancing with the old basilica behind. Bells, whistles, feathers, castanets, flutes, pipes, clowns, and choirs erupted in different exchanges of performance around us. It was a sea of faith, hope, celebration, and expression. We were at the basilica for 32 hours straight. It was an exhausting day and night.

Getting out of there proved extremely difficult, but Kojak managed to drive the rental car close enough so that we didn't have to walk too far; and we inched our way through the throng of humanity, dressed in multicolored outfits, walking shoulder to shoulder, all of them clutching a replica of Juan Diego's cloak under their arms or on their heads as they started the long trek home to their villages and their simple, happy lives.

IT WASN'T UNTIL A COUPLE OF DAYS LATER when we visited a local university that I was able to throw light on something that had been nagging at my unconscious. I'd wanted educated, young-adult Mexican perspectives on God. We were on the campus, and I was shooting the students in the same way I'd filmed the Indian schoolkids.

A young girl stepped into the frame, and with Vishnu translating, we started to shoot. "What is God?" I asked her.

The girl hesitated. She smiled; and I imagined her young, educated brain churning some fresh ideas around behind her youthful face. She made a sound: "Ehhh."

It's okay, I thought. *She's going to have a great perspective on the matter. She's just a little nervous.*

"God is . . ." She inhaled. "God is . . ." She exhaled, casting her eyes up toward heaven, as if seeking inspiration. "God is . . ." she started again, and then immediately rattled off a torrent of words in Spanish.

"What did she say?" I asked Vishnu.

He cleared his throat. "She just asked, 'What was the question again?'"

"This is a university, isn't it, Vishnu?" I asked my friend.

"It is," he answered.

"She's a student, right? Not a janitor or something?"

"Yes, she is."

"How did someone with such an, er, limited intellect get into such a nice university?" I waved my hand to indicate our sumptuously beautiful surroundings.

Vishnu fired up a fresh Camel. "'Cause, me old mate, her parents are very, very . . . rich."

"Ahh." I understood.

We ushered the young lady out and the next student in. He wasn't much more intelligent. I was starting to get frustrated. Thankfully, my frustration was short-lived. The next young man was extremely smart.

"God is something created to manipulate people," he pronounced confidently. "God, for me, was created to control the masses, dividing society into different religions, with different gods all with the same goal, which is to maintain control and cohesion of that society. I think God is a business. I think God is money." He paused and cocked his head, and then said in English as if to hammer the point home: "*I mean, God is money.* They don't just collect money; they are monopolies. They control society at a world level. That's mainly what I think."

And there it was: the young man had just nailed what had been bothering me about the whole Our Lady of Guadalupe feast day.

We'd read in the news that just short of 13 million peasants had turned up to see the cloak with the miraculous image of the Virgin upon it. These peasants had saved up all year to attend the pilgrimage, and what did they do while they were waiting? They reached into their pockets to pay a priest to splash them with holy water. I had filmed the activity—fat, stubby fingers reaching out time and time again, gathering and stuffing precious pesos in a big metal box. And what had they offered in return? A few Hail Mary's and a few drops of holy water flicked over wide-eyed farmers in from the fields, clutching overpriced souvenirs.

And inside the church, outside the church, and everywhere around the square were big donation boxes, and lines of poor peasants, digging ever deeper into their pockets to offer up their savings to the establishment. No wonder the monsignor had been so happy. We worked out that the religious festival had probably netted the basilica more than $25 million.

Abdesalam's words from that night in Marrakech echoed in my head . . . *Men with money are dangerous.* Imagine the church, the mosques—all the religions—with all the money they have: they are a million times more dangerous.

An old friend of mine, Bobby Klein, a counselor and teacher, echoed my concern when he told me later in an interview, "You know, Peter, religion has become business. Big business. And the moment that kind of organization takes place, people want more territory, they want more power, they want more money. They want to be able to do more than they've done before. You know this thing about property and territories and borders, and people saying, 'Well, this is mine, and this is yours. That's my God; I can't believe in your God.' Try to have ownership of that? We own nothing. We're caretakers."

IN EVERY COUNTRY WE VISITED, I would always try to get footage— cement, I called it—that put across the soul, the spice, the mindset, and the individuality of a country. The people, portraits, landscapes, bicycles, pedestrians, graffiti, mail carriers, butchers, barbers, and horsemen—you name it, I wanted to capture that fragrance, preserve it in my hard drive, shake it about a bit, and spit it out into the film so the audience could feel in their bones as if they had traveled with us on this journey, and were so involved that they could almost smell the essence of wherever we were. Mexico City was no exception.

Kojak took us to the seedy part of town. In the red-light district, a hubbub of activity, I was amazed by the sight of the prostitutes—they were everywhere, waiting on street corners, in archways, tucked in alleys, and sitting patiently outside shops. They were all pretty buxom, with big behinds and tree-trunk legs, and they would just sit or stand there, still as statues for the most part, only moving every now and then to maybe spark a twinge of lust in a potential customer's loins.

It was fascinating. They told such a visual story, so for my "cement," I wanted to capture them on film. I sprawled out in the back of our rental car and angled the camera in such a way that the lens was poking out through the bottom of the window as Kojak drove as smoothly as he could around in circles. But these girls had eagle eyes and could spot us a mile off. Every time we approached one of them, she would turn her back or hide her face. We drove around and around and around. The other problem was that the roads were so full of potholes that it was not a very stable environment from which to shoot. In one of the denser, most prostitute-populated streets, I announced that it just wasn't working. We would have to get out.

"Not a good idea," warned Kojak.

"Why?"

"Gangs. They control this area. They control the girls. They're not going to like some gringo pointing cameras in the wrong direction."

"Oh," I said. "Well, I guess we'd better not get caught, then. What do you think, Vishnu?"

"Give it a go. It's broad daylight. Wouldn't do it at night."

Kojak tut-tutted in a disapproving tone, but didn't try to stop us.

"Come on, then." I was rather excited.

It's a big camera. I really should have used the little B camera, but I wanted the quality, so off Vishnu and I went in search of prostitutes. I hid behind a barrow, until the owner shooed us away. I strolled down some streets holding the camera so that it pointed upward, as if I was just wandering nonchalantly home . . . I couldn't work out why everyone seemed to be staring at us, until I realized that we were the only European people around, and Vishnu was in another HM Envoy white baggy suit, but this time with a bright pink shirt underneath it.

I positioned myself in the shadows at the entrance of an alleyway opposite a row of shops with five or six prostitutes dressed in white hot pants waiting outside for a "bite." I supported the camera by balancing it on my shoe and started to shoot.

"Not many police around here, unlike the town center," I casually remarked to Vishnu.

"No, there aren't any police here," Vishnu replied.

"Why not?"

"They're not really allowed."

"Not allowed?" I questioned naïvely.

"Nah. Everything's controlled by gangs—they're really the police here."

"Oh," I said. I was trying to pull focus from a flower vendor to a bouquet of platinum-blonde hair behind it when I noticed it had darkened somewhat, yet I knew the sun couldn't have disappeared, as my exposure hadn't changed.

Vishnu and I both glanced up at the same time, to be confronted by the sight of about six shirtless gang members with their heads cocked left and right, standing in the alley, sizing us up. What was most disturbing about them was the number of horrifying tattoos that adorned their bodies and faces.

"Run," Vishnu mumbled.

"What?" I genuinely didn't hear him.

He cleared his throat and exclaimed, "Run!"

I must say that when adrenaline hits, it hits. Before we knew it, Vishnu and I were tearing down the street at an unbelievable pace. When we realized we'd somehow outrun them, we paused for breath.

"Bugger me!" he huffed. "Don't wanna mess with those chaps."

"I think we lost them anyway."

"They're nasty MS-13 members. Tattoos, you know," he explained. MS-13 is an abbreviation for Mara Salvatrucha—a very malicious transnational Central American criminal gang, which is famous for its members' distinguishing tattoos, and notorious for its use of violence and merciless revenge.

"They seemed okay. I mean, I think they were probably quite nice guys under all that insignia—they certainly seemed pretty interested in the camera. I think you overreacted. They're probably trying to work out why we suddenly took off. Maybe we hurt their feelings."

"Run."

"What?"

"Run," Vishnu squeaked again.

I looked up to see that three of the "quite nice guys" were tearing toward us.

"I think this way!" Vishnu exclaimed as he changed direction down a side street.

"Won't this make us more visible?" I gasped.

We rounded a bend and realized we were in an alley. It stank. It was strewn with rubbish. I suddenly felt like I was in a living cliché—alleyway, gang members, Mexico. Cliché or not, I started to feel the first wave of a rather nasty emotion creep up from my stomach. Mr. Chou was priming the nuclear arsenal. Our feet squelched through detritus. Heavy-duty industrial trash cans spewed rotting contents left and right. I hoped the living cliché ended right there. All I could think was: *I hope the alley isn't a dead end.*

"Do you have your money belt on you?" Vishnu shouted as we continued to run.

"Yep."

"Oh dear," he shot back.

We rounded another corner, and continued on for a few more yards. I'd just avoided stepping on a dead cat when there was the most frightening of noises that made Vishnu and me come to an abrupt stop as if we'd reached the edge of some great precipice.

As far as we were concerned that's exactly where we were.

The good news was, the alley led out onto another busy street. But there was a big problem—a *very* big problem. In keeping with the cliché, there was an ominous-looking door on our right. It looked like the entrance to some seedy underground club. But that wasn't the real problem. Beside the door, cemented into the wall, was a metal ring . . . attached to which, straining at the end of a long chain, was a very large and extremely mean-looking Rottweiler. Its legs were splayed, its teeth were bared, long strands of spittle drooled from its mouth. . . . My mind instantly flashed back to the night in the British pub with Billy from Bristol, when I'd avoided a beating by asking him if he wanted to be in the movie. But something told me this puppy wouldn't make a good interview.

The Rottweiler started to growl. The growl turned into a snarl. The snarl turned into a deep and vicious earsplitting bark. As if that didn't make me nervous enough, my ears picked up the distinct sound of several pairs of heavy feet pounding the ground behind us. Vishnu and I stared at one another, the same thought transparent on both our faces. With a very expensive 22-pound camera swinging in my hand and $7,000 in cash strapped to my waist, this wasn't looking very good.

The MS-13 guys were crowding into the alley behind us. We were trapped.

Just at that moment, Kojak appeared in the car on the street in front of us. He honked noisily and waved us over, blissfully unaware that the Hound of the Baskervilles stood between him and us. I have to give Vishnu credit for what happened next. It was a stroke of genius.

"The cat!"

I immediately understood.

"Here, give me the camera," he said.

"I can hold the camera. Go and get the cat!" I fired back.

"I have a white suit," he protested.

The MS-13 gang was now edging closer toward us. I could almost feel them breathing down my neck. With no time to waste, I threw the camera to Vishnu with a grimace and ran back. Grabbing the dead cat gingerly, I flung it at the wall to one side of the alley so that it was within easy reach of the dog. The hungry animal immediately broke off for lunch, which didn't last long once he realized how unappetizing it was. But it gave us enough time to scuttle past and reach the safety of Kojak's car.

I waved to our tattooed friends as we took off in a squeal of tires. Furious at being thwarted, one of them made the sign of a pistol with his hand and mimed firing it at me. It reminded me of when I'd said good-bye to Abdesalam at Tangier airport—same pistol shape, same miming gesture, but a different person and a complete antithesis of message.

To give Kojak his due, he took it all in his stride and never so much as mentioned a word about what we had been doing in the alley. He merely drove us away from that part of town and inquired if either of us were hungry. I could still smell the dead cat.

CHAPTER 31

On a Plane

"What you lose is for you to find—
what you find is for you to lose."

— NAPKIN #31

It was another beautiful morning in Mexico City. Kojak drove us to the airport. I was returning to Los Angeles, and Vishnu was going home to Acapulco. As I was saying good-bye to Vishnu and Kojak before disappearing into the international terminal, Pink Floyd chimed out.

As soon as I put my cell phone to my ear, everything went into slow motion. It was surreal, as if somebody had flipped a switch. In a flash, fast-moving traffic seemed to drift to a halt. I can still see the expressions on the faces of the people around us as, like a piece of old film that had come to the end of its life, everything around me began to distort and then fade into the background. I listened to Soumaya's voice on the phone. She was calling me from Morocco. Abdesalam had died.

He was in his billionth of a second. It was one year to the day, I realized, since he had told us about that. And he was gone.

It wasn't a surprise. He had been sick for a while, which was why Soumaya was in Morocco. But still, the news of the inevitable never comes without a hammerhead knock. Abdesalam was there, I guess, flapping his sparrow wings against the snowy, rocky, icy-cold slopes of Everest.

I closed my eyes, and when I opened them, time had kick-started itself again. I breathed.

THAT FLIGHT HOME WAS SURREAL, LIKE A TIME WARP. Thank God I had a window seat. I gazed out at the blue-black sky and fluffy-white clouds below me as we floated through the air. I thought about the moment of death that Abdesalam had just encountered—the bullet had been inside him, a meningitis virus—*that billionth of a second as the bullet hits the brain.* I wondered about the second of death and the consciousness—or lack of consciousness—he might have had as his life had slipped away. It was beautifully impossible to conceive.

The closest I had ever come to the understanding of space and time was when I was eight years old. We were in France, camping. My brother, Jon; my father; and I would sleep on brown World War II canvas camp beds under the stars in a meadow of long, lush green grass. There was a river nearby, and the sound of the water gushing just yards from where I lay would usually lull me to sleep. But one night it didn't. I just gazed up at the stars. I asked myself a very simple question: *What is beyond the universe?*

I imagined what would happen if I could take off, right then, and travel up to those stars and beyond. I imagined that I had no restriction of movement—however far it was, I could go there. However fast I wanted to travel, I could reach that speed. The question I had was: Would I ever come to the end? Would it be like one day happily traveling through space at my own desired, incredible speed, enjoying the view, admiring the myriad colors refracting from countless sources of light, and then suddenly bumping into the end? Bouncing off it, like hitting the inside of a sphere? Would it be like rubber or plastic, malleable with a cushioning effect, or would it be like hitting a concrete wall at the speed of light? And then what would happen? Where would my energy go? Or would I just carry on forever, marveling at the sights and finding new colors I never knew existed, and never bump into the end at all, because the end wasn't there? Then the questions became: *If the end isn't there, where am I? Who is my father? Who is my brother? Who is Peter? Who am I?*

Aha! It was at that moment that I'd felt an incredible lifting sensation . . . and there I was, staring back at myself, lying on that camp bed in a meadow in France, from out there looking in. Just for a second—maybe not even a second, more like a fraction of a second, perhaps a billionth of a second—I saw what a tiny speck of a thing I was. But that little speck down there was me. And then

I was back inside myself again, confused. *Where is Earth?* I wondered. *And what are we in?* Everything around me had a beginning, middle, and end; but what exactly did that mean when I didn't even know where we were?

I stared at the clouds through the window of the aircraft and thought about Abdesalam and about my own father. They had shared the same birthday, March 19. I found myself thinking about what had happened in 1995.

I hadn't been getting along with my father; and he had been sick for a long time, almost two years of a slow, spreading cancer that was weakening him incrementally. There was a lot of *stuff.* I'd noticed that what Rana and I had termed *The Thing*—that melancholic heaviness that dragged him down like treacle—was back, stronger than ever.

The Sunday Times magazine wanted to do an article on my father and me for a series called "Relative Values." The journalist, Ann McFerran, had asked him about me and me about him, without either of us knowing what the other had said. During the interview, I'd been very honest and had talked about all the things that I couldn't say to his face, but which needed to be said. Personal stuff—very personal stuff. To put it mildly, I had hung our dirty laundry out for all to see, but it was truthful and painful and forgiving all at the same time. And it was full of love.

My father had been sick for so long, and we really hadn't wanted to go anywhere, just in case. But it was my son Elliot's fourth birthday, and my then-wife, Chin, was pregnant with our daughter, Georgia, so we decided to go to Greece to get away. It just happened that the day we flew was the one when the article was published. I'd bought a stack of copies at the airport, but it wasn't until we sat down in our seats that I'd found the courage to read them. *But which part should I read first? His or mine?* I decided to read mine.

Everything I'd said was there, and at the end of the piece, I'd forgiven my father for not being God and accepted him for being a man.

And then I read his. It was beautiful. It was as full of love as you could get. He told me, as I had told him, all the things he couldn't say to me face-to-face.

I looked forward to getting back home and having a laugh with him over this one. I even remembered looking out that plane window back then, just as I was doing now, recalling those thoughts.

We'd celebrated Elliot's birthday in a beautiful *taverna* in a tiny village. We'd sat outside, and I had ordered some wine. The owner's wife, a big, smiling Greek mama, said that I had to go inside to choose which bottle of wine I wanted. "Please don't worry," I assured her. "I don't know Greek wine that well—would you mind choosing it for me?"

She refused, insisting I go inside. I walked in, and there on the wall was a poster of one of my father's photographs. It was a picture he'd taken in Italy three days before I was born: a picture of gondolas berthed on a misty quay with the skyline of Venice behind. The poster had large letters spelling out: GEORGE RODGER, VENICE 1965. I mentioned this to Big Mama and explained that I was the son of the photographer. She almost keeled over in excitement, and ran inside the kitchen to fetch her husband. He was a keen photography fan, and my father was one of his heroes. They gathered everyone around and started a fiesta. They sent their son off to the village to collect musicians for a party, and Big Mama danced and wobbled her hips. It was a great night, and when it was time to leave, they wouldn't let us pay for any of it.

The next morning, my head was a little thick. I was awakened very early by someone knocking at the door. I opened it. It was the owner of the little cabana we were renting. Speaking not one word of English, he'd put his hand up to his ear to mime a phone. I followed him along the beach, up a cliff, and to his house above. It was a peaceful, perfect morning. There in the house, sitting on the table, was an old-fashioned phone with the receiver off the cradle. He gestured to me to take it.

I cleared my throat, "Hello?" It was Jinx, my mother. My father had passed away the night before.

I could remember the scene, like the faces of the people outside Mexico City airport when I heard the news about Abdesalam. But that time, it was the sea. Very deep blue . . . miraculous, even. There were primary colors only. I didn't seem to remember any shift in time—just the sea and the harsh green contrast of the bushes lining the cliff.

I was concerned when we got home about the dirty laundry I had hung inside the U.K.'s most popular Sunday supplement. I took Rana aside and explained how I felt. What had I said? I would never be able to have that laugh with our father about it now. What had I done?

But Rana just said, "Oh no. You said the truth. You let him go. Don't you see? I was here. He read the article, smiled, went outside, and pruned the roses. It was a sunny day. He joked around. He smiled a lot, and then he left us."

We later worked out, factoring in the time difference, that the precise moment I saw that poster on Big Mama's wall was exactly when my father had passed away.

I suppose one could chastise me for ridiculing a flare in a camera lens or an image of a woman on a peasant's cloak when I relate things that happened under circumstances that mathematical probability would most certainly calculate as infinitely unlikely. But who cares? It was true, and as infinitely unlikely as bouncing against the wall of the universe.

I stared out the window, thinking about these two icons of my life, watching infinity and the blueness of the sky, the orange of the horizon, and the whites of the clouds. Where were they now? *They must be in the same place*, I thought. *They shared the same birthday, after all.* They had never met on Earth. Was I admitting that I felt there was life after death, or was life after death the memory of them I was experiencing now, as Dr. Demartini had hinted at? Or had they lived many new and different lives in the vast number of billionths of seconds that had passed since they both died?

I decided they were in the same place that my thoughts transported me to when I spent that night under the stars all those years ago in a meadow in France.

CHAPTER 32

Orange County, California

●

"It's easier to appreciate something when you've experienced having nothing."

— NAPKIN #32

A lot of people turn to God when they just can't cope anymore. Maybe it doesn't matter if God is real; what matters is that the person *believes* that He is real. Maybe it is their faith that counts.

When we are born, we show no signs of discrimination. In preschool, no child would turn his or her back on others because of their gender, the color of their skin, or the fact that they are disabled. Those attitudes are conditioned into us by society; and are influenced by our parents, friends, culture, and religion. I don't think many people would argue with me that a newborn child is the epitome of innocence and purity, and therefore, to use a loaded term, perhaps even godliness. It is only when children grow up that they begin to dislike others because of their differences.

These thoughts were what took me to the Jonathan Jaques Children's Cancer Center at Long Beach Memorial Medical Center. It seemed to me that the clearest, cleanest, and most poignant answers to questions about God would come from children. But what about a child who, instead of running around at school, experiencing and learning wonderful new things about life every day, was in a hospital room facing the possibility of death? What would such a child have to say about God?

Adam Krentzman found Teddi Softley, Ph.D., a dedicated pediatric psychologist. Dr. Softley understood intuitively what I wanted to achieve and invited us to meet some of her patients. Adam and I drove to Long Beach, in Orange County. It turned out to be one of the most rewarding days of the entire project.

I hate hospitals. They are usually always painted green; they smell of disinfectant; and there is no doubt that the residue of worry, loss, despair, and dashed dreams lingers in those busy hallways. But then so does care, hope, love, and the quest for strength. The air in hospitals is always thick with these kinds of emotions, old and new, and the Jonathan Jaques Children's Cancer Center was no exception.

A pink scarf covered her bald head. She wore red silk pajamas with floral greens and petals in the shapes of hearts. Her name was Kayleigh Scott. Behind her head was a large, colorful pillow depicting Tinkerbell holding her arms high in the joy of a moment, long lashes on wide blue-black eyes.

Kayleigh smiled. She looked angelic, with little fairy ears sticking out either side of her scarf. Beside her was a stand holding an ominous-looking electronic contraption, out of which ran tubes carrying all sorts of fluids. Attached to the machine was a plastic see-through bag containing chemotherapy drugs.

"I'm Kayleigh, and I just turned 11. I'm at Memorial hospital, and I'm here because I have cancer . . . well, *had* cancer—and this is my last day of chemo!" She smiled and threw her head back in joy. Her eyes sparkled beneath bald eyebrows.

"Kayleigh, what is God?"

"God is Jesus, our Savior, and He's helped me get through this a lot."

"How has He helped you, Kayleigh?"

The little girl spoke very slowly and thoughtfully. "Oh, like I've prayed to have the nausea stop, and stuff, and now they've figured out what works for the nausea; that now I get to see my friends. And I haven't seen my cousin in a long time, and I prayed for her to come down, and now she's coming down."

"When you pray to God, what do you visualize?" I paused. I started to speak as thoughtfully as Kayleigh . . . "Do you visualize a man? Do you visualize a spirit? A guy with a white beard?"

"I don't know. I really don't know," she answered, still smiling.

"How do you know that God listens to you?"

"Because I pray for stuff, and either that day or the day after, it will start to happen. Like, with the chemo, I get mouth sores, and so I pray for them to go away, and the next day I can finally eat again."

"And do you think because of the results of your prayers, that's how you know that God is with you?"

"Yeah, I think that because I prayed and He answered my prayers that He is with me, and He's helping me get through this a lot."

"What happened when you found out that you were sick?"

"Well, it was kind of like . . . it was so long ago I forget. But it was surprising because we thought it was something else."

"How long ago did it happen?"

"Well, my legs started to hurt about two years ago, and a lump formed about a year and a half ago. And so our doctor had us go to an oncologist, and he told us that I had some sort of tumor. And then we went to a surgeon, and he said it was a cancer tumor."

"Did that scare you?"

"Yeah." Kayleigh smiled like she had lived for thousands of years. "It kinda did."

"Did you pray more often after you realized that you were sick?"

"A little bit more, I think, but not really that much, because I do pray a lot."

"What do you think paradise is?" I asked her.

"Being done with cancer."

"Imagine that the whole world is listening to you right now, and you have the opportunity to say something straight into the hearts of people. Is there anything that comes to mind?"

"Just that, when you believe in God and when you pray to Him, He can really help you, and He gets you through tough times." She paused and added, *"Oh my God, thank You for everything, and thank You for letting this be over."*

And she never stopped smiling. While I was there, the hospital gathered the staff together and everyone piled into the room. Someone came in bearing presents and a massive card saying, "Way to go, Kayleigh." Kayleigh was going home after months in the hospital. Everyone clapped.

"Congratulations for your end of treatment," someone said. "You did a great job."

Kayleigh threw her head to the side and smiled wider. "Thank you."

ON THE OTHER SIDE OF THE CORRIDOR, mother Leslie Hernandez and grandmother Carmen Martinez led me into Christian Hernandez's hospital room.

Christian had been diagnosed with a very nasty form of leukemia less than a month before. He was obviously in a lot of pain. His grandmother sat beside him on the bed. His eyes widened, and he put his hands on both side of his temples and groaned.

"You got headache again?"

A nod. Christian cradled his head in his hands and whimpered. His grandmother put her hand on his, above his head, and muttered a prayer quickly, like a mantra, in Spanish.

We were all set to shoot, but I was concerned that we were being too intrusive. Christian vomited into a metal bowl. I looked to his mother, my eyes asking whether we should leave, but she gestured for us to stay. Christian had some water. I asked him if he felt okay for us to continue. He nodded.

"Christian, what is God?"

"He's . . . He's . . . He is the creator of the earth. He's the one Who loves all of us, even the bad people in the world. No matter what they do, He will still always love us. And no matter what, He will always try to protect you from . . . from sickness or any pain or suffering that you're in, and He loves you very much."

"When you were first told you were sick, how did it make you feel?"

"Sad, sad, but I knew God was going to protect me, so I'm fine."

"And has God helped you through this time?"

"Yes."

"Can you tell me how, maybe?"

"Like, by helping me—He helps me whenever I feel nauseated; He helps me recuperate from that, and a lot of other stuff."

"Do you pray to God?"

"Yes. I pray in the morning, every time before I eat, and at night; and then at around midday, and at three o'clock." Then Christian said all his prayers in English and in Spanish.

"When you pray to God, does He answer you?"

"Yes."

"Where do you feel it?"

"In my heart. I feel it all throughout my body. When I'm weak, He helps. He makes me stronger."

"What is your biggest wish today?"

There was a momentary pause. When he answered, his words sent shivers down my spine: "For all the wars and, and for all of the fighting that's going on in the world to stop." Then Christian looked straight into the camera. There was so much truth that came out of those eyes that I couldn't help thinking, *If there is a God, then this moment, out of all the experiences I've encountered making this movie, just might be the clearest indication of His/Her/Its existence.*

He could have asked for his cancer to go away so that he could be free, so that he could experience being a child and live to be a man. But he didn't. Christian wasn't thinking about himself; he was thinking about the suffering of humankind. He was using his space, his voice, his presence, to put that message across with a sincerity that no one could deny.

CHAPTER 33

Onwards

———————————————●———————————————

*"A napkin is a piece of cloth, or paper, used at a
table to wipe the lips or fingers and protect clothes."*

— NAPKIN #33

There is a saying that once you finish a film, the work has just
begun. It's true. Once you have a print, you then have to market
it. You have to build awareness through public relations, and you
have to find distribution. And all of that became much more of a
job with *Oh My God* than the actual making of the film itself.

The same theme can apply to my subject matter. The more
I questioned, the more answers I wanted, and the more people I
wanted to ask.

I *didn't* want to be opinionated, and I didn't want to preach. I
didn't want to tell anyone what I personally thought. I just wanted
to ask questions—the same questions of different people.

I had made so many new friends. I'd had the privilege of traveling around the world. I'd had many ups and downs, and lefts
and rights. I'd experienced danger, without realizing it, and I had
experienced fear. I'd had a road trip with Abdesalam. I'd heard
music and song, and I had learned about cultures and humanity. I
had traveled with Vishnu, Adam Krentzman, and Colonel Boobs.
I'd discovered the dispossessed, the brainwashed, those living in
happiness, and those living in hell. I had been betrayed; I had received kindness and gifts. I had been ripped off, and I had gained
something that no amount of money could buy. I had chased and
been chased. And I had found the crocodile in Smarden Church.

I had spent three years—and all my money, time, and energy—
traveling across 23 countries, asking people "What is God?"
I'd collected more than 200 hours of footage, which had taken

John Hoyt over a year to edit. This project had overwhelmed my life, and consumed me. It had separated me from my wife and children, whom I can never thank enough for giving me the freedom to do it.

Humankind has attempted to cross many gaps. I had tried crossing just one of them. I had stepped off the cliff edge, fueled by faith and hoping—well, no, *expecting*—there to be a hidden bridge that would be revealed by a change of perspective. Had my foot even touched the bridge? Maybe I was already on the other side of the ravine. Maybe the chasm was in my imagination. Or perhaps it is a canyon that I have yet to discover.

And, finally, Mr. Chou was beginning to settle down. He would still flap about and cause a scene from time to time; sometimes he would enter my dreams. But the closer I got to the finish line, the more he sat still and folded his gracious multicolored wings.

BUT THERE IS ONE THING THAT I CANNOT HIDE FROM. Everyone is now asking me: "Well, Peter, what is God?"

And I think, *Boy, that's one helluva question!*

That's what's so great about this experience—life is full of questions. Questions make us tick; they make us grow. Questions make us human.

Bobby Klein, my counselor friend, told me, "God—it's the thing that binds us all together. It's glue."

Ringo had said, "God, to me? My God in my life? God is love."

When I was in London, I posed the question to Jerry Hall, the American actress and model, on the phone. She replied, "When God invented man, she fucked up!"

Tom Maxwell, a musician friend and self-confessed agnostic, admitted, "I don't know that I can tell you what God is. But I will say that, having said that, when the jet plane takes off, I always say a prayer."

Dale Launer, my staunch atheist friend, told me, "I'm not a militant atheist. I'm not a passionate, hardcore-extremist atheist. I'm not an angry atheist. But I have been an atheist, and I've only lapsed when I've taken LSD."

Sir Bob Geldof had said, "It's rubbish. Why are you looking for a reason?"

Religious people are pretty certain they know what God is. But Chhote Bharany (the jewelry-store owner and philosopher in India) had cautioned: "Learn from Buddha, learn from Christ, learn from Krishna, learn from Mohammed, learn from everybody. But let it be from your own heart."

Benjamin Crème (the artist and author who believes Maitreya is alive with us today) had said, "Religion is like a ladder: It can help you to get onto the roof, but once you're on the roof, you don't need the religion. You can hand the ladder over to somebody else."

Rabbi Menachem Froman in Israel had declared, "The truth—the word of God—exists between us. God is freedom."

Hugh Jackman had remarked, "If you put Buddha, Jesus Christ, Socrates, Shakespeare, Arjuna, and Krishna at a dinner table together, I can't see them having any argument."

Mr. Gill had reminded us: "Our knowledge is very limited. We think we know a lot. We may be learned, but we are not wise. Try to access your scriptures by yourself. Let no priests stand between you and the scripture."

When I'd asked Jack Thompson, "Do you think God is within you, Jack?" he'd answered, "Yes. I think He's within *you*, Peter. I think God represents that which we all are."

And Dr. Lawrence Blair (the psycho-anthropologist in Bali) had said, "As soon as somebody tells you who God is . . . mistrust them!"

I often think of the fortune-teller dressed in red surrounded by many-limbed cows in a field outside Raipur, India, who'd told me: "The film will take a long, long time and will deplete all your resources; but if you are patient, it will be worth it in the end."

There was one thing that came out of this adventure that closed the holes in the land of holes for me, despite politics and people's stubborn belief systems. It is something all of us encounter every day, yet so many of us don't recognize: our humanity. I had experienced it everywhere I went, even in the eyes of the misguided.

We are all primitive little organisms on a large rock in a scary vacuum, driven by many sorts of emotions, the most common of which is fear. We are desperately trying to find something to hold on to, but what I came away with, after being on this journey, is that we can all hold on to something without having to push other people away.

When I was presenting the film at the Mill Valley Film Festival, near San Francisco, someone in the audience said, "There are many paths up the mountain, but the view from the top is always the same." I liked that. That would make a special napkin.

If Mr. Gill were to ask me a question today that I answered with a clipped *no* three years ago—"Now, if I point that monkey out to you, which is jumping up, and those monkeys that that man is trying to scare away, and I say, 'That is God,' would you recognize it?"—this time I would answer *yes*. But I would also add that God is the ant on my shoe, that Mr. Gill is God, and that I am God . . . and all the people in the world are God.

And if you put a gun to my head and say, "No, Peter, you're not going to get away with this. You've spent all this time and energy traveling the world to make this film, and you have to tell me, right now, what your answer is . . . what is God?" I suppose that answer would be: "God is a word that is overused, misused, and sometimes even abused to describe the magical balance of nature and the laws of the universe."

There you go. I let it out, and you can mistrust me if you want. Fine by me.

You might then ask me if I believe in spirituality, and whether or not I believe we have a soul. My answer would be *absolutely yes* to all of the above.

As the psychic said to me all those years ago in London: "Yesterday's breath is memory, tomorrow's breath is contemplation, but the air in your lungs now is what is keeping you alive." Well, I've finally exhaled what was in my lungs throughout this entire adventure; and have breathed my hopes, frustrations, findings, and testimony into this book. Now I am very much looking forward to the next breath.

So, over to you. Go and make up your own mind. And if one day you come back to me and tell me you know the answer and it's different from mine, I would love to hear it. But please—don't try to make me change *my* mind.

ACKNOWLEDGMENTS

Without making the film *Oh My God,* there would be no book; therefore, there are hundreds of people all across the world whom I wish to thank. From those in the film to those who were quoted in the book—and to all my family, friends, strangers, and champions of the project (some of whom I haven't even met)— thank you.

I particularly would like to thank my editor, Sandra Sedgbeer, who dropped everything to mold the book into what it is. I'd like to thank my publicist, Jill Mangino, for introducing me to Hay House and Sandra. You wouldn't be reading this without her. I'd like to thank the team at Hay House for doing such a great job and being there for me. I'd like to thank Will McFadden for all that transcribing, and Carol Holaday for making it presentable and double-checking me.

I'd like to thank Adam Krentzman, my manager, for putting not only the book together, but also the film, and for sharing some of the adventures. Horacio Altamirano, Metin Anter, and Penny Karlin—who were the financiers and executive producers of the film—without their support, I'd have nothing to write about. I'd like to thank my lawyer, Howard Frumes, who has always stood by me through thick and thin; and MJ Peckos for distributing the film. I'd like to thank my business manager, Bernie Francis; my bookkeeper, Valerie Kuhns; and my accountant, Preston Sadikoff, for being very financially creative to help me through. I'd like to thank John Hoyt, the editor of the film, who started making sense of it all.

I'd like to thank the characters who shared the journey with me. Patrick (Vishnu) Ellis; Alexander (Colonel Boobs) van Bubenheim; Peter Ker; Jack Ker; John Munroe; Dr. John Halpern;

K. P. S. Gill; Chandi Duke Heffner; Elizabeth Warner; Anthony Russell; Mark Lecchini; Rina Shantil; Abdesalam Akaaboune; Khadija El Hamam; Abel Damoussi; Francisco (Kojak) Torregrosa; Doris La Frenais; Simon Astaire; Graham Bradstreet; Teddi Softley, Ph.D.; Robert Norton; Jon Rodger; Rana Rodger; Jinx Rodger; and my late father, George Rodger.

I would like to thank the following for supporting me, believing in me, giving up their time, and providing such wonderful words: David Copperfield; Dr. John F. Demartini; Sir Bob Geldof; Hugh Jackman; Baz Luhrmann; HRH Princess Michael of Kent; Seal; Ringo Starr; Jack Thompson; Dr. Tim LaHaye; Rabbi Yitzchok Adlerstein; André Azoulay; Mark Standing Eagle Baez; Calvin Little Eagle Baez; William Barton; Sami Hall Bassam; Chhote Bharany; Alex Bienfait; Professor Meir Bozolo; Dr. Lawrence Blair; the children and teachers of St. Paul's Church Higher Secondary School in Raipur; Lobsang Chodak; Father Michael Collins; Benjamin Crème; Ayman Daraghmeh; Ibrahim Ahmed Abu El-Hawa; Rabbi Menachem Froman; Fujimori-san; Christian Hernandez; Abdullah Irzek; Rev. Peter Ole Kasingi; Robert Klein, DD; Dale Launer; John Langoi; Nolan Lowery; the Maasai tribe of Shompole; Maharaja Ram Chandra Singh; Carmen Martinez; Tom Maxwell; David Ngoombujarra; Ruriko Nitta; the Offray brothers; Monseñor Diego Monroy Ponce; Steve Robertson; Adrian Rooke; Ahmed Saad; Kayleigh Scott; Will Stevens; Charli Stokes; Sonkyo Takito; Ida Pedanda; Gede Putra Telabah; Imam Jihad Turk; Antonio Tutarro; Nathaniel Williams; Galarrwuy Yunupingu, AM; and Father Zambara.

I'd like to thank the following for supporting us while doing all that traveling, oiling the wheels of the journey, and providing all sorts of things along the way: Masashi Sasaki, Kaori "Little Typhoon" Fujimoto, Jason Hancock, Bean Ellis, Mark Elsdon-Drew, Uri and Cat Fruchtmann, Selin Barlas, Richard Horowitz, Loud Mo, Lorrie Mannie, Leslie Hernandez, Michelle Scott, Carlii Lyon, Thom McFadden, Monella Kaplan, Mika Nitta, and the organizers of the Garma Festival in Australia.

Finally, I would like to thank my family, who gave up more than I to create both the film and the book—they made sacrifices that cannot be expressed in words: Elliot Rodger; Georgia Rodger; Jazz Rodger; and my beautiful wife, Soumaya.

ABOUT THE AUTHOR

Peter Rodger grew up looking through a camera lens. As a teenager, the award-winning British director and photographer honed his skills by assisting his father, George Rodger, the renowned photojournalist and co-founder of Magnum Photos.

Peter's skill with the lens has made him one of the most sought-after advertising talents in both Europe and the U.S. He's filmed and photographed numerous car, clothing, and cosmetics companies' commercial and print campaigns in more than 40 countries.

Following an epic three-year journey producing, directing, and filming across 23 countries, Peter's nonfiction film *Oh My God* (and the inspiration for this book) is now available on DVD (Hay House).

In addition to winning numerous awards for his filmed work, and exhibiting his fine art all over the world, Peter has penned seven screenplays: *Bystander, Here Again, Mrs. Carr, Swapped, Publication Day, The Ban,* and *Comfort Of The Storm,* which he is directing and is currently in preproduction.

Peter resides in Los Angeles with his wife and children.

Websites: **www.OMGMovie.com** and **www.PeterRodger.com**

NOTES

NOTES

NOTES

NOTES

NOTES

NOTES

NOTES